INDIA AND THE APOSTLE THOMAS

AN INQUIRY. WITH A CRITICAL ANALYSIS OF THE *ACTA THOMAE*

BY

A. E. MEDLYCOTT

BISHOP OF TRICOMIA

LONDON

DAVID NUTT, 57–59 LONG ACRE

1905

Publishing Statement:

This important reprint was made from an old and scarce book.

Therefore, it may have defects such as missing pages, erroneous pagination, blurred pages, missing text, poor pictures, markings, marginalia and other issues beyond our control.

Because this is such an important and rare work, we believe it is best to reproduce this book regardless of its original condition.

Thank you for your understanding and enjoy this unique book!

PREFACE

BEFORE commencing the perusal of these pages, the reader may find it useful to be put in possession of some of its principal features. A close inspection of the List of Contents would no doubt outline the information; yet it may not be inappropriate for the general reader to have the chief lines briefly traced, and the aim the writer had in view indicated.

The book will fall into the hands of at least two classes of readers: those who, accepting in a general way the ecclesiastical tradition that Thomas the Apostle had preached the Gospel in India, desiderate that the subject should be threshed out and placed on a solid historical basis; others—and these may be the more numerous—who look upon such traditions as legendary and void of foundation, and therefore give no further thought to the subject.

The writer, who held the former opinion, ventures to offer the result of his researches on the question; he hopes the treatment of the Apostle's connection with India here submitted may be of interest to both classes of readers, and helpful to the formation of a correct opinion.

The inquiry opens with the earlier contact of St. Thomas with India; this would fall within the period that may be termed the first tour of his apostolate, when he conveyed the glad tidings of the Gospel to the Parthians, as the oldest written record attests. It would have been then that he came in contact with Gondophares, the Parthian, who, during the middle of the first century A.D., ruled over Afghanistan and the borderland of India.

The subject is, next, more fully discussed in a close examination of all available records supplied by the East and the West having reference to the Apostle and his mission to India.

It is confidently hoped that the evidence adduced will uphold the truth of the tradition that Thomas suffered martyrdom in India : thence it will follow that his tomb ought to be found in India. In fact a long chain of witnesses will be produced extending from the sixth century to the landing of the Portuguese on the shores of India, attesting that the tomb was really in Mylapore.

The subsequent history of the Remains of the Apostle will show that, at an early period, these had been removed from India to Edessa; evidence from the writings of the Fathers will attest that they were known to repose in that city during the fourth century; and that, in fact, they remained there until the city was sacked and destroyed by the rising Moslem power.

To remove all doubt as to whether the Apostle Thomas was the first to evangelise India, the claims brought forward on behalf of certain alleged Apostles of India are likewise submitted to a close scrutiny.

This closes the historical part of the Inquiry. The reader will find what is historical and what is traditional regarding the Apostle classified in the Index under the word " Thomas."

In the course of the previous discussion mention had to be made more than once of the story which has come to us regarding the Apostle named the " Acts of Thomas." These form part of a class of writings known as the " Apocryphal Acts of the Apostles." It had not been the writer's original intention to handle this subject separately; but, later, it appeared advisable to undertake it in order to ascertain what further historical data it might yield beyond that of St. Thomas's contact with King Gondophares; and also because this class of literature has of late years claimed the attention of several scholars both in England and in Germany.

As Professor Carl Schmidt has made a special study of the Apocryphal Acts of the Apostles, it will be interesting to learn the outcome of his

special researches in this line. He deals[1] with
a group of the Acts of Peter, John, Andrew, and
Thomas; those of Paul he reserves, but has since
treated them very fully in a new work.[2] He
commences by making it clear that Lipsius had
wrongly assigned an heretical origin to the above
writings, and he blames him for adducing the
authority of Philastrius in support of that view,
which, he says, Lipsius had done by giving a
wrong punctuation to the words of Philastrius and
by interpolating words of his own into the text
of the former. For this statement the authority
of Zahn is cited in support. The Professor next
gives his own views on the original texts; he
admits that some had been manipulated, but maintains that such additions and corrections as were
made did not so alter the writings as not to allow
the primitive text to be clearly discerned—in fact,
remained transparent, is his expression; further,
the matter introduced was not so extensive as to
change the substance of the writings. He then
goes on to say that he has the greatest confidence
and is very optimistic in regard to the faithful
transmission of the ancient texts so far as they
have come down at present. He draws also a
comparison between the present state of the text

[1] *Alten Petruskaten im Zusammenhang der Apocryphen Apostellitteratur*, Leipzig, 1903, p. 73, ff.

[2] *Acta Pauli*, Leipzig, 1904.

of these Acts and that of those of the Martyrs, and concludes to the effect that no deliberate corrections or alterations had been made with a view to change the nature of the texts, but that what was done was due to the arbitrary act of individuals, or to the personal taste of amanuenses, or of translators.

After a full discussion of the Acts of Peter, he passes to review those of John (of all writings of this class these are held by some as of undoubted Gnostic origin); he then formulates his general opinion (p. 129): "My discussion has been longer than I expected; but I have full confidence that more accurate researches will support my thesis for the catholic character of the Acts of John, provided we keep in view the peculiarities of their ideas, their age, and their origin. However, before all else, I wish to insist that we should not work with general Gnostic ideas [in our minds], nor should we forget the deep and radical differences which, at bottom, separate the writings of a Gnostic mind from those of a catholic. A Gnostic romance of the Apostles is to me a phantom."

It would not be a difficult task to compile a long list of ancient documents which had once been rejected as apocryphal and legendary, but have since been acknowledged as reliable and historical documents. We submit, on this subject, the opinion of another modern scholar of great

research and erudition, the Rev. Dom H. Leclercq :[1] " Il n'y a presque pas de document hagiographique de l'antiquité chrétienne dont on n'ait
mis en question l'authenticité. De cette suspicion
générale il est sorti un groupe compact d'écrits
sur la valeur desquels nous sommes pleinement
assurés." [2]

The ground for a critical handling of the Acts
of Thomas was, in a way, quite prepared ; critical
editions of the early Greek and Latin versions
had been issued, as also an edition of the original
Syriac text with an English translation by the
late Dr. Wright.

This portion of the book, as a whole, may
perhaps not sufficiently interest the general reader
—it should, besides, be read with a copy of the
Acts in hand ; but even the ordinary reader will,
it is hoped, find certain sections attractive. He
will realise that the Acts of Thomas were, at an
early date, extensively interpolated and adapted
for doctrinal purposes by certain sects ; and that
this manipulation of the text was carried out

---

[1] *Les Martyrs*, vol. iii. pp. cxliv–cxlv.
[2] In a note the reader is referred to the following authorities :—
For documents of the Ante-Nicene period—list by A. Harnack,
Geschichte des Altechristlichen Litteratur, Leipzig, 1893, vol. i., parts
i. and ii. ; for subsequent period—O. Bardenhewer, *Patrologie*, Freiburg, 1894 [and his later and fuller work, *Geschichte des Altkirchlichen
Litteratur*, Freiburg, 1902]; for hagiography—the *Analecta Bollan-
diana*, Bruxelles, 1892 ; and after 1892, *Bulletin Hagiographique ;
Nuovo Bullettino di Archeologia Cristiana*, Rome ; and others.

according to the system employed in the case of an earlier writing, the Acts of the Virgin-Proto-martyr, Thecla, tending to prove that the Acts of Thomas had an early and independent position.

Following on this the reader will be prepared to accept the fact that, besides the historical inci-dent mentioned previously, they embody in a portion of the narrative, which has all the appearance of offering an historical account of events, the men-tion of usages and customs which are found to be purely Indian and Hindu. This would natu-rally suggest that they cannot be considered as merely legendary ; further, that they yet retain portions of an original narrative which must have come from India, though this earliest text now bears marks of gross disfigurement as it appears in the text and versions.

The writer assumes all responsibility for the English renderings of quotations given in the book, unless they are assigned to others.

A coin-plate and a sketch-map of Mylapore and its environs accompany the Illustrations ; these will help to place before the reader such memories of the Apostle as survive.

The writer's best thanks are offered to Mr. W. R. Philipps for continuous help during the several years occupied in collecting the material for the evidence here produced : it is, however, a matter of some regret to him to feel bound to express in the book dissent on two points from opinions published by his friend. He has also to express his acknowledgments to the Rev. Dom H. N. Birt, O.S.B., for most useful assistance while reading the last proof-sheets.

The Author desires to record his great appreciation of the liberality of the Marchioness Dowager of Bute in enabling him to go to press with his work.

NICE, *August* 1905.

CONTENTS

CHAPTER I

CHAPTER II

THOMAS, THE APOSTLE OF INDIA

CHAPTER III

SAINT THOMAS'S TOMB IN INDIA

CONTENTS

CHAPTER IV

FURTHER HISTORICAL AND TRADITIONAL RECORDS OF THE APOSTLE

CHAPTER V

THE ALLEGED APOSTLES OF INDIA

CHAPTER VI

APPENDIX

A CRITICAL ANALYSIS OF THE ACTS OF THOMAS

SECTION I

PREAMBLE

SECTION II

PRELIMINARY QUESTIONS

b

SECTION III

THE ACTS OF THOMAS DISCUSSED

LIST OF ILLUSTRATIONS

Explanation.—Top row: Christ and Angels.
Second row, left: (1) Thomas puts his finger into Christ's side. (2) Christ consigns Thomas to Habban. (3) Habban and Thomas embark for India.
Third row, right: (1) Banquet scene, dog in front gnawing the cup-bearer's arm. (2) Habban presents Thomas to King Gondophares. (3) Thomas distributes the King's money to the poor. (4) (Imperfect) Thomas blessing, probably Mygdonia.

INDIA AND THE APOSTLE THOMAS

CHAPTER I

THE APOSTLE THOMAS AND GONDOPHARES THE INDIAN KING—CONNECTION PROVED FROM COINS AND INSCRIPTION

'THE Acts of Thomas,' to adopt an appellation now become general, contain certain statements which discoveries made in recent years have enabled us to test in the light of actual history. The narrative tells us that the Apostle Thomas, much against his will and inclination, had to undertake the work of preaching the Gospel to the Indians ; and that to induce him to obey the mandate he had received, our Lord appeared to him in person, and sold him to Habban, a minister of King Gondophares of the Indians, who had been sent to Syria in search of a competent builder, able to undertake the construction of a palace for his sovereign. Thomas in his company left by sea for India, which was reached after a rapid passage. Both proceeded to the court, where Thomas was presented to the king, and undertook the erection of the building. Several other incidents are narrated regarding the Apostle, mixed up with much fabulous matter ; these we pass over for the present.

In the second half of the story Thomas is in the

A

dominions of an Indian king, named in the Syriac text *Masdai*, in the Greek version Μισδαῖος, and in the Latin *Misdeus*. It was in this country that he brought his apostolic labours to a close by receiving the martyr's crown. The facts connected with his martyrdom will be dealt with subsequently. We now propose to examine if there be any, and what, foundation for coupling the name of King Gondophares with that of the Apostle.[1]

Did a king of the name of Gondophares reign over any portion of India, and was he a contemporary of the Apostolic age? Where was his kingdom situated? Was it practicable for the Apostle Thomas to have had access to it?

Should the above questions receive an affirmative solution, they would justify the inference that the recital in the Acts of Thomas in this point was based on historical knowledge; and further, that on this account the Acts themselves deserved closer study and examination.

The name of King Gondophares appears in the Syriac text of the Acts as *Gūdnaphar;* in the Greek version as Γουνδαφορος : codd. Rand S of a later date give Γονταφορος and Γουνδιαφορος ; the longer Latin version, *De Miraculis*, does not reproduce the name of the king : he is throughout styled 'rex'; it appears in the shorter Latin version, *Passio*, as *Gundaforus* : codd. QGR of Max Bonnet's *Acta Thomae* give *Gundoforus*.

It was only about the middle of the nineteenth century that it became possible to say whether a king of that name ever existed and had reigned in India.

---

[1] The reader will find in the Appendix *A Critical Analysis of the Acts of Thomas*. We would suggest that whenever the Acts are referred to in the text he should turn to the Appendix for further information, and consult the list of contents for same, given to facilitate such reference.

In 1854 General Alexander Cunningham, writing in the *Journal of the Asiatic Society of Bengal* (vol. xxiii. pp. 679-712), was able to say that in the preceding twenty years no less than thirty thousand coins bearing Greek and Indian legends, and extending over a period of more than three centuries, had been found in Afghanistan and the Punjab. A large, if not the greater, number belong to Greek princes who ruled over the country as inheritors of and successors to the conquests of Alexander the Great. Another portion bear the evidence of Scythian conquerors, confirmed also by other authorities, and of Parthian kings and rulers who had become masters of these territories. The coins of Gondophares, the king with whom we are concerned, belong to the latter category.

The first specimen of a coin of this ruler was discovered by Masson in Afghanistan about 1834. Since then many others have come to light, and specimens are to be seen in public collections at the British Museum, the Bibliothèque Nationale, Paris, and the Berlin Museum. We had opportunities of examining the specimens of the two former collections from which the types, reproduced in this book, are taken.

H. H. Wilson in his *Ariana Antiqua*, London, 1841, gives a history of these discoveries, and he and James Prinsep did much towards deciphering the then unknown characters in which the Indian legends on the coins appear. After the death of James Prinsep, his brother, H. T. Prinsep, published in 1844 a work on the same subject—*Note on the Historical Results deducible from Recent Discoveries in Afghanistan* in continuation of James Prinsep's labours. But these works are now obsolete, and many of the early readings of the legends have had to be discarded.

What General Cunningham wrote in 1854 in the

periodical above named, pp. 711–712, may here be quoted with advantage :—

'The coins of Gondophares are common in Kabul and Kandahar and Seistan, and in the western and southern Punjab. All these countries, therefore, must have owned his sway. He was, besides, the head and founder of his family, as no less than three members of it claim relationship with him on their coins— ORTHAGNES, his full brother ; ABDAGASES, his nephew ;[1] and SASA or SASAN, a more distant relation. The coins of Orthagnes are found in Seistan and Kandahar ; those of Abdagases and Sasan in the western Punjab. I presume, therefore, that they were the Viceroys of those provinces on the part of the great King Gondophares, who himself resided at Kabul.[2] All the names are those

---

[1] Cunningham here styles Abdagases the nephew of King Gondophares. One of the bi-lingual coins proclaims this relationship in both legends—Greek and Indian. By good luck, coin No. 5 on the plate, which is a coin of Abdagases, gives this reading in Greek incorrectly, but yet sufficiently clear to indicate the reading βασιλευ [—] Υ[νδ]ιφερο αδελφιδεως. The name of Abdagases is given in an incorrect abbreviated form, Aoa [for Aβa], representing (if we rightly surmise) the Indian form the name bears on the reverse legend Avadagasa (see also Silvain Lévi's *Notes*, ut infra, p. 35). The Indian legend leaves no room for doubt.

[2] This should be regarded as a purely personal opinion of the writer. The question of the capital of Gondophares' kingdom has yet to be decided. The royal cities that then existed in Northern Afghanistan and North-Western India, and have since been identified, are : (1) *Kabul*, alias *Ortospana* (Cunningham, *Ancient Geography of India*, London, 1871, pp. 32–36), to the Chinese *Kao-fu* [a mistake for *Tou-mi*] (Vincent A. Smith, *The Kushan, or Indo-Scythian Period*, ut infra, p. 21). (2) Chinese *Ki-pin* identified with *Kapisa*, Northern Afghanistan, where the king of the kingdom of *Kapisa-Gandhāra* passed the summer, while the winter was spent in the latter province Gandhāra), possibly at (3) *Pushkalavati* or *Peukelaotis*, the former, the Sanscrit, the latter the Greek form of the name ; also *Prokalis* (in *Periplus Maris Erythraei*, and Ptolemy's *Geography*), now known as Hastinagar (Cunningham, *ut supr.*, pp. 49–51 ; also Beal's *Hiuen-Tsiang*, i. p. 109 ; *cf.* Vincent A. Smith, *ut supr.*, pp. 24–29). (4) *Taxila*

of Parthians, but the language of the coins is Indian
Pali.   Abdagases is the name of the Parthian chief who
headed the successful revolt against Artabanus in A.D. 44.
The great power of Gondophares and the discovery of
a coin of Artabanus counter-marked with the peculiar
monogram of all the Gondopharian dynasty,' &c.[1]

The reader will find reproduced on the Plate select
specimens of the better preserved coins of the Gondo-

---

or *Takshasila*, captured by Alexander the Great.   If Gondophares'
capital be removed to the south, there would be Kandahar.

The shorter Latin version of the Acts offers the following variants
of the names of Gondophares' capital : *Elioforum, Hienoforum, Hyro-
forum, Yroforum, Inforum ;* nothing, of course, can be made out of
this medley.

[1] We omit what follows, as we are unable to agree with what
the learned archæologist says—' That the Indo-Parthian Abdagases
was the same as the Parthian chief whose revolt is recorded by Tacitus
and Josephus.'   On careful examination of the texts referred to, it appears there is no ground to assume identity of person in the two cases.
Tacitus, *Annales,* xv. 2, quoted, refers to A.D. 62–65 and not A.D. 44,
and has no mention of Abdagases.   But bk. vi., A.D. 32–37, mentions
Abdagases only incidentally.   In A.D. 35 (chap. xxxi.), Sinnaces, son of
Abdagases, is mentioned ; he caused some Parthian nobles to be sent
secretly to Rome, to have Artabanus, their king, deposed; and the
same Sinnaces drew Abdagases into open revolt (chap. xxxvi.).   Under
a new king, Tiridates, Abdagases became practically the ruler of the
country ; Tiridates was soon turned out (chap. xliii.), and Abdagases
fled with him, when Artabanus, the lawful king, was restored.   All
this would seem to have occurred in A.D. 36.   Beyond a similarity of
name, it is doubtful if there was any connection between this Abdagases and the nephew of King Gondophares.

The second quotation from Josephus' *Antiquities,* xxiii. 2, is equally
faulty.   Josephus' *Antiquities* of the Jews has but twenty books ; the
only mention of Abdagases occurs in bk. xviii. chap. ix. sec. 4, p. 71,
where Artabanus, the King of Parthia, is mentioned in connection
with ' Abdagases, one of the generals of his army,' who asked to be
allowed to kill Asineus and his brother Anileus, Jews, who had succeeded in establishing a sort of independent position around Babylon ;
but this the king would not allow, as they were his guests, and he had
pledged his word to them for their safety (see *The Works of Flavius
Josephus,* translated from the Greek by William Whiston, in 2 vols.,
London, 1838, vol. ii.).   Here there would also seem to be only a
coincidence of names, and no connection between the two Abdagases.

phares series existing at the Bibliothèque Nationale and the British Museum. Impressions of the four coins on the left were kindly supplied by M. Jean de Foville, Sous-bibliothécaire au Cabinet des Médailles de la Bibliothèque Nationale. Those on the right were similarly obtained through the kindness of Mr. E. J. Rapson, Assistant Conservator, Department of Coins and Medals, British Museum; he has also very kindly corrected the Greek and supplied the Indian legends given in the text. Coin No. 1 at the top of the plate comes from the Berlin Museum.

COINS OF KING GONDOPHARES

1. *Obv.* Gondophares. Bust of the king wearing Arsacid tiara, diadem.
   Rev. King seated on throne holding sceptre; behind, Nike crowning him. Greek legend—

   BACIΛEⳫ BACIΛEⲰN MEΓⳭ
   YNΔⲟ⳨EPHⳭ AYTⲟKPATⲟ

2. *Obv.* Bust of king crowned. Greek legend, part legible—

   BACIΛEⲰⳭ Ⳮ[——]

   Rev. Nike offering crown. Indian legend—
   Goṃdapharnasa tratara[sa——]

3. *Obv.* Bust of king crowned (different type from No. 2). Greek legend—

   [BAC]IΛ[EⲰ]Ⳮ ⳭⲰTHPⲟⳭ YN[. . . .]

   Rev. Nike offering crown. Indian legend—
   [—] harajasa Goṃdapharnasa[. . . .]

4. *Obv.* King on horseback, flowing turban, whip in hand. Greek legend—

   [B]ACIΛEⲰN BACIΛEⲰN [Γⲟ]NΔⲟ⳩ⲀΓⲟY

   Rev. Siva; right hand holding trident, left extended over symbol. Indian legend—
   Maharaja-rajarajasa-mahata-dramia-devavrata |
   Gudapharasa.

5. [Abdagases' coin]—

Obv. King on horseback (type No. 4). Greek legend—

BACIΛEV AΠA V[NΔ]I◆EPO ΔΔEΛ◆IΔEШC

Rev. King standing; right hand over symbol. Indian
legend—
[Gudaphara-bhrata-putrasa] maharajasa tratarasa
Avadagaśasa.

6. *Obv.* King wearing an ornament in the form of a diadem.
Greek legend—

BACIΛEΩC CΩTHГOC VNΔOΦEГГΠV

Rev. Nike holding crown. Indian legend—
Gom[da]pharnasa tradarasa maharajasa.

7. *Obv.* King crowned. Greek legend—

BACIΛE [. . . . .]ГOC VNΔOΦEГOV

Rev. Nike as in No. 6. Indian legend—
Gomdapharnasa tradara[sa . . . .] jasa.

8. *Obv.* King on horseback, facing left. Nike standing in
front with crown. Greek legend—

[—]EГAΛΠY ГΠNΔ[—]ΦAГΠY

Rev. Indian symbol and legend—
Maha[———]dramiasa apratihatasa devavratasa
Gudapharasa.

9. *Obv.* Same as preceding. Greek legend—

[B]ACIΛE[Ω]N [—]BACIΛEШ[—

Rev. Indian symbol and legend—
[———a] pratihatasa deva[———].

Professor Percy Gardner, in his *Catalogue of the Coins
of Greek and Scythic Kings of Bactria and India in the*
British Museum, edited by Reginald Stuart Poole, London, 1886 (Introd., pp. xliv–xlv), observes : ' In the inscription of the Gondophares coin we find the epithet
Αὐτοκράτωρ, which is found in the money of only two

Arsacid kings—Sinatroces, B.C. 76 to 69, and Phraates IV., A.D. 8–11. This particular coin of Gondophares, then, would seem to have been struck not later than the middle of the first century A.D. The period mentioned would suit the other coins of Gondophares.' At p. xlvi he offers the following additional data : '(Epigraphy of the Coins.) On referring to the coins of the Arsacidae, we find that in the series the square [*omicron*] ◻ and Ⲥ [*sigma*] come in some twenty years B.C. On the other hand, ⨿ [*omega*] does not take the place of Ω until 8 A.D. It is in keeping with these facts that Maues uses round letters only ; Azes and Azilises, Spilirises and their contemporaries, use the square ◻ with Ω ; Gondophares and Abdagases use the forms ◻ and ⨿ . We have thus a series of kings covering B.C. 50 to A.D. 50.'

Mr. E. J. Rapson of the British Museum (*Indian Coins, with Five Plates*, Strassburg, 1897, p. 15, § 61) confirms the above chronology : 'Indo-Parthian Coins— Date of Indo-Parthian Dynasty. The Indo-Parthian dynasty, the best known member of which is Gondophares, seems to have succeeded the dynasty of Vonones in Kandahar and Seistan, and to have at one period extended its territories eastwards into the Punjab and Sind, which, at an earlier date, formed the kingdom of Maues. With regard to the chronological limits— (1) the foundation of the dynasty seems to be after 1 B.C. (Von Gutschmidt, *Gesch. Ir.*, p. 134); and (2) the date of one of the latest kings, Sanabares, after 77 A.D. (Von Sallet, *Z. f. N.*, 1879, p. 364). For a coin, bearing the name of Aspavarma (*v. supra*, § 34), which seems to join in some manner as yet unexplained the two branches represented by Gondophares and Azes (§ 31), *v.* Rodgers, *N. Chr.*, 1896, p. 268.'

The French savant, M. Sylvain Lévi, who wrote about the same time, concurs in the views given above (*Journal Asiatique*, tom. ix., Neuvième série, 1897, Jan.,

Févr., p. 41): 'Du côté de Gondopharès, l'hypothèse concorde avec d'autres données. Gondopharès prend sur les légendes grecques des monnaies le titre d'*auto-kratôr*, comme font les empereurs romains à partir d'Auguste. Les Parthes Arsacides, intermédiaires naturels entre le monde romain et l'Inde, marquent avec précision l'époque où ce titre passe d'Occident en Orient : Phraates IV, qui règne de 8 à 11 après Jésus-Christ, est le seul (en dehors de l'incertain Sanatrokès) à prendre le titre d'*autokratôr*. C'est également à partir de Phraates IV que l'oméga carré se substitue à l'oméga arrondi dans les légendes grecques ; les monnaies de Gondopharès montrent la transformation accomplie déjà dans l'Inde.'

The latest writer who treated the subject, Mr. Vincent A. Smith (*Journal of the Royal Asiatic Society*, January, 1903, 'The Kushan, or Indo-Scythian Period of Indian History, B.C.165 to A.D. 320,' quotation taken from separate reprint of the paper, p. 40), is also in full agreement with preceding scholars : 'On the obverses of his coins his name in Greek characters assumes the forms of Gondo-phares, Gondaphares, and Undophares, which last is perhaps to be read as beginning with an aspirate. The reverse legends in the Kharoṣṭhī script give the name as Gudaphara, Gadaphara, or Gudaphana.[1] This mon-arch . . . was clearly of Parthian origin, and his coins are closely related to those of other Indo-Parthian kings. All the indications of his date taken together show that he must have reigned in the first half of the first century A.D. He uses the title αὐτοκράτωρ, which was introduced by Augustus, who died in A.D. 14, and was adopted by the Parthian king Phraates, A.D. 8–11. The square

[1] M. Sylvain Lévi (*ut supr.*, p. 36), draws attention to another variant of the name Gondophares offered in the Indian legend of a Berlin coin, with the termination Gudu/*pharna;* the reading is also found in the Indian legends (Plate) in our coins Nos. 2, 3, 6, and 7.

omega and square *omicron*, which were not definitely
adopted by the Arsacidae before A.D. 8, frequently
occur in his coin legends. . . . The relation of his
coins to those of Azes, Soter Megas, and other rulers
on the Indian frontier, agrees with the other data which
indicate his reign as lying in the first half of the first
century A.D.'

Besides the legend-bearing coins an inscription has
also been discovered offering the name of King Gondophares. As some doubt had been cast on the reading
of the inscription, it will be best to give the reader
an historical account of the stone and of the readings of
the inscription.

The Takht-i-Bahi stone, to give it the name by which
it is known, is now in the Lahore Museum, where the
writer had occasion to inspect it several years ago. It is
a large thick block, not a slab, with a flaw at the top
centre ; a large piece was apparently chipped off.
General Cunningham in the Archæological Survey
Report for the years 1872–73 (vol. v., Calcutta, 1875,
pp. 58–59) gives the following account: ' The stone
itself was discovered by Dr. Bellew, and has been presented by him to the Lahore Museum. We are indebted,
however, to Dr. Leitner for bringing it to notice. I have
repeatedly examined it in different lights, and have made
numerous impressions of it, from which, with the aid
of a large photograph, I have prepared the accompany-
ing copy. Before seeing Professor Dowson's notice
[published in *Trübner's Literary Record*], I had read the
name Gondophares, together with the year of his reign
and the name of the month Vesákh, &c., in a small
photograph. But an inspection of the stone showed me
that there were two distinct dates—the first of which I
take to be the year of the king's reign, and the second
the Samvat year. As the stone has been used for

many years, perhaps for centuries, for the grinding of
spices, all the middle part of the inscription has suffered
and become indistinct, and some portions have been
obliterated altogether. But the top and bottom lines
and the left-hand portion of the three middle lines are
generally in very good preservation. The stone is 17
inches long by 14¼ inches broad. [It has six lines.] . . .
In the first line it will be observed that there is a rough
space in the middle of the king's name. From the
appearance of the stone I am satisfied that this gap
existed when the record was inscribed. There is, however, the trace of a peculiar flourish still visible in the
left half of the broken space, which curiously enough
is the very same that is now used by English clerks
to denote a blank space. . . . I consider that it is a
very good illustration of the practice of the old
Indian masons when they met with a flaw in the
stone.

'I read the opening of the inscription as follows :—

'"In the 26th year of the great King Guduphara, in
the Samvat year three and one hundred (repeated in figures)
100 + 3 = 103, in the month of Vaisákh, on the 4th day."

'Its last words: *sapuyaĕ, matu pitu puyaĕ*—"for his
own religious merit, and for the religious merit of his
mother and father"—show that it is only a simple record of the building of a *stupa* or *vihar* by some pious
Buddhist.'

We follow up this clear account of the stone and
its inscription by what Professor Dowson has to say
on the subject (see *Journal of the Royal Asiatic Society*,
New Series, vol. vii., 1875). His first reading appeared
in *Trübner's Record*, June 1871, mentioned above. Of
the six lines he found only the first two legible, containing name of a king and a date, and towards the

end the word *puyae* twice inscribed.   The reading he
gave was the following :—

> 'In the 26, twenty-sixth year of the great King Guna . . .
> pharasa, on the 7, seventh day of the month of Vaisákha.'

He considered the identification of the king's name
doubtful, as three letters were obliterated.   He afterwards saw Cunningham's reading reproduced in the
Journal of the Royal Asiatic Society, August 1873, p. 242.
Cunningham there says the inscription ends with the
words: 'for his own religious merit, and for the religious
merit of his father and mother.'   Professor Dowson
then took up the inscription again, and his new reading
of the first line was :—

> 'In the 26th year of the great King Gunu . . . phara
> (Gondophares).'

Second line :—

> 'In (the year) one hundred of the Samvat on the day
> of the month Vaisákha.'

He declares himself doubtful about the first part of
the second line.

The reader will observe, comparing the Professor's
second reading with that given by the General, that
the differences are (1) the first portion of the king's
name is read 'Gunu' by Dowson and 'Gudu' by
Cunningham ; then (2) the Samvat year is read 100 by
Dowson and 100+3 by Cunningham ; (3) in the month
Dowson omits the date given by Cunningham.   These
differences, even if they can be sustained, do not vary
the substance of the record.

The General on his return to England took up
the inscription once more, and gives his matured
opinion (*Coins of the Indo-Scythians*, pp. 16–17) : 'An

inscription of *Gadaphara* or Gondophares, found at Takht-i-Bahi, to the north-east of Peshawur, is dated in the 26th year of his reign. There is also a date of Samvat 103, as I read it. The numeral for 100 is certain, and as this is followed by three upright strokes, the whole date would appear to be 103. The era, however, is quite unknown. If referred to the Vikramâditya Samvat it would be 103−57=46 A.D. This date would place the beginning of the reign of Gondophares in 46−25=21 A.D., and as his coins are very numerous, he must have had a long reign, perhaps thirty or forty years, or down to A.D. 50 or 60. The reading of the name Gadaphara in the Takht-i-Bahi inscription is thought to be doubtful by those who have not seen the stone. I have examined the inscription many times, and I reassert that the reading of the name is most certainly *Gadaphara*, the separation in the middle of the name being simply due to an original fault in the stone. I may note here that there are many similar faults in the great Kâlsi inscription of Asoka.'

M. Senart, member of the Institut de France (*Journal Asiatique*, Huitième série, tom. xv., Fév.-Mars, tom. i., 1890) is the last scholar who has written fully on the Takht-i-Bahi inscription, *Notes d'Épigraphie Indienne*, accompanied by a print of an impression taken from the inscription. He gives his reading at p. 119, fully supported by detailed remarks given in the text. The following is the reading he offers :—

'L'an 26 du grand roi Gudupharas, 103 du comput continu, le cinquième jour de mois Vaiçakha . . . en l'honneur de . . . en l'honneur de ses père et mère.'

'The 26th year of the great King Gudupharas, the one hundred and third of the continuing (running) era, the fifth day of the month of Vaisâkh . . . in honour of . . . in honour of his father and mother.' The reader

will not fail to observe that the reading in substance
gives the same result as that proposed by Cunningham
in 1875, with the correction that a 'continuing era' is
quoted, and the date of the month is read 'fifth' instead
of fourth. In his reading of the era date M. Senart
agrees with Cunningham in opposition to Professor
Dowson ; he adds (pp. 115–117): La lecture des
caractères suivants ne laisse aucun doute sur l'interpré-
tation de la date; c'est bien l'année 103 comme l'avait
admis le general Cunningham. Un second example
du chiffre 100 est déjà connu par l'épigraphe de
Pandjtar (*Archæological Survey*, iii., Pl. XVI., Fig. 4);
see Fleet, *Corpus Inscript. Ind.*, iii.

The last remark is aimed at a theory put forward
by Mr. Vincent A. Smith that in writing the figures of
an Indian era the numerals of hundreds and thousands
were omitted. Since then Mr. Vincent Smith in a
recent paper, 1893 (*ut supr.*), has expressly excluded the
Takht-i-Bahi inscription from the number of those
which he reckons as belonging to the Laukika era, to
which he restricts at present the theory he had put
forward. We reproduce his latest opinion on this
inscription, p. 40 : 'One of the most famous of these
rare Karoṣṭhī inscriptions is that from Takht-i-Bahi (or
Bahaï), north-east of Peshawar, which was published
by Cunningham in an incorrect form, and has been
revised by M. Senart. The record, although too imperfect to admit of continuous translation, is certainly
a Buddhist votive inscription record in the 26th year
of the Maharaya Guduphara on the 5th day of the
month Vesākha of the year 103 of an unspecified era.
It is impossible to doubt that the Maharaya Guduphara
mentioned in this record is the well-known King
Gondophares, whose coins are abundant in the Pañjâb
and Eastern Afghanistan. [The intermediate passage has
been given above.] If, on this evidence, the conclusion

be accepted that the accession of Gondophares must be placed somewhere about A.D. 25, it follows that the unnamed era of an inscription, dated in the year 103 of that era and in his 26th regnal year, must run from about the middle of the first century B.C. The only known era, starting from that point, is the Mālva or Vikrama era of B.C. 57, and in order to avoid the assumption of the existence of another unknown era with approximately the same starting-point, we are justified in provisionally treating the Takht-i-Bahaī inscription as being dated in that era. This theory is, as Mr. Rapson has observed, "supported by every recent discovery" (*Journal of the Royal Asiatic Society* for 1900, p. 389).

'On this assumption, the date of the Takht-i-Bahaī inscription is 103 − 57 = A.D. 46, the 26th year of the reign of King Gondophares. His accession therefore occurred twenty-five years earlier, or in A.D. 21. This date, which is certainly close to the truth, is a most valuable resting-place in the troubled sea of Indian chronology.'

In the light, then, of the present-day advance in Indian archæological research, the Vikrama era, which began in B.C. 58, February or March, the first year ending in B.C. 57, is, we may now say, almost unanimously accepted to be the era of the Takht-i-Bahi record, though at one time there had been some doubt. Since Indian chronology only reckons completed years, the beginning of Gondophares' reign falls in A.D. 21 and that of the inscription is A.D. 46. If the reign of Gondophares be extended to forty years—no exceptional reckoning for that period—it would bring us down to A.D. 60. From what has been shown above, the numismatic tokens on the Gondophares coins demand approximately a similar date—the middle, or a little after, of the

first century; the date fits in mutually with the proba-
bilities of the case and the possibility that the Apostle
Saint Thomas may have come in contact with the king
then reigning.

But did they meet ?

To suggest an answer to such a question the reader
should first bear in mind that, until the coins were
found, no historical or other indication was known to
exist that there had ever been a king bearing the name
of Gondophares, or that he had reigned over any part of
India, except and only in the Acts of Thomas.   Whether
that statement was true or false, nothing could fairly be
said for or against it, though—as has often happened in
similar cases—it had been put down to legendary fiction.
Now, when suddenly, about the middle of the last century,
that name is deciphered on coins found in India and the
borderland, and when this is further supported by the
discovery of an Indian inscription bearing the name in
ancient Gandhāra, it is impossible to resist the conclusion
that the writer of the Acts must have had information
based on contemporary history.   For at no later date
could a forger or legendary writer have known the
name.   It is impossible to suppose that a later writer,
drawing on his imagination for facts, persons, localities,
and incidents, could have brought about the coincidence
of two personages, one of whom was unknown to living
history, fitting the circumstances of place, persons, duty,
and time, so aptly as occurs in this case.   On this ground
we maintain there is every reason to conclude that the
Apostle Thomas had entered King Gondophares' dominions in the course of his apostolic career.

The credit of first[1] drawing the attention of scholars

[1] Not conscious of this earlier discovery by the French savant
of the connection between the newly-discovered coins of the king and
the record of the Acts, Cunningham thought himself justified in supposing that he 'was the first to draw attention in 1854' (his *Coins of
the Indo-Scythians*, p. 16) to that connection,

to the connection between the coins of Gondophares and the Acts of Thomas is due to M. Reinaud, who put it forward in 1848, in his *Mémoire Géographique Historique et Scientifique sur l'Inde* (*Mémoire de l'Institut National de France*, tom. xviii., ii. partie—tirage à part, 1849, p. 94 f.). He therein says that 'of the number of Indo-Scythian kings who reigned in the valley of the Indus shortly after Kanerkes, coins recently discovered offer the name of a prince called Gondophares. Specimen coins of this series are to be seen at Paris in the Bibliothèque Nationale. A tradition, according to the first centuries of the Christian era, asserts that the Apostle Thomas went to preach the Gospel in India, and that he suffered martyrdom on the Coromandel coast. Now the Acts of Thomas, which have come down to us both in Greek and Latin, mention the name of a king of the interior of the peninsula called Gondaphorus, Γονδαφορος. . . . But the name of Gondophorus is only to be found in a certain class of coins ; and the Acts of Thomas are the sole written document which reproduces it. Are we then not authorised to believe that here we are really dealing with the Apostle Thomas, and with an Indo-Scythian prince, his contemporary ? '

B

CHAPTER II

THOMAS, THE APOSTLE OF INDIA

I.—THE WITNESS OF ST. EPHRAEM AND OTHERS

OWING to the frequent wars waged between the Roman Empire and the powers ruling east of the Euphrates, whether Parthian or Persian, from some time before the dawn of Christianity to even after the fifth century and later, communication between Europe, Western Asia, and the countries beyond the Euphrates was generally cut off for long periods, and, when open, was of the most fitful character. In ecclesiastical history we find a singular fact which illustrates the truth of this statement. In the year A.D. 139 Achadabues and Kam-Jesu, *alias* Job-Jesu, were, at the dying request of Jacob, the Bishop of Seleucia-Ctesiphon, sent to Antioch in order that one of the two might be chosen and appointed his successor (Barhebraeus, *Chronicon Ecclesiasticum*, Abbeloos and Lamy's edition, 3 vols., Lovanii, 1872–77, vol. iii., col. 24; and Assemani, *Bibliotheca Orientalis*, in 4 vols. fol., Romae, 1719–28, vol. ii. p. 396, and vol. iv. p. 41), for the ecclesiastical usage then prevailing required that the person elected to the see should receive consecration at the hands of the Bishop of Antioch. On their arrival at Antioch, the two candidates were denounced as Persian spies to the authorities. Both were seized, but Achadabues escaped to Jerusalem, while his companion, Kam-Jesu, and his host were executed as spies by the prefect or governor of the city. This sad event naturally led to a change

of the ecclesiastical rule in the case of the see of
Seleucia-Ctesiphon.

The occurrence shows how political difficulties
hindered and made it impossible to keep up any intercourse between the churches within the Roman Empire
and those under barbarian sway beyond the border in
the Far East. It is owing to this, no doubt, that so
little of regular history has been handed down to us
through the ordinary channels of Western Church
records regarding the preaching of the Apostles, the
doings of their disciples in the sub-apostolic age, and
the foundation of churches outside the Empire, especially
in the Far East. On the other hand, regarding such
apostles and their disciples as worked within the
boundaries of the Roman Empire—even apart from
what the canonical books mention — a good deal of
general history and some circumstantial details have
found their way down to us ; though on looking closely
into the subject, it will be noticed the limits of even
such information do not extend beyond the basin and
the shores of the Mediterranean.

If, then, any morsels of information regarding the
apostolic and sub-apostolic age have escaped the general
havoc wrought by the Mahomedan and Mongholian
hordes in the East, we can only hope to recover them
by careful search among the Syriac records still existing
in the far eastern churches and monasteries. Guided
by this conviction we have for years devoted our efforts
towards recovering from Syrian sources whatever may
cast a gleam of light upon the Indian Apostolate of
Saint Thomas. Though it has involved long and patient
research to follow up every clue and to collect
together every scrap of information recovered from
the treasure-house of the East, and to re-set it in its
proper place, we now feel ourselves in a position to
place before the reader results which we believe to be

well worthy of serious attention. These results, we think, will throw new light on a subject which—owing largely to contentious discussions—appears to have become more and more involved in doubt. In this we may well see a just retribution of Providence. The Apostle who had stood in the full light of the public life and miracles of our Lord was nevertheless capable of doubt when His resurrection was announced; so also the field of the same Apostle's labours has been shrouded with unnecessary doubt. It will be an ample satisfaction if we can remove all reasonable doubt as to the main facts.

The earliest author of the Eastern Church, whose recovered writings serve to remove it, is the Deacon Saint Ephraem, the Great Doctor of the Syrian Church. He was a native of the city of Nisibis, and had lived there up to A.D. 363, when the surrender of that town by the Emperor Jovian to Sapor, the King of Persia, took place after the death of his predecessor, Julian the Apostate, and the partial defeat of the army under the same. The Saint then retired to Edessa, which had become the frontier town of the Empire (see Ammianus Marcellinus, *History*, Bohn's ed., 1862, bk. xxv. chap. viii. p. 397). As the Relics of the Apostle Thomas had been treasured in that city from an early period, and as Ephraem had lived there for fully ten years till his death, which occurred in the summer of 373, it certainly seemed strange that in the numerous published works of so prolific a writer—in those which fill six folio volumes of the Roman edition by Assemani, and in minor works subsequently published—no direct evidence could be found regarding the Indian labours of the Apostle, so specially venerated in the very city in which Ephraem resided, the city which, largely owing to his influence, became the general centre of Syrian literature. It was not until past the middle of the nineteenth century that such evidence was forth-coming.

The first writing of Ephraem which threw clear light on this subject appeared in 1866. It is No. 42 of his *Carmina Nisibena*, so styled by the editor Bickell, because they refer chiefly to the city of Nisibis. The hymn in question consists of ten strophes, and is composed in form not unlike that of Greek and Latin odes, with a 'refrain' to be sung after each strophe. Ephraem composed most of his hymns that they should be sung at the public services of the Church. Bickell (*S. Ephraemi Syri, Carmina Nisibena,* Lipsiae, 1866, Introduction, p. 33) remarks : ' These refrains which always contain a prayer, or a doxology, were undoubtedly sung by the people in chorus, while the hymn was sung as a solo by a cleric.' This style of singing took its origin in the Syrian Church, and Ephraem composed his hymns in order to prevent the people continuing any longer to sing those tainted with Gnostic errors composed by Bardaisan and his son Harmonius.[1]

---

[1] The history of the origin of the singing of St. Ephraem's hymns is as follows. The saint had noticed that the people were in the habit of singing the hymns composed by Harmonius, the son of Bardaisan, and he feared that, attracted by the melody, they would gradually imbibe the errors of father and son. He therefore set himself to master the art of poetical composition in his mother tongue, and in the rhythm of Harmonius. Eventually he became so great an adept in the art, that the bulk of his numerous writings are actually in metre. In the composition of the *Madrāshās*, or hymns, St. Ephraem adapted his to suit the tunes already in popular use—juxta numeros Harmonii alios composuit libros (odas) ; cujusmodi sunt ea quae in Hymnis et Encomiis Sanctorum virorum ab illo sunt elaborata—Ex eo tempore Syri juxta numeros canticorum Harmonii scripta Ephraem psallere solent (Sozomen, *Hist. Eccl.,* lib. iii. cap. xvi.).

Theodoret, after saying that Ephraem successfully refuted the writings of heretics, adds (*Hist. Eccl.,* lib. iv. cap. xxix.) : ' Et quoniam Harmonius Bardesanis filius cantica quaedam olim composuerat, et modorum suavitate impietatem admiscens, auditorum animos demul-

The collection of hymns edited by Bickell is from British Museum Add. MS 14572. The MS consists of 117 folios, and is assigned by Bickell to the sixth century; some folios of the text have been lost, but the deficiency is supplied from Add. MS 17141 (of which more will be said further on), and from MS 1457.

We give a translation of the first three strophes of Hymn 42 ; the remaining strophes have no direct bearing on our subject. We may remark here that in our English rendering of this hymn and of others that follow we have endeavoured to retain the divisions of the original as far as has been possible ; this, however, was found impracticable in the first and fourth hymn quoted :—

I

'(Thus) howled the devil: into what land shall I fly from the just?

'I stirred up Death the Apostles to slay, that by their death I might escape their blows.

'But harder still am I now stricken: the Apostle I slew in India has overtaken me in Edessa; here and there he is all himself.

'There went I, and there was he : here and there to my grief I find him.

---

cebat et ad exitum pertrahebat; ipse modorum compositione ab illo mutuatus pietatem canticis permiscuit et suavissimum simul ac utilissimum medicamentum audientibus exhibuit. Atque haec cantica festos martyrum dies laetiores ac splendidiores etiamnum efficiunt. St. Jerome subjoins (*De viris illustr.*, cap. 115): 'Ad tantam venit claritudinem ut post lectionem Scripturarum, publice in quibusdam ecclesiis ejus [Ephraemi] scripta recitentur.' See also Assemani, *Bibl. Or.*, i. pp. 47-48. For further proof that St. Ephraem taught the singing of hymns in the churches, see Lamy, *S. Ephr., Hymni et Sermon.*, iv., praef., p. xx. See also Rubens Duval's *La Littérature Syriaque*, Paris, 1900, pp. 18-21 of 2nd ed.

II

'The merchant brought the bones:[1] nay, rather! they brought him. Lo, the mutual gain!

'What profit were they to me, while theirs was the mutual gain? Both brought me loss.

'Who will show me the casket of Iscariot, whence courage I derived?

'But the casket of Thomas is slaying me, for a hidden power there residing, tortures me.

---

[1] That the removal of the Relics of Thomas from India to Edessa was effected by a merchant is asserted not only in this hymn but also repeatedly in the quotations that follow. St. Ephraem does not give us the name of the merchant, but it is found in the Chaldean Martyrology, preserved by the Nestorians. The Rev. A. J. Maclean in the last chapter of his book, *The Catholicos of the East and his People* (London, 1892), treating of the 'Kalendar, Fasts and Festivals, Sundays' of the 'Eastern Syrian Christians (known also as Nestorians),' gives at pp. 346–352 the contents of the 'East Syrian Kalendar.' We reproduce from the feasts of saints (p. 350) the first section of the Kalendar to enable the reader the better to judge of the antiquity and authority of the same :—

OLD STYLE

January 1.—Mar Shalita (obsolete ; see September 19).

January 24.—St. George's companions, martyrs (obsolete).

March.—First Wednesday. St. George, martyr.

April 15.—Mar Shimun Barseba'i, Catholicos (obsolete).

April 24.—St. George, martyr. A great festival.

April 27.—St. Christopher, martyr, and St. George (obsolete).

May.—First Tuesday. Sons of Shmuni (2 Macc. vii.). Universally observed.

May 15.—St. Mary.

July 3.—St. Thomas, who 'was pierced with a lance in India. His body is at Urhai (Edessa), having been brought there by the merchant Khabin.' A great festival.

July 15.—St. Cyriac ('Mar Quriaqus, whom Halinus killed in Persia, and Diuliti, his mother.') Ruinart in his 'Acta Martyrum Sincera' (p. 477) says that Cirycus and Julitta died at Tarsus about 305 A.D. The Greeks keep their festival on this day, but the Latins on June 16.

July 29.—St. Peter and St. Paul (obsolete).

The reader will understand that the remarks between brackets are those of the editor, and the dates in italics represent the Syriac dates

III

'With profit Moses, the elect, in faith transported bones.[1]

'If then so great a Prophet held that help from bones could be obtained, rightly did the merchant believe the same, and rightly a merchant he styled himself.

'The merchant has made a profit, has become great and rules.

' His treasury has greatly impoverished me, for to Edessa it is open, and the great city by his aid is enriched.'

The second quotation we give is, like the preceding, from a *Madrâshâ*, or Hymn of St. Ephraem.   It is

of the MS., while those bearing the sign of quotation, as at July 3 and 15, are verbatim quotations of the MS.   In the extract given above three festivals bear the note 'a great festival'—(1) that of Thomas the Apostle, (2) that of St. George, and (3) that of St. Cyriac. SS. George and Cyriac are both greatly venerated among Syrians, and their names are very commonly borne by the Christians.   The extract, we venture to think, will of itself disclose the fact, that these festivals are those of primitive martyrs venerated in the East, for only such were entered in the earliest Church Calendars.   The MS used by Mr. Maclean is dated A.D. 1443, 14th May, but it is obviously a copy of an ancient Kalendar.

Mention is also made of the removal of the Apostle's Relics from India to Edessa by Solomo (Solomon), bishop of Bassorah *c.* 1222 (*The Book of the Bee*, edited with English translation by E. A. Wallis Budge, Clarendon Press, 1886, being part ii. vol. i. of Semitic Series of 'Anecdota Oxoniensia').   He writes (chap. 48, p. 105) : 'Thomas . . . because he baptised the daughter of the King of the Indians, he (the king) stabbed him with a spear and he died.   Hâbban, the merchant, brought his body and laid it in Edessa.'   This is the name of Gondophares' messenger, who is said in the Acts of Thomas to have taken him to India, and likely enough wrongly introduced in place of Khabin.   In such matters the reading given by a Martyrology must carry greater weight ; besides, the similarity in sound may have induced a transcriber to make the substitution.

[1] Regarding the removal of the bones of Joseph (see Gen. l. 24, 25 ; Exod. xiii. 19 ; Josh. xxiv. 32, referred to in Acts vii. 16), the authority of Moses is brought forward in support of the practice of the Church in venerating the remains of God's martyrs and saints, and the words of St. Ephraem disclose the early practice and belief of the Syrian Church.

published by the learned Syriac scholar, Monsignor Lamy, of the University of Louvain, in his *S. Ephraemi Syri Hymni et Sermones*, four volumes in quarto. He devoted to his researches for the material and to the editing of the last volume, from which the further quotations are taken, ten years of labour (vol. iv., Mechliniae, 1902, col. 694 *seq.*). The hymn we are now going to quote is taken from British Museum Add. MS 17141, folio 85; Wright (*Catalogue of Syriac MSS in the British Museum*, pp. 359–363) assigns the MS to the eighth or ninth century: it contains a large collection of hymns ascribed to Ephraem, Isaac of Antioch, and Jacob of Batnae (Sarug).

The *Breviary according to the Rite of the Church of Antioch of the Syrians*, seven quarto volumes, published 1886–1896 at Mosul, at the press of the Dominican Fathers, also contains strophes 1–2, 6–7, 10 of this hymn in vol. vi. p. 631. This *Breviary*, compiled from ancient codices, was edited chiefly by a learned Eastern scholar, the late Clement David, Archbishop of Damascus, a student of the Propaganda College. After his death the work, the materials for which he had prepared, was carried through the press by his collaborators. These volumes contain a large collection of hymns and liturgical prayers of great value, and, as Monsignor Lamy remarks, they offer a better text than even the old Nitrian codices of the British Museum. We take this early opportunity to express our deep and sincere acknowledgments for his kindness in sending us advance sheets of the fourth volume above mentioned, containing the hymns we are going to quote from; we also wish to thank him for much additional help given without stint whenever applied to.

The hymn now in question contains seventeen

strophes or stanzas; we offer an English version of the
last seven :—

ON THOMAS THE APOSTLE

.   .   .   .

XI

'Blessed art thou, Thomas, the Twin, in thy deeds! twin is
thy spiritual power; nor one thy power, nor one thy name:.
'But many and signal are they; renowned is thy name among
the Apostles.
'From my lowly state thee I haste to sing.

XII

'Blessed art thou, O Light, like the lamp, the sun amidst
darkness hath placed; the earth darkened with sacrifices' fumes
to illuminate.
'A land of people dark fell to thy lot that these in white
robes thou shouldest clothe and cleanse by baptism: a tainted
land Thomas has purified.

XIII

'Blessed art thou, like unto the solar ray from the great orb;
thy grateful dawn India's painful darkness doth dispel.
'Thou the great lamp, one among the Twelve, with oil from
the Cross replenished, India's dark night floodest with light.

XIV

'Blessed art thou whom the Great King hath sent, that India
to his One-Begotten thou shouldest espouse; above snow and
linen white, thou the dark bride didst make fair.
'Blessed art thou, who the unkempt hast adorned, that having
become beautiful and radiant, to her Spouse she might advance.

XV

'Blessed art thou, who hast faith in the bride, whom from
heathenism, from demons' errors, and from enslavement to sacrifices thou didst rescue.
'Her with saving bath thou cleansest, the sunburnt thou hast
made fair, the Cross of Light her darkened shades effacing.

XVI

'Blessed art thou, O merchant, a treasure who broughtest where so greatly it was needed; thou the wise man, who to secure the great pearl, of thy riches all else thou givest;
'The finder it enriches and ennobles: indeed thou art the merchant who the world endowest!

XVII

'Blessed art thou, O Thrice-Blessed City! that hast acquired this pearl, none greater doth India yield;
'Blessed art thou, worthy to possess the priceless gem! Praise to thee, O Gracious Son, Who thus Thy adorers dost enrich!'

The third quotation we offer is from another hymn given in the same *Breviary*, vol. vi. p. 635, and is taken from col. 704 of Monsignor Lamy's fourth volume. The hymn consists of eight stanzas; we omit two :—

ON THOMAS THE APOSTLE

I

'Thomas, whence thy lineage,
That so illustrious thou shouldst become?
A merchant thy bones conveys;
A Pontiff assigns thee a feast; [1]
A King a shrine erects. [2]

---

[1] This is a reference to the institution of the annual festival at the church of Edessa in honour of the Apostle: from Edessa the celebration of this festival spread over the whole Christian world. The feast kept by the Syrian churches is not the festival of the martyrdom, but that of the translation of his Relics to Edessa, and this feast is kept on the 3rd of July, the same day as in former times, as is shown by the Nestorian Calendar quoted above, and by others that will follow. It cannot be supposed that this festival is the commemoration of the translation of the Relics under Bishop Cyrus, when they were, as will be shown later, removed from the old church, in which they had previously reposed, to the great new church erected in honour of St. Thomas. The *Chronicon Edessenum* assigns the translation to A.D. 394, and gives the day of the month as the 22nd of August. So the feast of the 'Translation,' kept on the 3rd of July by the Syrian churches, must refer to the first arrival, or the 'Deposition' of the Apostle's Bones in that city.

[2] This possibly refers to the concluding statement in the Acts

II

The bones the merchant hath brought,
Over them an outward watch he kept,
They from within guard over him keep.
Since on divers trades he embarked
Nothing so priceless did he acquire.

III

In his several journeys to India,
And thence on his returns,
All riches, which there he found,
Dirt in his eyes he did repute
When to thy [sacred] bones compared.

.   .   .   .

VI

Neither promised nor hoped for,
One thing more did he [the creator] give.
Lo, in India thy wonders,[1]
In our land thy triumph,
Everywhere thy festival.

---

of Thomas. King Mazdai (Misdeus) is there stated to have opened the grave of the Apostle, and not finding his bones, took some of the dust and applied it to his son, and thus delivered him from the devil's possession. After this the king may perhaps have become a Christian, and have joined the brethren under Sifur. If so, he would probably be the founder of the first church built over the original tomb of the Apostle at the town now known as Mylapore. It is to some such tradition that Ephraem appears to refer.

[1] From this it would appear that in Ephraem's time merchants who had visited the Indian shrine brought back reports of miracles wrought there, and of favours obtained : this is also implied in the Nisibine hymn quoted above. Thus also Marco Polo and others bear witness to similar occurrences at a later period, as will be seen in a subsequent chapter. Ephraem moreover expressly affirms that the inhabitants of Edessa were aware of miracles and favours granted in their city, and that the fame of St. Thomas had spread far and wide.

VII

Wonders during life thou performest,
These, after death, thou still continuest :
Under great bodily fatigue
In one region only didst thou heal.
Now, everywhere, without labour thou dost cure.

VIII

As thou wast taught [by the Lord],
With the sign of the Cross and oil thou didst heal ;
But now, without speech, demons thou expellest ;
Without speech human ills thou curest ;
Without prayer the dead do arise.'

Our fourth quotation from St. Ephraem comes also from the *Breviary,* vol. vi. p. 638. In Monsignor Lamy's fourth volume it will be found at col. 706. It consists of six strophes ; we quote only three :—

On Thomas the Apostle

I

'The One-Begotten his Apostles chose,
Among them Thomas, whom he sent
To baptize peoples perverse, in darkness steeped.
A dark night then India's land enveloped,
Like the sun's ray Thomas did dart forth ;
There he dawned, and her illumined.

II

What dweller on earth was ever seen,
But Thomas, the Lord's Apostle,
On earth designing and a dwelling in Heaven erecting ? [1]
Or on earth who so wise was found
Here of his genius essaying
What in Heaven a crowning secures ?

.   .   .   .

[1] Ephraem refers to a vision related in the Acts of Thomas. It was the vision of a beautiful building in heaven which the Apostle

V

The client of Thomas needs not men his praises to sing :
Great is the crowd of his martyred followers.

had erected by his preachings and good works in India. See Wright's
translation of the Syriac Acts, p. 162 ; and pp. 141-142 of Max
Bonnet's *Acta*. In the Acts the building to be erected is called a
palace, while Ephraem speaks of a dwelling ; the reader will keep in
mind that while Thomas saw a palace in heaven in a dream, he was
asked by the king to build him a mansion for his dwelling.

It is hardly probable that stone houses existed in Southern India
in those days. There seem, however, to have been stone temples,
and possibly there may have been some of these even in Malabar.
Buildings of burnt brick are of comparatively recent date. Prior
to the arrival of the Portuguese on the Malabar coast the houses
of a superior class were built of teak-wood, and used to last
upwards of 400 years when kept well tarred on the outside, in
spite of the very heavy annual rainfall (120 inches) in that part
of India. In support of our statement we may quote two authorities—Jarric (*Indicarum Rerum*, tom. iii. lib. ii. cap. v. pp. 50-51)
gives part of a letter by James Fenicio, a Jesuit missionary in
the Zamorin's territory. This letter is our earliest authority ;
as quoted above it has no date, but evidently belongs to the
period between 1600 and 1607. The missionary had obtained permission to erect four churches in the Zamorin's territory : ' I devoted
all the remaining available time to the erection of these churches,
and to the Christian inhabitants of this village [Palur]. I used to give
them instructions as I chanced to meet them. As the church of
Palur dedicated to Saint Cyriac [*Syr*. Quriaqus], which was the oldest
(*primus*) among all the churches in Malabar, and renowned for
favours and graces obtained, and for this reason much frequented,
I devoted myself more especially to it. The stone church which I
began two years ago [enclosing, apparently, within it the primitive
building] had risen to the height of the windows. At this stage no
one would dare to pull down the old wooden building, fearing to be
struck down by sudden death : it stood surrounded by the walls of
the new erection, but after I had prayed and removed their timidity,
the old structure was pulled down, and the new building stood out in
such fine proportions that the Hindus, the Mahomedans, and the Jews
flocked to see it.' This is one of the *Seven* churches traditionally
assigned to the time when Saint Thomas preached in Malabar. The
wooden structure must undoubtedly have been very old, and constructed no doubt of teak, which formerly grew all over the country,
even in comparatively recent times : at that early age the supply must
have been very plentiful. Our second authority is the Carmelite mis-

Lo, his Bones, his Passion, his Work proclaim ; [1]
His Miracles, him yet alive assert ;
His Deeds the rough Indian convinced.
Who dares doubt the truth of his Relics ? '

The passages given above from the four *Madráshás*
of Ephraem establish certain points as matters of history.
This they do in spite of the limitations imposed by
poetical language.   The points established are the following :—

A.—*By the Nisibine hymn 42.*

(1) Thomas the Apostle suffered martyrdom in India (Strophe
i.).
(2) His body was buried in India (i.).
(3) His bones were thence removed by a merchant to the
city of Edessa (ii.–iii.).
(4) His power and influence were felt in both places (i.–ii.).

B.—*By the first hymn given by Monsignor Lamy.*

(1) Thomas was a lamp placed in darkness to illuminate the
earth filled with the smoke of false sacrifices (xii.).
(2) It was to a land of dark people he was destined, to clothe
them by baptism in white robes, and to purify the
tainted land (xii.).
(3) His grateful dawn dispelled India's painful darkness (xiii.).

---

sionary Paulinus a Sancto Bartholomaeo (often wrongly quoted as
Poli) in his *Viaggio alle Indie Orientali* (Roma, 1796, pt. i. chap. viii.
p. 112 f.) : ' The greater part of the houses in Malabar [this was written
at the close of the xviiith century] are built of teak-wood, which in
weight [and durability excels oak. This wood is imperishable.   I
have seen many houses built 400 years back, which showed no signs
of decay.'

[1] In these words Ephraem brings us practically face to face
with realities.   There is no longer anything vague or general as in
the preceding reference to the ' building ' the Apostle was erecting :
but now we come to the realities of his martyrdom, his preachings,
his conversion of the Indians, his miracles after death.   No wonder,
then, that St. Ephraem exclaims : ' Who dares doubt the truth of
his Relics ? '

(4) He, one of the Twelve, like a great lamp with oil from the Cross replenished, flooded India's dark night with light (XIII.).

(5) It was his mission to espouse India to the One-Begotten : this he did by making the unkempt beautiful and radiant for the Bridegroom's acceptance (XIV.).

(6) He had faith in the Bride, so he rescued her from demons' errors; the sunburnt he made fair with light from the Cross (XV.).

(7) The merchant is blessed for having brought so great a treasure to a place where it was greatly needed (XVI.).

(8) Edessa thus became the blessed city by possessing the GREATEST PEARL India could yield (XVII.).

C.—By the second hymn given by Monsignor Lamy.

(1) Thomas suddenly attains great honour, because his Bones are conveyed from India by a merchant; a Pontiff assigns a Feast in his honour; a King erects a Shrine to his memory (I.–III.).

(2) Thomas works miracles in India and at Edessa; and his festival is kept everywhere (VI.).

(3) During his life, with great bodily fatigue, he did good and healed the sick in one region only, but now without labour he does the same everywhere (VII.).

(4) The traditional apostolic custom, as taught or ordered by the Lord, of healing with blessed oil and the sign of the cross, is mentioned (VIII.).

D.—By the third hymn given by Monsignor Lamy.

(1) Thomas is destined to baptize peoples perverse and steeped in darkness, and that in the land of India (I.).

(2) Thomas, the Lord's Apostle, has the singular power of designing an edifice on earth, and erecting it in heaven (II.).

(3) Thomas' praises are well known : the result of his apostolate is attested by his martyred followers; his work attests his teaching; his miracles proclaim him living in heaven; the rough Indians are converted by the deeds they have witnessed. Who, then, can possibly doubt the truth of his Relics? (V.).

In order to seize the full weight and importance of the above evidence, it is most important for the reader to bear in mind that the facts relating to the Apostle in connection with his evangelisation of India, here set forth, are not attested only by the one individual, Ephraem, but carry with them the assent of a whole Church, that of Edessa.   Ephraem was not putting forward his personal views on the subject, as an ordinary writer would do, but he embodied in these hymns the local tradition and facts which were of common knowledge among the people.   Moreover, as these hymns in great part became incorporated in the Liturgy of the Syrian Church, and were sung in that Church, first at Edessa, they have received the most emphatic support a Christian people can give to facts, the knowledge of which regards them in some special manner.

The ancient Syriac document entitled 'The Doctrine of the Apostles,' edited by Cureton (*Ancient Syriac Documents*, London, 1864), and previously by Cardinal Mai (*Scriptorum Veterum Nova Collectio*, Romae, 1838, Latin translation by A. Assemani, vol. x. pp. 3–8, text pp. 169–175), also by Lagarde (*Reliquiae Juris Eccles. Antiquissimi*, Syriace, Vindobonae, 1856), is akin to Διδασκαλία τῶν ἀποστόλων; there are besides the *Constitutiones Apostolicae* in Latin ; also the *Didascalia*, or ' Apostolic Church Ordinances,' in Coptic, Ethiopic, and Arabic.   These documents incorporate the Διδαχή, or ' The Two Ways,' but cover more extensive ground.   The primal *Didaché*, to distinguish it from others bearing the title, was discovered in a monastic library by the Greek bishop, Philotheus Beryennios, at Constantinople, and published in 1883 ; it may aptly be termed the primitive Manual or Catechism of the Church.

The 'Doctrine of the Apostles' in Syriac, which here concerns us, is earlier than others of this class, the

Greek alone may contend with it for priority. If the
Coptic can be assigned to the third century, the Syriac
may well be dated half a century earlier.[1]

These writings contain a collection of ancient ecclesiastical ordinances which obtained eventually the force of
Church canons. Though the Syriac, Greek, and others
are akin, each has its characteristic traits. The Syriac
heads the compilation of Synodal Canons by Ebed-Jesu
of Soba, *alias* Nisibis, the Nestorian Patriarch, and bears
the title *Epitome Canonum Apostolicorum;* Barhebraeus
includes it in his *Nomocanon* (also printed by Mai, *ut
supr.*, vol. x. pt. ii. p. 31 ff.)

Cureton took his text verbatim from the British
Museum Add. MS 14644, folio 10 ff. He supposes the
Nitrian MS to be the identical one which J. S. Assemani
saw at the monastery at Scete, when he visited
that place in order to obtain MSS for the Vatican
Library. Assemani described the MS as *pervetustus*
(for details see *Bibliotheca Orientalis*, iii. p. 19, note).
As to its date, Cureton writes (p. 147) : ' Its age appears
to be certainly not later than the beginning of the
fifth century.' Dr. Wright in his *Catalogue of Syriac
Manuscripts in the British Museum*, pt. ii. pp. 1083-1084,
describes the same MS (14644) as follows : 'Vellum,

---

[1] The following are some of the recent editions of these documents :—*Syriac—The Didascalia Apostolorum*, edited from a Mesopotamian MS, with Readings and Collations of other MSS, by Margaret
Dunlop Gibson, Cambridge University Press, London, 1903 ; the translation in English by the same lady (*ibid.*), 1903 ; the Syriac text of
the *Teaching of the Twelve Apostles, Journal of Theol. Studies*, vol. iii.
pp. 59-80, with notes—the text is taken from the Mesopotamian MS of
the Syriac Bible recovered from Malabar by Rev. Claud Buchanan, and
left to the Cambridge University. *Ethiopic—Didascalia Æthiopum*
desumptum ex Londinensi, Thomae Pell Platt, 1834, new edition,
London, 1879. *Boharic* text, edited by Tattam ; *Sahidic*, by Lagarde ;
Latin (fragment), by Hauler ; *Arabic*—by Rev. G. Horner, *The Sta-
tutes of the Apostles*, or *Canones Ecclesiastici*, translation and collation
from Ethiopic and Arabic MSS ; also a translation of the Sahidic, &c.,
London, 1904.

about 9⅜ in. by 6, consisting of 94 leaves, many of which are much stained. . . . The quires are 11 in number, but only one or two are complete, leaves being wanted in the beginning, &c. This volume is written in a fine regular Edessene hand of the vth or vith century, with the exception of folios 44 and 45, which are comparatively modern and palimpsest.'[1] For such a document to have attained importance enough to be incorporated in this ancient MS, it might belong to the third or very early fourth century.

We can legitimately use these collections as witnesses to the ancient usages, customs, and belief of the Church which adopted them to her service. It is then, in support of the ancient belief of the Syrian Church, that we quote from Cureton's translation the following passage bearing on the traditional knowledge by that Church of the apostolic labours of Saint Thomas.

At p. 32: 'After the death of the Apostles there were Guides and Rulers in the churches, and whatsoever the Apostles had committed to them, and they had received from them, they taught to the multitudes all the time of their lives. They again at their deaths also committed and delivered to their disciples after them everything which they had received from the Apostles; also what James had written from Jerusalem, and Simon from the city of Rome, and John from Ephesus, and Mark from the great Alexandria, and Andrew from Phrygia, and Luke from Macedonia, and Judas Thomas from India; that the epistles of an Apostle might be received and read in the churches, in every place, like those Triumphs of their Acts which Luke wrote, are read.'

Again at p. 32: 'India and all its own countries,

---

[1] A later British Museum Add. MS 14531, 'written in a good clear Estrangêlo of the viith or viiith century,' says Cureton, also contains the text.

and those bordering on it, even to the farther sea, received the Apostles' Hand of Priesthood from Judas Thomas, who was Guide and Ruler in the church which he built and ministered there.'

The text in Mai's edition of the above passages is identical.

A third passage which we give below, though it does not refer to St. Thomas, will be found useful in illustrating what follows and, moreover, will help the reader to understand better the early traditions of this Church regarding apostolic and sub-apostolic preachings and missions. The passage runs thus (p. 34) :—

'The whole of Persia of the Assyrians and Medes, and of the countries round about Babylon, the Huzites and the Gelae, even to the borders of the Indians, and even to the country of Gog and Magog, and again all the countries from all sides, received the Apostles' Hand of Priesthood from Aggaeus, maker of golden chains, the disciple of Addaeus the Apostle. But the rest of the other fellows of the Apostles went to the distant countries of the Barbarians,' &c.

This is confirmed and expanded by what is mentioned in the life of St. Mares, Bishop of Ctesiphon, in the sub-apostolic age, and a disciple of the above-mentioned Addaeus. The Syriac text of this life, with a translation in Latin, was published by J. B. Abbeloos at Brussels in 1885. We read at p. 85 : 'These were the towns where lived the traders from Huzai (Susiana, see note *in situ*) as they also do now ; there were also traders among the Persians ; and from both countries they would go to the west for trade ; and it was there that they were brought to the worship of God by the blessed Apostle Addaeus. And as these Huzites and Persian converts used to return from the west they used to make numerous conversions in the neighbouring countries ; and from that time dates the origin of the

Church among the Huzites and in Persia. When Mar
Mares reached the country of the Huzites, and found
believers there, and heard of the conversion of the
Persians, his heart was filled with joy to find a small
quantity of wheat in extensive fields of tares. He
preached through that country and converted many.
Then he descended still further (or went still further)
until the perfume (or odour) of Mar Thomas, the
Apostle, was wafted unto him ; and there also he
added great numbers to the fold, and left behind him
a disciple named Job, to minister to them.' The
biographer then makes Mar Mares retrace his steps to
Ctesiphon. On approaching the then outer boundaries
of India the biographer discloses the knowledge that
Mares had come into close proximity to the region
where the Apostle's labours had been fruitful.

We need not give here the testimony of Jacob of
Sarug as to the tradition that the Apostle preached to
the Indians, as Jacob's poem on the palace built by
Thomas is restricted to the events narrated in the
first two acts or chapters of the Acts of Thomas, and
will be found utilised in another section of this book.

Salomo gives the tradition of the Nestorian section
of the Syrian church in his *Book of the Bee*. This work
was edited with an English translation by E. A. Wallis
Budge, Oxford, Clarendon Press, 1886, and forms part
ii. of vol. i., Semitic Series of *Anecdota Oxoniensia*. Mar
Solomon was Metropolitan of Perath-Maishan—that is,
Bassorah (Al-Basrah). Budge says in his preface that
the author is very little known ; he became metropolitan
on the right bank of the united streams about A.D. 1222,
in which year he was present at the consecration of the
Catholicus or Nestorian patriarch Sabr-Ishô (*Hope in
Jesus*). (See Assem. *Bibl. Or.*, tom. ii. p. 453, no. 75 ;
also Barhebraeus, *Chron. Eccl.*, tom. ii. col. 371). A
Latin translation of the book was published by Dr. J. M.

Schoenfelder, at Bamberg, in 1866, based on one MS.
We quote from Budge's translation, p. 105, chap. xlviii. :
'Thomas was from Jerusalem, of the tribe of Juda.   He
taught the Parthians, Medes, and Indians [Oxford MS.,
in India and Sind and Persia]; and because he baptised
the daughter of the King of the Indians, he stabbed him
with a spear and he died.   Habbân, the merchant,
brought his body, and laid it in Edessa, the blessed
city of our Lord.   Others say that he was buried in
Mahlûph, a city in the land of the Indians [the Oxford
MS says he was buried in India].'

II.—THE WITNESS OF THE LITURGICAL BOOKS AND CALENDARS OF THE SYRIAN CHURCH

The extracts from the hymns of St. Ephraem, given
in the preceding pages, some of which are embodied also
in the Breviary above quoted, have already demonstrated
to us what was known and believed by the Edessan
Church, then the head and centre of the Syrian Christians, in regard to the connection of the Apostle Thomas
with India.   Through the kindness of Mgr. Lamy, we
have been favoured with additional extracts from the
same Breviary, which we now place before the reader
(*Breviar.*, tom. iv. pp. 427–484) :—

The feast of Saint Thomas is fixed on the 3rd of July.

FROM THE *Sedra* :—

'O blessed Apostle, valiant Mar Thomas, whom the violent
threats of the King on account of the palace thou didst build for
him in heaven, did not affright.

'Blessed Apostle, be thou praised, O Mar Thomas, thou
whose slavery secured freedom to the Indians and the Kushites
[Ethiopians] blighted by the evil-doer.'

And further on :—

'O Apostle Thomas, athlete of the faith, who preachest the
Gospel and convertest peoples from their errors, and who for the
love of Christ sufferest scourges and wounds and enterest the
abode of joy.'

A prayer ascribed to Jacob of Sarug, in verses of twelve syllables, like his other metrical compositions, contains the following :—

'The Apostle Thomas on leaving for India, parting from the apostles, wept and moved them to tears.

'He asked them to implore the mercy of our Saviour to assist and support him in his preachings.

'Behold, he said, I go now to a darkened (blind) land as architect, pray that I may erect a palace that may rise to the Kingdom above.

'Join me in prayer that my building may not be cast down by the flood.

'O blessed Thomas, whom thy Lord hath sent as a torch to illuminate the land shrouded in the darkness of error.

'O blessed one, thou goest forth as a ray of the sun to dissipate the dark night of India.

'O blessed Thomas, whom the heavenly bridegroom hath sent to unite unto him the dark bride whom thou hast cleansed and made whiter than snow.'

At Matins, after the hymns of Ephraem, given above, a prayer composed by the same saint is given. It is in seven-syllable verse, and contains the following :—

'Blessed be he who solemnises thy commemorative feast, O bright Apostle Mar Thomas.

'Of thee He has made a source of blessings ; a refuge for all who are in pain.

'By thee He has converted the Indians to the true faith and has baptised them in the name of the Trinity.'

Again in the *Sedra* of the morning we read :—

'Kings and judges attend his preaching, are converted, and quit their evil ways, and plunge into the celestial waters of baptism ; from black they become fair. When the sick and the paralysed approach him his word restores them to health ; they come to him void of sight and depart with sight restored. As the sun lights up and gladdens the world, so Thomas the Apostle brightens and gladdens dark India by his numberless blessings. The heavenly hosts and the souls of the just are charmed with admiration when he measures and marks out the earthly palace, while his Lord completes it in heaven. While that celestial beauty expanded itself the king believed and was baptised with the children of his house and the nobles of his court.'

THE CHURCH OF THE JACOBITE SYRIANS

The following quotations from the service-books of this church are taken from Assemani, who gives the traditions of the Syrian churches connected with the Apostle Thomas (*Bibl. Or.*, iv. pp. 30 ff.).

In the Office of the feast of Saint Thomas, kept on the 3rd of July :—

'The Lord sent him to preach the Gospel in the East Indies [*in India Orientali*],' etc.

And also :—

'This Thomas whose memory we celebrate, on being sent to India, was sold as a slave. . . . While he was designing the splendid palace, the Lord was raising it up in heaven.'

Again :—

'Like unto his Master, pierced by a lance, with the honour of the Apostolate, he gained a martyr's crown.'

THE NESTORIAN SECTION OF THE SYRIAN CHURCH

Up to the close of the fourth century the Syrian Church was one, with its literary head-centre at Edessa. Some time after the outbreak of Nestorianism, the extreme eastern section of the Syrian Church, outside the Roman Empire, was captured by the rising sect of Nestorius. Later, Eutychianism, or the Jacobite heresy, as it was subsequently named from Jacob Baradaeus, its ardent upholder, made a second breach in this church. Centuries later, the Maronites broke off from the Jacobites, and returned to the centre of church unity. This divided state explains how the Nestorian section, more than any other church, became and remained closely related by position and intercourse with the centres of Christianity beyond the Euphrates. The continued evidence borne by that church therefore carries much additional weight.

In the Office for the feast of Saint Thomas, kept on the 3rd of July, at Vespers (*Bibl. Or. ut supr.*), we read :—

'The Indians inhaled the odour of life by thy doctrine, O Thomas, and discarding all pagan customs at heart and externally, they commenced to cultivate chastity.'

And lower down :—

'The Lord has deigned to grant Saint Thomas to his faithful church as a treasure found in India. . . . who for the faith was by a lance pierced.'

The following occurs in the Canticle :—

'As Christ had anointed Peter to the High Priesthood of Rome, so thou [O Thomas] to-day among the Indians [hast received the same honour].'

In the Nocturn we read :—

'Thomas took the route to India to demolish the temples of demons, and to extirpate immorality prevailing among men and women.'

We append some further quotations from non-Catholic Syrian calendars, published by Assemani (Bibliotheca Vatican. Codicum Manuscriptorum Catalogus, tom. ii., from a Jacobite calendar, codex xxxvii. p. 250) :—

'(1) Tesri—October, die 6, Coronatio Thomae Apostoli et regis Indiae et Misadi, ejusque filii Johannis—et decem, &c. p. 266.—Tamuz—Julius, die 3, Thomae Apostoli. p. 271.—Elul —September, die 16, S. Thomae Apostoli.

'(2) From another Jacobite Calendar, codex xxxix.: p. 275. —Mensis Tesri prior—October, die 6, Thomae Apostoli.

'(3) From a Syrian Calendar of Saints, codex xxx. pp. 114 ff. —p. 117.—Tisrin prior—October, die 6, Coronatio Thomae Apostoli. p. 131.—Julius 6, S. Thomae,' etc.

These entries will show that the old principal feast of Saint Thomas, kept on the 3rd of July, gradually fell off in importance; this happened, no doubt, after the destruction of Edessa, and the disappearance of the Relics from the city. Things have come to such a pass, that now, even at Edessa, the present Urfa, no particular

feast, in the popular sense, is any longer kept in honour
of the saint. This we learnt lately at Rome from Syrians
who had newly arrived from Urfa. The commingling of
the Syrians and Greeks under the new conditions prevailing under Mahomedan rule, brought about the keeping of the feast on the same day, October the 6th, by both
communities, though, as should be remarked, the old
date yet retains its place in the later calendars. The
Armenians also now keep the feast with the Greeks on
the 6th of October.

III.—THE WITNESS OF THE FATHERS OF THE WESTERN CHURCH

We pass on now to review the testimony given by
the Fathers of the Western Church to the Indian apostolate of Saint Thomas.

St. Gregory of Nazianzus[1] (Homil. xxxiii., *Contra
Arianos et de seipso*, cap. xi., Migne, *P. Gr.-L.*, vol. xxxvi.,
2nd of Gregory Naz. col. 227): 'What ?   Were not the
Apostles strangers [foreigners] amidst the many nations
and countries over which they spread themselves, that the
Gospel might penetrate into all parts, that no place might
be void of the triple light or deprived of that of truth,
so that the cloud of ignorance among them even who sit
in darkness and the shadow of death might be lifted ?
You have heard what Paul says : *to me was committed*

---

[1] Gregory was born A.D. 330, and ordained priest in 361 ; he
was consecrated bishop by his friend St. Basil ; he did not take up
the work of a bishop, but retired into solitude.   In 372, however, his
father, the bishop of Nazianzus, induced him to share his charge ;
his father died soon afterwards, and the death of his mother followed
in 375. Gregory then quitted Nazianzus, and in 379 the people of
Constantinople called him to be their bishop.   In 381 he resigned
his see and returned to Nazianzus.   There he again exercised the
episcopal office till 383, when Eulalius was named bishop. Gregory
died between 389–390. By the Greeks he is emphatically termed the
'Theologian' (Bardenhewer, *Les Pères de l'Eglise*, French transl., in
3 vols., Paris, 1898, ii. pp. 90–105).

the gospel of the uncircumcision, as to Peter was that of the circumcision. Peter indeed may have belonged to Judea ; but what had Paul in common with the gentiles, Luke with Achaia, Andrew with Epirus, John with Ephesus, Thomas with India, Mark with Italy ? Not to speak of each separately, what had the other Apostles in common with the people to whom they were sent ? '

St. Ambrose [1] (*Opera omnia* edidit Paulus Angelus Ballerini, Mediolani, 1876, tom. ii., *Enarratio in Psalm. xlv.* § 21, cols. 389–390), after mentioning the civil wars among the Triumviri, continues : ' *Making wars to cease even to the end of the earth, he shall destroy the bow, and break the weapons, and the shields he shall burn in the fire* (Ps. xlv. 10). And in very deed before the Roman empire became expanded, not only were the kings of each city mutually at war, but the Romans themselves were constantly weakened by civil strifes.   Whence it came to pass that wearied of civil wars the supreme Roman command was offered to Julius Augustus, and so internecine strife was brought to a close.   This, in its way, admitted of the Apostles being sent without

[1] Ambrose, the son of a Pretorian Prefect of Gaul, was born *c* 340, and was chosen bishop of Milan, while acting in his official capacity as Governor of Æmilia and Liguria in maintaining order between the Catholics and Arians then assembled in the church for the election of a bishop. He was then only a catechumen, but was forced to accept the office ; he received baptism on the 30th of November 374, and was consecrated bishop on the 7th of December following. He sold his patrimony, and on assuming episcopal charge distributed the proceeds among the poor. There were two important incidents in his life. The first was the conversion and baptism of Augustine in 387, who was destined to become the great light of the Western Church, and whose conversion was largely due to the prayers of his mother, St. Monica. The other incident occurred in 390, when St. Ambrose forbade the great Theodosius to enter the church, and made him humbly do public penance for the massacre of the people of Thessalonica, which had been ordered by him in revenge for the murder of some imperial officers by the populace, during a tumult. St. Ambrose died on the 4th April 397 (Bardenhewer, *ut supr.*, ii. pp. 317 ff.).

delay, according to the saying of our Lord Jesus : *Going therefore, teach ye all nations* (Matt. xxviii. 19). Even those kingdoms which were shut out by rugged mountains became accessible to them, as India to Thomas, Persia to Matthew. This also (viz., the internal peace) expanded the power of the empire of Rome over the whole world, and appeased dissensions and divisions among the peoples by securing peace, thus enabling the Apostles, at the beginning of the church, to travel over many regions of the earth.'

St. Jerome[1] (Epist. lix. *ad Marcellam*, alias cxlviii. Migne, *P.-L.*, vol. xxii., 1st of Jerome's, cols. 588–589) : 'The last sheet contained the following question, Did our Lord after his resurrection abide with his disciples for forty days and never go elsewhere ? or did he secretly go to heaven and thence descend, at no time denying his presence to the Apostles ?

'If you consider our Lord to be the Son of God, of whom it is said, "Do I not fill the heavens and the

---

[1] Jerome was born at Stridon, a small village on the frontier between Dalmatia and Pannonia, either in 331, or, more probably, in 340 ; he went to Rome at the age of twenty to commence his literary studies ; he received late baptism at the hands of Pope Liberius. From Rome he went to Treves, then renowned for its school of theology; later he was at Aquileia, whence he went to the East, and arrived at Antioch in 373. On the death of an intimate friend he retired into solitude. During this period he studied the Hebrew language. He was ordained priest at Antioch *c.* 378. Called to Constantinople by St. Gregory of Nazianzus, he went there before the close of 379. 'Ecclesiastica necessitas,' as he terms it, made him give up his exegetical studies, and he went to Rome, where he attended the council held on account of the schism of Antioch, and acted as the Pope's secretary. It was during this stay at Rome that he commenced the revision of the old Latin text of the Scriptures, and this formed the turning-point of his life. On the death of Pope Damasus he decided to quit Rome, which he left in August 385 for Antioch ; thence in company with the noble Roman ladies, Paula and Eustochium, he went to Palestine, and settled down the next year at Bethlehem, where he wrote most of his works and letters, till his death in 420 (Bardenhewer, *ut supr.*, ii. pp. 364-394).

earth, saith the Lord"? . . . You certainly need not
doubt that even before the resurrection the true God-
head so dwelt in the Lord's body, as to be in the Father,
as to embrace the expanse of the heavens, and to per-
vade and circumscribe all things, that is, so as to be
within all things, and, without, to contain all things. It
is foolish to limit to one small body the power of him
whom the heavens cannot contain ; and yet he who was
everywhere, was also all entire in the Son of Man. For
the Divine nature and the Word of God cannot be par-
celled out, or divided by place, but, while everywhere,
is all entire everywhere. He was indeed at one and the
same time with the apostles during the forty days, and
with the angels, and in the Father, and in the uttermost
ends of the ocean. He dwelt in all places : with Thomas
in India, with Peter at Rome, with Paul in Illyricum, with
Titus in Crete, with Andrew in Achaia, with each apostolic man in each and all countries.'

St. Gaudentius, bishop of Brescia (died between
410–427). Extract from Sermon xvii., Migne, *P.-L.*,
vol. xx. cols. 962–63. This sermon was delivered on
the occasion of the dedication of a church named
' Basilica Concilii Sanctorum ' — Assembly of the
Saints, at Brescia in 402. For this church the relics of
Saints Thomas, John the Baptist, Andrew and Luke had
been secured—hence the title. ' We possess here the
relics of these four who having preached the kingdom
of God and his righteousness were put to death by un-
believing and perverse men, and now live for ever in
God, as the power of their works discloses. John at
Sebastena, a town of the province of Palestine, Thomas
among the Indians, Andrew and Luke at the city of
Patras are found to have closed their careers (consum-
mati sunt).' [1]

---

[1] A friend once wrote to us : ' All I know at present is that St.
Paulinus had relics of St. Thomas at Nola, and St. Gaudentius at

St. Paulinus of Nola[1] (Migne, *P-L.*, vol. lxi. col. 514) : 'So God, bestowing his holy gifts on all lands, sent his Apostles to the great cities of the world. To the Patrians he sent Andrew, to John the charge at Ephesus he gave of Europe and Asia, their errors to repel with effulgence of light.   Parthia receives Matthew, India Thomas, Libya Thaddaeus and Phrygia Philip.'

St. John Chrysostom.[2] This Doctor of the Greek

Brescia, but I could not find anything to show how they obtained these relics, which they placed in their respective churches.' No doubt many another among the readers of these pages would feel inclined to ask the same question.   An excellent little essay was written for academical honours by Mathias H. Hohlenberg of Copenhagen, entitled, *De originibus et fatis Ecclesiae Christianae in India Orientali, disquisitio historica ad finem saeculi decimi quinti perducta*, Havniae, 1822. The title is rather high-sounding, but his effort to establish that the first evangelisation of India was by the Apostle Thomas, is not only commendable, but on the whole is the best thing yet published on the subject, and we have found it often suggestive. The writer (p. 82), referring to Bolland. *Acta SS.*, die 18 Febr. et 22 Jan., adds that, besides at Nola and Brescia, the relics of Thomas were also deposed in the 'basilica Apostolorum' at Milan.   There are thus three places, all in upper Italy, where relics of this Apostle appear at about the same time.   The mention of the relics of Thomas at Milan will be found also in the *Martyrologium Hieronymianum* [details of this important Martyrology will be given presently] (p. lxxiv. and p. 57, first col., bottom) : *vii. id. Mai, Mediolano, de ingressu reliquiarum Apostolorum Johannis Andreae et Thomae in basilica ad portam Romanam.* If we bear in mind that in the year 394, as mentioned above, the relics of the Apostle Thomas were, at Edessa, removed from the old church to the new magnificent basilica erected in his honour, it will be noticed that an opportunity would then offer itself to extract from the urn or sarcophagus that held them some portion of the relics, and morsels or fragments from these could be obtained by pious pilgrims and conveyed to Italy, where precisely they are found in the cities of Nola, Brescia, and Milan, in the possession of their bishops, Paulinus, Gaudentius, and Ambrose, after 395.

[1] Paulinus was born at Bordeaux in 353; his devotion to St. Felix of Nola led him to that city, to which he was accompanied by his wife, who was now a sister to him; he was made bishop of Nola in 409, and died in 431 (Bardenhewer, *ut supr.*, ii. pp. 344 ff.).

[2] John, the son of a general of the Eastern empire, born at Antioch in 344 (or perhaps as late as 347), was surnamed 'Chry-

Church does not expressly state that Thomas the Apostle preached the faith to the Indians, but as he says they were evangelised by an Apostle and with the gift of tongues, we can see that some one apostle was present in his mind. We may almost legitimately infer that that apostle was Thomas, for such was the evidence of the saint's contemporaries, as we have shown above. The well-known fact that the Relics [the Bones] of the Apostle were then at Edessa, a fact which Chrysostom himself attests elsewhere (*Homily* 26 *on the Epistle to the Hebrews*, Migne, *P. Gr.-L.*, vol. 63, col. 179), and the general knowledge of the Apostle diffused from that city, make the inference most probable (see also his testimony quoted in Chapter IV.). We should remember also that the saint was a younger contemporary of Ephraem.

In the first of the three passages St. John Chrysostom asserts that in the Apostolic age the Indians, in common with the Scythians and others, accepted the mild yoke of the Gospel teaching. In the second passage he speaks of the gift of tongues conferred on the Apostles, and mentions the Apostle of India as one endowed with the gift. In the third passage he mentions that the apostles erected altars everywhere, and among the Scythians, Persians, and Indians. The three passages will be found below.[1]

sostom' or 'Golden-mouthed,' because of his great eloquence. As deacon and as priest he occupied the pulpit at Antioch from 387 to 397, during which time his most famous homilies were preached. He was chosen for the Patriarchal see by the people of Constantinople, and consecrated by Theophilus of Alexandria in 398. After a few years he incurred the displeasure of Eudoxia, and was exiled by the feeble Arcadius, but again soon recalled by the Emperor and Empress, owing to a tumult among the people. Exiled a second time in 404, through intrigues of Theophilus and others, he died 14th September 407 (Bardenhewer, *ut supr.*, ii. pp. 164 ff.).

[1] The following are the passages from his works as they appear in a Latin version (*S. Joan. Chrysost., Opera omnia*, edit. Montfaucon, Parisiis, 1735, tom. i., *Quod Christus sit Deus*, § 6, p. 566) :—

I. *Tunc pascentur simul lupus cum agno.* On this he writes : De

St. Gregory of Tours bears strong and clear testimony to the Apostle's martyrdom and burial in India, as will be seen in the quotation given in our next chapter.

St. Bede the Venerable [born *c.* 673, died 735], *Opera omnia*, Coloniae Agrippinae, 1688, tom. iii., Excerptiones Patrum, Collectanea, &c., col. 485 : 'The Apostles of Christ, who were to be the preachers of the faith and teachers of the nations, received their allotted charges in distinct parts of the world.   Peter receives Rome ; Andrew, Achaia ; James, Spain ; Thomas, India ; John, Asia ; Matthew,' &c.   Further evidence from his Martyrology will be found below.

IV.—THE WITNESS OF THE ANCIENT CALENDARS, SACRAMENTARIES, AND MARTYROLOGIES OF THE LATIN CHURCH

Each Church from ancient times had its own list of feasts, *ferialia*, containing 'dies natalis martyrum,' the anniversaries of the martyrs of that particular church ; and 'depositio episcoporum,' the anniversaries of the demise of its bishops ; besides special feasts.   Two

feris hominibus id dictum est, de Scytis, Thracibus, Mauris, Indis, Sauromatis, Persis. Quod autem omnes illae gentes sub uno jugo futurae essent, alius propheta declaravit his verbis : *Et servient ei sub jugo uno*, &c.

II. (p. 567) : Et quomodo illos omnes, dicit quispiam, attraxerunt Apostoli? Qui nonnisi unam linguam habebant, nempe Judaicam, quomodo Scytam, Indam et Sauromatam docere potuit? Accepto nempe per Spiritum Sanctum linguarum multarum dono.

III. (pp. 574-575). Speaking of the preaching of the Apostles he says : Ubique altaria excitarent, in regione Romanorum, Persarum, Scytharum, Maurorum, Indorum ; quid dico? vel extra orbem nostrum.

IV. (Tom. xii., *Commentar. in Epist. ad Hebr.*, *homilia xxvi.*, § 2, p. 237) : Aaronis autem, Danielis, Jeremiae, et Apostolorum multorum, nescimus ubi sita [ossa] sint. Nam Petri quidem et Pauli et Johannis et Thomae manifesta sunt sepulcra. Aliorum autem cum sint tam multi, nusquam sunt nota.

separate lists were kept, one for the 'depositiones' and
the other for the 'dies natales' and festivals.   The
Roman church had thus a similar *feriale*, which in the
past has been called by different names.   The Roman
feriale, containing the two lists under the headings
'depositiones episcoporum' and 'depositiones martyrum,' was first discovered and published by the Jesuit,
Bucher (De Doctrina Temporum, c. cxv. pp. 266 ff.
Antwerp, 1634), and thus came to be called the *Kalen-
darium Bucherianum*: it was reproduced by Ruinart in
Acta Sincera Martyrum.   It was subsequently found
that this Calendar formed only a part of a larger compilation bearing the name of Furius Dionysius Philocalus, and comprising a variety of elements, such as
an Almanac might contain, and had been prepared for
one Valentinus.

The latest development of the discoveries of this important document is given by the late Professor Theodore
Mommsen in *Monumenta Germaniae historica*, tom. ix.,
ed. in 4°, Berolini, 1891, which contains his second edition of this ancient Roman Calendar.   Mommsen shows
that Philocalus was not the author, but being a celebrated caligraphist of the age he transcribed the compilation, and appended his name to it.   Quoting De
Rossi, Mommsen shows that Philocalus inscribed himself the 'cultor' and 'amator' of Pope Damasus :
*Damasi s[ui] pappæ cultor atque amato[r] Furius Dionysius
Filocalus scribsit.*   Under these circumstances Mommsen
thought it best to style the compilation—*Chronographus
anni CCCLIIII.*

This Calendar, or rather Almanac, is partly civil and
partly ecclesiastical, and a long chronology is attached
to it, which has no doubt undergone very considerable
enlargement since its first appearance.   The civil part
comprises eight sections :—dedication to Valentinus ;
pictures representing principal cities, Rome, Alexandria,

Constantinople, &c.; an imperial dedication, the birth days of the Cæsars—*in his d(omini) n(ostri) Constantii;* figures of the seven planets, &c.; the signs of the Zodiac; representations of the months, &c.; pictures of the two emperors of the day, one seated and crowned, the other standing uncrowned; the complete fasti con- sulares *A. U. C.* 245 to 753; and *post Christum* from annus 1 to 354. Then commences the ecclesiastical part con- taining: (ix) the Paschal cycle from *p. Chr.* 312 to 358, and with some omissions continued to 410; (x) a list is here intercalated of the Prefects of the city; (xi) the 'depositiones' or burials of the bishops of Rome, the last mentioned being Julius who died A.D. 352; (xii) the feriale of the Roman Church 'depositiones marty- rum'; (xiii) a list of the bishops of Rome ending with Liberius elected in 352; (xiv) the divisions or *regiones* of the city of Rome; and lastly (xv), the chronology or *Liber generationis,* &c. Of section (xiii) Mommsen gives a critical text from existing MSS, and supplements defects or omissions from a reconstructed text prepared by Mgr. Duchesne in his *Liber Pontificalis.*

This compilation was first prepared in 336, and was made public with later additions in the year 354. Mgr. Duchesne (Bolland. *Acta SS.,* November, vol. ii., ' Martyrologium Hieronymianum, ediderunt Joh. Bapt. de Rossi et Ludov. Duchesne,' pp. xlviii.–xlix) observes that the list 'depositiones episcoporum' contains the names of only some of the Popes; and the 'de- positiones' or 'dies natales martyrum' also contains only some of the Roman martyrs, while others are omitted. He concludes that what has been given in this compilation is only an excerpt of the Roman feriale now lost.[1]

---

[1] For full particulars regarding this ancient document the reader is referred to the following authors who have ably and fully discussed it in recent years: De Rossi, *Roma Sott.,* tom. i. p. iii; tom. ii. p.

A similar calendar belonging to the Church of Carthage was discovered and published by Mabillon. It was also incorporated by Ruinart in his *Acta* above mentioned. It opens with the following heading : Hic continentur dies natalitiorum Martyrum et depositiones episcoporum quos ecclesiae Cartaginis anniversaria celebrant.[1] This Carthaginian calendar is rather provincial than diocesan, and belongs to the beginning of the sixth century, and is not much later than A.D. 502.

Next in antiquity to the Philocalian is another Roman calendar found attached to the Leonine Sacramentary Codex of Verona, the date of which is *c.* 488. The third calendar in order of date is the Gelasian *c.* 495, so called after Pope Gelasius and found attached to his Sacramentary. The fourth is the Gregorian attached to the Sacramentary of Pope Gregory the Great, *c.* 591.[2] The *Sacramentarium* formed the *Missale* of the ancient church, and the calendar was attached to it, as now to our modern Roman Missal. The same practice pre-

vi ; Mgr. Duchesne in his edition of *Liber Pontificalis*, tom. i. pp. vi. and 10; and Mommsen, *Monumenta Germaniae: Scriptores Antiquissimi*, tom. ix. p. 13, Berolini, in 4to, 1891 ; articles 'Calendar' and 'Martyrology' in the *Dict. of Christ. Antiquit.* Philocalus' Calendar will also be found in Bolland. *Acta SS.*, June, vol. vii. pp. 178–184 ; and Migne, *P.-L.*, vol. xiii., col. 675, where it is printed side by side with the Calendar of Polemeus Silvanus, dated 448, but these two publications contain only the civil portion of the Calendar, and not what is termed the Roman *feriale.*

[1] The ancient custom in this matter is stated by St. Cyprian of Carthage (*Epist.* xxxvi.), when he asks the clergy to make known to him the day on which each confessor suffered : Dies eorum quibus excidunt nuntiate ut commemorationes eorum inter memorias martyrum celebrare possimus. Quamquam Tertullus . . . scripsit et scribat et significet mihi dies quibus in carcere beati fratres nostri ad immortalitatem gloriosae mortis exitu transeunt, et celebrentur hic a nobis oblationes et sacrificia ob commemorationes eorum.

[2] For the three *Sacramentaria* of the Roman Church see Muratori, *Liturgia Romana Vetus*, in 3 vols., published with his *Opere*, Arezzo, 1771 ; or separate in one vol.

vails in the Syrian Church as may be seen from its printed Missals.   Intermediate between the Gelasian and Gregorian calendars comes the *Martyrologium Hieronymianum*, of which more later.

The earliest calendar, the Philocalian or 'Chronographus anni CCCLIIII.,' contains the names of only two Apostles, St. Peter and St. Paul, *III. Kal. Jul. Petri in Catacumbas et Pauli Ostiense*, with the commemoration *de Cathedra Petri* assigned to the 22nd of February ; the feast of the Nativity is given on the 25th December.   It contains a scanty list of Roman martyrs, and also the names of Cyprian and of one or two non-Roman martyrs.

The MS of the Leonine calendar is defective, and the leaves containing three and a half months are missing ; the manuscript now begins with *XVIII. Kal. Maias*, the 14th April.   The feast of our Saint George is found in this calendar on *IX. Kal. Maias*, the 23rd of April.   The existence at Rome, *in Velabro*, of an ancient basilica dedicated to the saint accounts for the inclusion of his name in this ancient calendar, and attests the early diffusion of his festival.   Of the Apostles, besides St. Peter and St. Paul, we have Saint Andrew, Peter's brother, *Prid. Kal. Dec.*, 30th of November, and Saint John, *VI. Kal. Jan.*, 27th of December : the Holy Innocents are also commemorated and two dedications of basilicas, *Angeli in Salarium*, and another which, though marked *Natale sancti Stephani in Coemeterio Callisti Via Appia*, is not the feast of the saint himself, but of the dedication of his basilica, as Muratori (*Litur. Rom. Vetus, ut supr.*, vol. I., col. 70) points out. The missing portion of this calendar would probably not have contained the names of any of the other Apostles, as none of their festivals fall between January and the middle of April.

The Gelasian calendar has *kalendis Maii*—1st May,

Philippi et Jacobi Apostolorum,[1] *Natale Apostolorum Petri et Pauli,* and Saint Andrew on the usual days, and *XII. Kal. Jan. Sancti Thomae Apostoli,* on the 21st December ; it gives also St. John the Evangelist.

The Gregorian calendar, as might be expected, contains more names than any of its predecessors. It gives the following feasts of the Apostles : St. Philip and St. James, St. John *ad Portam Latinam,* St. Peter and St. Paul jointly, as also a separate feast of St. Paul on the day following, St. Andrew and St. John the Evangelist.

These Sacramentaries, even the earlier Leonine, generally give more than one mass for each of the above mentioned Apostles. For the festival of St. Thomas the Gelasian has a special mass (*ut supr.* lib. II., § LXXI.), *In Natali Sancti Thomae Apostoli;* it gives three proper prayers for the same. The first of these is the prayer now named 'Collect,' which in the ancient Sacramentaries bore no name; the second is marked in the text 'Secreta'; and the third 'Post Commun.' or post-communion. The primitive first prayer or collect of this mass remains unchanged in the Roman Missal to this day, but in the Secret a few verbal changes have been introduced, and a new post-communion has replaced that of the Gelasian. There is no proper preface to this Gelasian mass, though several

[1] With reference to a similar double entry of the two Apostles occurring in the *Martyr. Hieron.,* Duchesne makes the following remarks (p. lxxvii) : Jacobus qui hic cum Philippo jungitur . . . neque aliquo vinculo cum Philippo conjunctus est, ut pronum fuerit ambos simul uno festo celebrari. Sed *Jacobi pariterque Philippi* basilicam Romae aedificaverunt pontifices Pelagius I. et Johannes III. circa annum 561 ; hic fuit initium festi communis, ea causa Jacobi post Philippum in Kalendaria inserendi. Quod quidem in hieronomyano factum est, sed non ubique ; nam neque in Indice Apostolorum Philippo Jacobus sociatur neque, &c. For the principal statement he gives a reference in a note to his *Lib. Pontif.,* tom. i. p. 306, No. 2. The inference to be drawn is that the insertion of the double feast is posterior to the issue of this Calendar.

of the other masses have, in addition to the three prayers, also their special preface. These ancient prefaces, like those still retained in the Roman Missal, always contain some special reference to the mystery, or the saint commemorated.

Though the existing text of the Gregorian Sacramentary does not mark the feast of Saint Thomas in the calendar, or contain a mass for the same, there is proof available that it formerly did contain a mass for the feast. In the collection of prefaces at col. 1044 (apud Muratori *ut supr.*), under the heading *Undecimo Kalendas Januarii,* NATALE SANCTI THOMAE APOSTOLI, a preface is given: ‘Vere dignum et justum est,’ &c. The editor remarks in a footnote that the above preface in the Vatican Codex is assigned *in unius Apostoli ad missam.* The date given above for the feast would place it on the 20th December; this must be due to an error of the copyist: the reader will observe that the date is written in words, not in Roman numerals, as in the previous quotations; probably the last character of the Roman numeral XII. was effaced by age, or inadvertently overlooked by the copyist who wrote ‘undecimo Kalendas’ instead of ‘duodecimo Kalendas.’   The calendars show no variation of this date, and it may be taken for certain that 21st December was the accepted date of the Apostle’s martyrdom. In the old ‘Secret’ of the mass in the Gelasian Sacramentary occur the words, ‘Cujus honoranda confessione laudis tibi hostias immolamus,’ &c. These words, retained also in the present Roman Missal, imply that the Apostle suffered martyrdom, and so do the words of the heading, IN NATALI SANCTI THOMAE. In the Martyrologies the words *in Natali* or *Natalis* are only used for martyrs.

The Hieronymian Martyrology is anterior to the Gregorian Sacramentary, and though never used for

Liturgical or ecclesiastical services, is a document of very considerable authority.   Compiled largely from ancient authentic documents existing in the fourth century, the primitive body of the compilation comprised three principal elements, viz.: A Roman calendar fuller than that which has come down to us through Philocalus; the eastern Greek calendar, probably of Antioch, comprising also that of the Church of Nicomedia; and nearly the entire African provincial calendar.   The Greek portion incorporated appears to have been derived from the same source from which the translation in Syriac was done, which has come down to us bearing the date 723 of the Seleucan era (A.D. 411–412), and which is the oldest Syriac dated MS extant.   This calendar, though styled by Dr. Wright, who discovered it in the British Museum, 'an ancient Syrian Martyrology,' is, in its principal part—from 26 Kânân (December), to 24 *Teshri*, November (pp. 423–431), a translation of a Greek calendar, closing, according to Wright's translation, with the words: 'here end the Confessors of the West.'   What follows bears the heading: 'the names of our Lords, the Confessors who were slain in the East'; this second portion, covering pp. 431–432, consists of one and a half pages of octavo in print (see *Journal of Sacred Literature*, London, January, 1866, pp. 423–432, where the translation first appeared).   The *Martyrologium Hieronymianum* (*ut supr.*) gives of the first above part the Syriac text, and in parallel columns offers also translations in Greek and Latin, pp. li.-lxiii., and so attempts to reproduce for the benefit of students the primitive text now lost.   Of the second part it gives the Syriac and a translation only in Greek, pp. lxiii.-lxv.   This Hieronymian Martyrology, as Mgr. Duchesne shows, incorporated also a considerable number of local feasts of the churches of northern Italy, which makes him suspect that the work was compiled in that locality. It first went under various names—of Eusebius of Cæsarea, of Jerome, and of Chromatius and Heliodorus; but is now generally known as the 'Martyrologium Hieronymianum.'

The existence of such a compilation was known to St. Gregory the Great. We have a letter (Ep. viii. 28, *J*. 1517) written by him (between 590–604) in reply to Eulogus, the bishop of Alexandria, who had asked him 'to send a collection of the acts of all the martyrs which had been compiled by Eusebius of Cæsarea.' The Pope replies that he does not know of such a work, and has searched in vain at Rome for such a collection ; but he adds, 'We have the names of nearly all the martyrs marked with their separate passion (martyrdom) for each day, gathered in one volume, and we daily offer the Mass in their honour. But this volume does not specify what each suffered, but gives only the name, place, and day of passion. Whence it comes that many (*multi*) from diverse lands and provinces are known to have been crowned on each day, as I have said. But this we believe your blessedness possesses.'

Prior to this, Cassiodorus (between 540–570) (*De Institutione divinarum litterarum*, c. 32) exhorted his monks to 'read regularly the passions of the martyrs, who flourished all over the world, which you no doubt will find — *inter alia* — in the letter of St. Jerome to Chromatius and Heliodorus, that moved by their holy example you may be led to things heavenly.' The letter here mentioned is that which prefaces this Martyrology, and is in reply to one by the bishops Chromatius and Heliodorus to Jerome. These two letters, which are acknowledged to be fictitious, it would seem were known to the writer as prefacing some codex containing the acts of martyrs which he recommends the monks to read ; and this may have led him to

suppose that other codices similarly contained the
letters and the acts. But the ordinary codices of the
martyrology which are prefaced with these letters contain no acts of martyrs, but answer the description given
by Pope St. Gregory, that is to say, they give the name
of each martyr and the place and date of martyrdom.
It follows that this Martyrologium was in existence in
Italy by the middle of the sixth century. Mgr.
Duchesne shows (*ut supr.* p. xliii.) that it was in France
towards the close of the same century; and he further
infers (p. lxxiv.) from a close analysis of the saints of the
churches of northern Italy found in the text, that
' nulla ratio est distinguendi inter collectorem illum (referred to by Cassiodorus) et martyrologium, quem ipsa
Chromatii et Heliodori cura Italiæ superiori adnectit.'

The existing MSS do not present the primitive form
of this Martyrology. De Rossi concludes, from a comparison with the texts of other martyrologies dependent
on this, that the older recension had entries of superior
value to those now found. In its present form the
martyrology contains a great many erroneous entries,
resulting from the incorporation of marginal notes on
older codices; these have become duplicated by insertion in wrong places and at different dates; names have
been misread; others have been split up and new entries
have thus been formed. These alterations and the non-
survival of primitive documents make it extremely difficult to reconstruct the Martyrology in its primitive form.
De Rossi was hopeful of doing this till disabled by
paralysis, and, if attempted, he has left no trace of his
work. Even his share in preparing the introduction for the publication of the Hieronymian text of the
Martyrology, was but partly completed, and his colla-
borator, Mgr. Duchesne, had to finish the work. The
arduous task of re-constructing the primitive text awaits
the enterprise of a competent scholar.

The edition referred to has been very carefully prepared. The oldest principal texts of the different recensions are given in three parallel columns, with the variants of a large number of subsidiary codices dependent on the Hieronymian Martyrology. The codex princeps occupies the middle column, and though now at Paris, it formerly belonged to the monastery founded about 698 by St. Willibrord, the Apostle of Friesland, at Epternac, in the diocese of Treves, and is therefore known as the *Epternacensis*. As De Rossi remarks, it was 'written by Englishmen for the use of Englishmen.' The Calendar attached to this MS was written for St. Willibrord himself, and holds an entry in his own handwriting : this Calendar is written in an Anglo-Saxon hand, and is not later than 702-706. The Martyrology to which it is now attached was written a little later, but the whole manuscript is probably well within the first quarter of the eighth century. Its text is remarkable for accuracy of entries and purity of readings.

The column to the left is occupied by an excellent codex, now known as *Bernensis;* it formerly belonged to Metz, and was written at the latter end of the eighth century ; the last quaternion is missing, and the text is incomplete from 22 November to 24 December. The remaining column contains what is now known as the codex *Wissemburgensis:* it belongs to the family of codices named after the monastery of Corbie in the diocese of Amiens, and was written late in the eighth century. A fragment is also given, all that now exists, of the codex *Laureshamensis* (of the convent of Lauresheim or Lorch, diocese of Treves); De Rossi terms it an 'insigne fragmentum.' It is important we should take note that, in the opinion of this learned Christian archæologist, it is 'the only existing sample of the fuller Jeromian text' now lost, containing also some historical details taken from the Acts of the Martyrs. This fragment was lost for a time in the Vatican Library till recovered by Mr. Henry Stevenson (see *Martyrol. Hieron., ut supr.*, pp. x.–xi., § 3).

We now proceed to show what the *Martyrologium Hieronymianum* contains regarding the Apostle Saint Thomas.

In the complete manuscripts, on a folio preceding the text of the martyrology proper, there is a list containing the festivals of the Apostles only. In the Epternac codex this list is headed : ' Notitia de locis Apostolorum,' and the entry regarding Saint Thomas is as follows :—

> xii. kl. ian. Nat. S. Thome apostoli in India et translatio corporis ejus in Edessa (V. K. Jul. 2*m.) [it should be v.n., July 3rd, *as the text shows*].
>
> NOTE.—This brief entry exactly sums up all that has to be said : the *Natalis* or martyrdom is kept xii. kl. ian. (21st Decr.), and the feast *translatio corporis ejus in Edessa*, on July 3rd.

In the body of the Martyrology (cod. Epternac) there are two entries :—

> (I.) v. Non. Jul. Translatio Thome apostoli in Edessa (*a*).
> (II.) xii. Kal. Jan. Passio Thomae apostoli in India (*b*).

The above are the readings given *in situ*, but the editors in a summary of the Apostle's festivals (p. lxxvii.) add the following explanatory notes :—

> (*a*) Ita E. [Epternac], cett. [caeteri] : In Edissa Mesopotamiae, transl. corporis S. Th. ap. qui. passus est in India.
> (*b*) Ita E. ; N. [for 3rd col. of print] : In Mesopotamia, civitate Edissa natl. et transl. corporis S. Thomae qui translatus est ab India, cujus passio ibidem celebratur v. non. iul.

The best and most accurate statement of the Apostle's festivals is given, as was to be expected, by the Epternac copy of the Hieronymian Martyrology :

thus on the 3rd of July—v. non. Jul. 'the translation
of Thomas the Apostle in Edessa,' and on the 21st of
December—xii. Kal. Jan. 'the Martyrdom (*passio*) of
Thomas the Apostle in India.' These entries represent
the real facts as to the two celebrations kept by the
Church in memory of the apostle. It should also be
noted as regards note (*b*) that N. (the third codex and
other readings of codices given there) distinctly says
that the feast was celebrated in India on the 3rd of July :
we shall recur to this later.

Besides the two entries (I.) and (II.) which we have
extracted from the Martyrology (pp. lxxvi.–lxxvii), there
are two others (*in corpore*) :—

(III.) v. Kal. Jan. In Edessa Translatio corporis S. Thomae
apostoli (*c*).

(IV.) iii. Non. Jun. Natalis S. Thomae apostoli.

(*c*) [Our note : ita codd. Bernen. fragment. Lauresh. et N.]

As regards (III.) v. Kal. Jan., 28th of December, " In
Edessa the translation of the body of Thomas the
Apostle," as this is a week after the feast kept on the
21st, it may be taken as a celebration of the octave.
The fourth entry (IV.) iii. Non. Jun. is obviously an
error, and is not supported by other texts. Duchesne
says : Ex Gregorio Turonensi scimus apostoli festum
ab Edessenis Julio mense celebratum fuisse; etiam nunc
a Syris Julii 3 Thomas recolitur, ergo dies v. non. Julii
recte, dies iii. non. iun. errore assignatus est. The reader
will have noticed that in some of the best texts of the
Martyrology, as shown by the editorial notes reproduced
under (*a*) and (*b*), some confusion or rather blending
of the 'natalis' and the 'translatio' has occurred,
though the same texts designate Edessa for the translation and India for the martyrdom. This point could
be further confirmed, if necessary, by entries in the
other codices. These double entries taken together, if

anything, confirm more fully the accuracy of (I.) and (II.).

As to the feast the Syrian Church keeps—not that of the martyrdom, but of the translation of the Relics—we have in the Roman Martyrology a parallel case of another Apostle. This Martyrology marks the feast of St. James the Apostle, the brother of the Evangelist John, on the 25th of July; this is not the feast of his martyrdom, which, as the Martyrology informs us, occurred at Jerusalem, about Easter, under Herod (*Acts* xii. 2), but of the transfer of his Relics thence to Compostella, in Spain : and this is the only festival of this Apostle in the Roman Martyrology.[1] So also the Syrians keep only one feast of Saint Thomas, the feast of his translation to Edessa ; more will be said on this subject in another part of the book.

De Rossi also treats fully (p. xvii., *ut supr.*) of the two ancient codices of Lucca, edited by Florentini, *alias* Florentius Franciscus Maria, *Vetus Occidentalis Ecclesiae Martyrologium D. Hieronymo tributum*, Lucae, 1668. Mabillon dated the older of these codices *c.* 800 ; De Rossi would assign it to the eleventh century. The following two entries of the festivals of Saint Thomas are taken from the printed edition :—

> xii Kal. Januarias. In Mesopotamia civitate Edessa Translatio corporis S. Thome apostoli, qui translatus est ab India ; cujus passio ibidem celebratur v Non. Julii.
>
> v Nonas Julii. In Edessa Mesopotamie translatio corporis S. Thomae Apostoli, qui passus est in India.

---

[1] The following is the entry *ad diem:* Sancti Jacobi Apostoli, fratris beati Joannis Evangelistae, qui prope festum Paschae ab Herode Agrippa decollatus est. Ejus sacra ossa ab Jerusolymis ad Hispanias hoc die translata, et in ultimis earum finibus apud Gallaeciam recondita, celeberrima illarum gentium veneratione, et frequenti christianorum concursu, religionis et voti causa illuc adeuntium pie coluntur. (*Martyrol. Roman.*, Romae, typis de Propaganda Fide, 1878, editio noviss., SS. D. N. Pio Papa IX., auspice et patrono, a S. Rituum congregatione ad haec usque tempora adprobata.)

The former entry blends the feast of the 'natalis' with that of the 'translatio,' an inaccuracy common to several MSS, but both entries distinctly specify (1) that the *passio* was in India, (2) that the *translatio* was from India, and one of them (3) specifies that the feast was kept in India 'v Non. Julii,' or the 3rd of July.

The *Martyrologium Bedae* (see critical discussion by De Rossi, *ut supr.*, p. xxiv.§ 15), according to the Bollandist edition, *Acta SS. Martii*, tom. ii. p. xlii.; and Migne, *P.-L.*, tom. xciv., *Oper. Bedae*, tom. v. col. 1137, gives the following entry :—

> (I.) xxi, xii Kal. Jan. Nat. S. Thomae Apost.
> *Florus addit in ATL* [Codd. Attrebatensis, Torna-censis, Laetiensis], qui passus est in India, lancea quippe transfixus occubuit. Hujus etenim corpus translatum est apud Edissam civitatem. T quinto nonas Julii.

From Bedae *Opera omnia*, Coloniae Agrippinae, 1688, tom. iii. col. 359; also Migne, *P.-L.*, tom. xciv., *ut supr.*, col. 1137, the *Martyrologium* as given there :—

xii Calend. Jan.

Natale beati Thomae Apostoli qui Parthis et Medis Evangelium praedicans, passus est in India. Corpus ejus in civitatem quam Syri Edessen vocant, translatum, ibique digno honore conditum est.

Martyrol. Bedae, Bolland. *Acta SS.*, ut supr., p. xxii. ; Migne, *ut supr.*, col. 965:—

> (II.) v Nonas [Julii]. Translatio S. Thomae apostoli in Edessa ex India.
> Addit B [Barberinianum] qui fuit passus in India 12 Kal. Januarii.

At same date the Cologne edition, *ut supr.*, and Migne, col. 966:—

v Nonas Julii apud Edessam Mesopotamiae translatio corporis sancti Thomae apostoli.

Bede supplies the following particulars regarding his Martyrology (at the close of his *Hist. Eccl.*, col. 390, Migne, tom. vi., *Oper. et P.-L.*, tom. xcv.): Martyrologium de natalitiis sanctorum martyrum diebus; in quo omnes quos invenire potui, non solum qua die, verum etiam quo genere certaminis, vel sub quo judice mundum vicerint diligenter [al. om. *diligenter*] adnotare studui.

The reader should be informed that in the discussion above mentioned De Rossi says that the Bollandist edition of Bede's Martyrology by no means reproduces all that the best texts of the same offer, and he repeats the caution, previously given by Scipio Maffei, that superior MSS of Bede's text exist in the Chapter House (of the Canons) at Verona; and, on his own account he adds, that he found there not one but two parchment codices of the ninth century, numbered LXV. and XC., which contain a text *fere absque additamentis;* he mentions also the existence of other ninth-century MSS of the text at the Vatican. The ' Florus,' named after our first quotation above given in the Martyrology, was a sub-deacon of the Church of Lyons, A.D. 830, who first enlarged Bede's work.

We are enabled through the kindness of the authorities of the Cathedral of Verona to further strengthen the above witness from Bede's Martyrology, by giving also the readings for the two festivals from the two ancient codices highly commended by De Rossi. The Cathedral Chapter is the fortunate possessor of 450 ancient codices, comprising these two :—

A.

Codex lxv. (63) *Venerabilis Bedae Martyrologium*, fol. 47ᵛ, line 11 :—

      (1) xii kl iān scī thome apti

        (Kalendas Januarias Sancti Thome apostoli).

Codex xc. (85) *Orationes Hymni Preces Martyrologium Bedæ*, fol. 109ᵛ, 3rd last line :—

      (2) xii k̄ iān nāt scī tŏme, apti.

N.B.—The letter *h* by a later hand of the tenth century.

B.

Codex lxv. (63) fol. 23ᵛ, line 12 :—

    (3) v n̄ īul Translatio thome, apti.

Line 13 :—

    In edissa passus vero In India.

Codex xc., fol. 103ᵛ, line 1 :—

    (4) v nŏn īul translatio thome apti.

Comparing A (1) and (2) with (I.) of Bollandist edition, we ascertain that the true reading of Bede's Martyrology at December 21 gives *natalis* of the Apostle with no additional remark. Comparing similarly B (3) with (II.) of Bollandist edition, the genuine reading of the text expresses two separate ideas or facts—in (II.) *translatio in Edessa ex India*, and in B (3) *translatio in edissa passus vero in India.* Thus Bede's Martyrology harmonises completely with the Hieronymian in placing the 'martyrdom in India,' and the 'transfer of the Relics to Edessa,' of the Apostle Thomas.

Codex lxv. contains the larger, Codex xc. the abbreviated *Martyrologium* of Bede.

We shall close this section, dealing with the Liturgical Books of the Western Church, with two quotations from the authorised *Martyrologium Romanum* in present use, and a short historical note on its revision and authorised edition.

Duodecimo Kalendas Januarii.

Calaminae natalis beati Thomae Apostoli, qui Parthis, Medis, Persis, et Hyrcanis Evangelium praedicavit, ac demum in Indiam perveniens, cum eos populos in Christiana religione instituisset, Regis jussu lanceis transfixus occubuit ; cujus reliquiae primo ad urbem Edessam, deinde Orthonam translatae sunt.

Quinto Nonas Julii.

Edessae in Mesopotamia Translatio sancti Thomae ex India, cujus reliquiae Orthonam postea translatae sunt.

The Roman Martyrology now sanctioned for use was prepared by Cardinal Baronius, and approved by Pope Gregory XIII. in a brief dated January 14, 1584; it is a new edition of the Martyrologies of Ado, Archbishop of Vienne, and of Usuard, revised and completed. As to the part which the Pope personally took in the revision, Baronius states in the *Tractatus*, which is prefixed to every edition, cap. viii.: 'Cui [videlicet Martyrologio] etsi ex nostris Notationibus levis certe aliqua accessit emendatio, vel si quid additum reperitur (quod quidem perraro factum invenies), id nos ejus, cujus summa est in Ecclesia auctoritas, constanti voluntate fecisse lector intelligat.'

Baronius speaks of three editions—the third, of 1584, is his work; the two preceding he styles faulty.

V.—The Witness of the Greek and Abyssinian Churches

The Liturgical Books of the Greek Church comprise among others :—

Τὰ Μηναῖα, the *Menaea*, used in the plural, denotes the entire series of Office books which are usually bound in twelve volumes, one for each month. A single volume of the compilation, for a month, is termed τὸ μηναῖον in the singular. The *Menaea* contain the variable parts of the Offices for fixed festivals, comprising a variety of elements.

Τὸ Μηνολόγιον, the *Menologium*, answers somewhat the purpose of the *Martyrologium* of the Western Church; it contains the acts and lives of martyrs and saints. One was compiled by order of the Emperor Basil (A.D. 867–886); and Constantine Porphyrogenitus (A.D. 911) directed Simeon Metaphrastes to compile the lives of saints and the acts of martyrs arranged in order according to the months of the year. This was the earliest

E

compilation of the sort; there is another in Latin by Surius, and that of Alban Butler in English is perhaps the latest.

Τὸ συναξάριον, the *Synaxarium :* Goar defines it ' sanctorum vitas volumen brevibus verbis complectens συναξάριον est.' In the plural, συναξάρια denote the twelve volumes for the year containing short lives of saints and acts of martyrs read in the Liturgical Offices.

The two first quotations given below are from the *Synaxarium ;* the other two are from the *Menologium,* compiled by order of the Emperor Basil.

The *Synaxarium Ecclesiae Constantinopolitanæ*[1] gives (col. 113 *seq.*) :—

'The same month [October] 6.'

'The conflict of saint Thomas the apostle, named also Didymus [the Twin]. He having preached the word of God to the Parthians, and the Medes, and the Persians, and the Indians, and having brought great multitudes to the faith of Christ by miracles innumerable, was put to death by Misdeus, King of the Indians, because Uzanes, his son, and Tertia, the mother, and Narkia had believed, and were by him baptised. On this account he was consigned to five soldiers, who, taking him up

---

[1] Edited by the Bollandists, ' *Propyleum ad Acta SS.*, November, Bruxelles, 1902, e codice Sirmondiano, nunc Berolinensi, Opera et Studio Hippolyti Delehaye.'

As to the value of the text, we reproduce for the reader's information some of the remarks of the editor *ex prolegomenis*, col. i.–ii. : ' Licet enim archetypum nequaquam dicendum sit Sirmondianum Synaxarium, caeteris omnibus quae inspeximus, tot commodis praestare visum est, ut facile palmam tulerit. Etenim vel hac sola ratione multis antecellit quod uno volumine duodecim menses complectitur, cum in aliis plerisque vel dimidia tantum vel etiam minor contineatur ; nec ita raro contingat ex genuinis fratribus alterum in nostris regionibus, puta Parisiis, commorari alterum non interierit in locis multum dissitis, puta Hierosolymis vel penes monachos Athonenses peregrinari. Integritate quoque alia pleraque superat . . . esto inter vetustissima non connumeretur, antiqua tamen ex stirpe procul dubio ortum est, simulque uberrimum, ita ut sanctorum nominibus festorumque commemorationibus affluet.'

the mount, covered him with wounds and made him attain his blessed end.   Nisifor and Uzanes remained on the mount ; the apostle, appearing, told them to be of good heart.   For he had ordained Nisifor a priest and Uzanes a deacon.

'After these things had happened, the son of the King was suffering from a mortal disease, and the King asked that a relic of the apostle might be brought to his son who was already beyond hope of recovery, and near death.   As the body of the apostle was not found, he ordered earth from the grave to be fetched.   On this earth touching the dying man he was cured at once.   But the King, even then not having believed, died a corporal and spiritual death.'

Col. 781 :—

'*The month of June*, 30.'

('Feast of the Commemoration of the Apostles.')

'5. The seventh Thomas, who is also named Didymus [the Twin].   He having preached the God-Word to the Parthians, the Medes, the Persians, and the Indians, was by these killed, transfixed with lances.'

The *Menologium.*—The subjoined extract is taken from the best edition of the work, one superbly illustrated ; divided into three parts with Greek text and Latin translation.[1]

Pars i., p. 97 :—

'October, the sixth day.—The contending of saint Thomas the Apostle.   After the Ascension of our Lord Jesus Christ when the Apostles each went to the countries which had fallen to them by lot to teach, to saint Thomas fell the country of the Indians, where he preached Christ.   Because he had brought to the faith of Christ the wife of the King of the Indians and her son, he is traduced before the King, who orders Thomas to be cast into prison with other convicts.   The King's son, with his mother and others, not a few, enter the prison by bribing the soldiers, are by him baptised, and, after a suitable delay, from

---

[1] Jussu Basilii Imper. Graece olim editum, munificentia et liberalitate SS. D. N. Benedicti XIII. nunc primum Graece et Latine prodit, studio Hannibalis Card. Albani, Urbini, 1727.

among them priests and deacons are ordained, who taught in the name of Christ. On the King coming to know this, being angered, he ordered the Apostle to be taken from the prison and consigned to soldiers to be executed. The holy man thus taken to the mount is by them transfixed with a lance and killed.'

Pars iii., p. 146 :—

' June the thirtieth.'

' Synaxis of the Twelve Apostles.'

' The seventh, Thomas Didymus, is by the Indians transfixed by lances.'

As regards the Abyssinian Church, we may quote from an Ethiopian Calendar of the twelfth century, which was published by Job Ludolf.[1] This Calendar contains the following entry for the feast of Saint Thomas :—

In mense Octobris 6, Thomas Indiae Apostolus.

The practice of the Greek Church of keeping the Apostle's feast on the 6th of October, as we have already seen, had affected other Eastern churches, and now we find the Abyssinian Church, which was dependent on the Church of Alexandria, observing the same date. As is known, even to the present day the Abyssinian schismatics receive their 'Abbuna' or bishop from the schismatic Coptic patriarch of Alexandria.

---

[1] *Commentarius ad suam Historiam Aethiopicam*, Francofurti, 1691, pp. 389–436.

CHAPTER III

SAINT THOMAS'S TOMB IN INDIA

ON the broad fact that Saint Thomas the Apostle, according to the evidence of antiquity, had preached the Gospel and sealed his teaching by his martyrdom in India, it should be taken for granted that if his tomb were to be discoverable anywhere, it would naturally be found within the limits of India proper. Yet this, which in itself is but an historical aphorism, has met with the strongest opposition ever since the Portuguese first announced the discovery of his tomb at Mylapore. This opposition has come first and chiefly from quarters which must cause an impartial historian, who patiently investigates the whole history of the case, to consider the same as being rather the outcome of 'odium theologicum,' than arising from insufficient historical evidence.[1]

---

[1] Basnage was amongst the first to deny the Indian Apostolate and martyrdom of Saint Thomas, and Assemani (*Bibliotheca Orientalis*, tom. iv. p. 25 ff.) gives a full refutation to his statements. La Croze (*Histoire du Christianisme des Indes*, Lahaye, 1724) rejects the tradition summarily. Tillemont (*Mémoires Hist. Eccl.*, Venice, 1732, tom. i. p. 359), on the erroneous supposition that the entire body of the Apostle was at Edessa, declines to accept the tradition ; in his additional Note 4 (p. 613) he accepts a statement of Theodoret, and thereupon builds a further supposition that Thomas, one of Manes' disciples, may have given occasion to the supposition that the Apostle had visited India ; a refutation of this will be found in Chapter VI. The Rev. J. Hough (*History of Christianity in India*, London, 1859, vol. i. p. 30 ff.) denies that any Apostle was ever in India. Sir John Kaye (*Christianity in India*, London, 1859) considers it a worthless legend. The Rev. G. Milne-Rae (*The Syrian Church in India*, London, 1892) rejects the tradition ; while Dr. George Smith (*The*

A plausible excuse for the general feeling of scepticism created by these writers was, in part, offered by the want of previous historical knowledge shown by the Portuguese authorities and writers in India who claimed to have discovered the body, or the entire remains of the Apostle, coupled with other uncritical details.

Once the opposition view, arising at first from the doubt regarding the tomb, was taken up and ruthlessly exploited, it was extended to the preaching of the Gospel by the Apostle within the geographical limits of India, and a widely extending prejudice was formed. It is only in more recent times, when men indifferent to that ' odium,' or guided by their familiarity with, or their long researches in India approached the subject, that they came gradually to admit the Apostle's mission to India, and to consider the strong historical claim of Mylapore to be the possible site of his martyrdom and burial, as not unfounded. Some of these expressions of opinion will be found in the course of this work.

Under these circumstances, and eliminating the con-

Conversion of India, 1903) ignores the subject altogether, dating the first conversion of India from A.D. 193.

As a sample of some of the absurdities put forward regarding the Apostle Thomas's connection with India, we take the following from this last writer's work, *Geography of British India*, by Dr. George Smith, London, 1882, pp. 370–371 : ' The southern suburb of Saint Thomé, two miles south of the Fort [of Madras], with an old Roman Catholic church, is identified by Heber and by H. H. Wilson with the Mailapoor, or Mihilapoor, where the Apostle Thomas is said to have been martyred on 21st December 58 A.D. The rocky knoll of the Little Mount, five miles south-west of the Fort, with church dedicated to St. Thomas, attracts crowds, under the belief that the Apostle perished there. A cave in which he concealed himself and a cell in which he worshipped are shown ; *but it has been proved that it is Thomas Aquinas whose name was given to this place.*' The gross absurdity of the last sentence, from a historical point of view, passes conception ; and yet this is the sort of stuff that is put before the rising generation in the Government and Protestant missionary schools in India, and, for all we know, it may yet be the text-book for geography in those schools ! The *italics* are ours.

troversial element from an historical investigation, it
has been thought best, after setting forth the available
evidence for the Indian Apostolate, to bring forward
such evidence as will uphold for Mylapore[1] the claim
to the tomb.

I.—The Visit of Theodore to the Indian Shrine of the Apostle Thomas before a.d. 590, as set forth by St. Gregory of Tours

Gregory of Tours, the best known of the writers of
the Merovingian period and the father of Frankish
history, born, probably on November 30 in 538, at
Clermont-Ferrand, the ancient Avernia, bore the name
of George Florentius which he subsequently dropped on
assuming that of Gregory from his maternal great-grand-
father, Gregory, bishop of Langres. He was educated
by his paternal uncle, St. Gall, bishop of Clermont,
546–554. In 573 he was elected to the see of Tours.
Fortunatus of Poitiers, the Christian poet, has left a
laudatory poem commemorating the event, addressed
'ad cives Turonicos de Gregorio episcopo.'

The Bishop of Tours in his *In Gloria Martyrum*,
a work which he revised in 590, shortly before his
death (which occurred on the 17th November, 593 or
594), writes : 'Thomas the Apostle, according to the
narrative of his martyrdom, is stated to have suffered
in India. His holy remains *(corpus)*, after a long
interval of time, were removed to the city of Edessa
in Syria and there interred. In that part of India
where they first rested, stand a monastery and a church
of striking dimensions, elaborately adorned and de-

---

[1] The now accepted form of writing the name in English is
Mylapore ; but this to a foreigner would not convey an idea of the
right pronunciation of the word. The Tamil, or current native form,
is given in English by Colonel Yule as *Mayiláppúr;* with the Latin
sound of vowels, termed the Italian, we would write *Mailápúr.*

signed. . . . This, Theodore, who had been to the place, narrated to us.'

Gregory's authority for the tomb of the Apostle Thomas being situated in India came from an eye-witness, Theodore, probably a travelled Syrian Christian, who had visited the Indian Shrine and venerated the Relics at Edessa as well : he may then have gone to Gaul making, or completing, a tour to the celebrated sanctuaries of Christendom, and may have so come to Tours also to venerate the renowned shrine of St. Martin. In the interesting evidence recorded by Gregory in the last quarter of the sixth century the following points are brought clearly to light : the existence of a narrative, or Acts of the martyrdom of the Apostle, 'historia passionis eius,' which declares that he suffered martyrdom in India, 'in India passus declaratur'; the existence of the first tomb of the Apostle, 'in loco regionis Indiae quo prius quievit'; a church of large dimensions covering the Indian tomb, 'templum mirae magnitudinis'; a monastery adjacent, 'monasterium habetur,' the monks of which, no doubt, conducted the services at the Shrine ; the further know-ledge that, after the remains of the Apostle had remained buried in India for a long time, they were thence re-moved to Edessa, 'corpus post multum tempus ad-sumptum in civitatem quam Syri Aedissam vocant'; and, finally, that they were buried anew at Edessa, 'ibique sepultum.' These several points, as the reader will remark, embrace all and even more than is necessary to establish the fact of the early knowledge of the existence of the Indian tomb of the Apostle.

The reader may be interested to know in what spirit Gregory undertook the task of writing the lives of the saints and martyrs of God, and of recording the miracles they worked. We extract for this purpose a short quotation from his introduction to his book *In Gloria*

Confessorum (*infra*, pt. ii. p. 748) : Nobis, ut saepe testati sumus, nec artis ingenium suppeditat nec sermonum facundia juvat, veniam temeritati libenter indulgeat (lector), quem non jactantia mundalis erigit ut scribat, sed depremit pudor ut sileat, amor timorque Christi impellit ut referat.

The reader may further desire to be acquainted with the pains he took to obtain direct information from eye-witnesses, and he is careful to indicate the source. Here is a list of some of those who brought him information from foreign lands which he incorporated in these writings; for fuller details the reader should turn to the editor's general introduction to St. Gregory's hagiological writings, pp. 456–461, written by Krusch. The sixth century was by no means wanting in pilgrims whose piety urged them to travel to far and distant countries to visit the places where reposed the mortal remains of God's faithful servants, and who came to Gaul as well, or started thence. Among such informants Gregory names the Deacon Agiulph, whom he sent to Rome in 590, who brought back thence relics of martyrs from the catacombs, and who gave him the particulars of the life of Pope John, of which he made use. Another deacon of Tours had visited Jerusalem, and had made the pilgrimage to the Holy Places, whose testimony Gregory quotes as that of 'our deacon' (*Gl. Mart.*, c. 1), the 'man named John' (c. 18), and again the 'deacon John' (c. 87.) There occurs mention of probably another pilgrim who had visited Jerusalem and had come to Tours (*ibid.*, c. 5). Theodore came to Gaul from India and met Gregory, and gave him the interesting historical details, part of which the reader has seen above. Gregory learns particulars concerning St. Julian, whose life and miracles he described 'fidelium fratrum relatione' (*Mir. S. Jul.*, c. 33). He is enabled to give the acts of the so-named 'Seven Sleepers' (martyrs who had suffered at Ephesus), from a Syriac MS, 'passio eorum quam Siro quodam interpretante in Latinum transtulimus'; another codex gives the name, 'interpretante Johanne Syro.' To him, probably, Gregory also owes other Eastern details incorporated in his works.

We now pass on to give the reader the sequel of Gregory's narrative concerning the Apostle Thomas. This describes a quite natural scene, not uncommon even in Europe in the early and later Middle Ages, when great fairs were held in certain places on the festival of some saint greatly venerated by the people : 'In the above named town, in which, as we said, the sacred bones (*artus*) were buried, there is on the feast day a great gathering, lasting for thirty days, of all classes of people, coming from different countries, with votive offerings and for trade, buying and selling without paying any tax. During these days, which occur in the fifth month, great and unusual blessings are conferred on the people. . . . While at other times you have to draw water from wells at a depth of over a hundred feet, now [at the season of the festival] if you dig to even a short depth you find an abundance of water, which is no doubt due to the favour of the blessed Apostle. . . . After that, there is such a supernatural downpour of rain that the entrance of the church and the grounds around are swept so clean of all defilement and dust that you would think the ground had not been trodden.' We shall examine the incidents of this account, and endeavour to bring out more prominently its special features.

First of all, mention is made of the town 'in which the sacred bones were buried'; this clearly points to Edessa, and has been so taken by subsequent writers. But do the climatic and other details given above suit Edessa and its surroundings ? We have grave reasons for suggesting they do not; to us it appears there has occurred a confusion in reporting these details, and that there has been a blending of the accounts given by Theodore of two festivals, one kept at Edessa and the other in India.   But these cannot be appropriately discussed until the date of the festival has been ascertained.

Gregory, after telling us that during the festival a fair is held, and a great gathering takes place lasting for thirty days, adds that these days occur 'in the fifth month.' As he does not offer any hint to make us suppose he is reckoning by a foreign calendar, we have no option but to conclude it must be the fifth month of the general calendar in use in Western Europe—that is, the Roman Calendar. The fifth month of this Calendar is the *Quintilis* (fifth), afterwards named Julius, or our July.[1] The feast, which lasted a month, occupied the whole of that month. Gregory continues: 'Decursis igitur festivitatis diebus,' &c. (this covers the whole of July). 'The days of the festival having passed,' &c. Thereafter, or from this time forth, 'there is such a supernatural downpour of rain,' &c. 'Dehinc emissa divinitus pluvia,' &c. This heavy rainfall witnessed by Theodore —for all these local details appear to have been communicated by him to the writer, it is difficult to see how else Gregory came to know them—occurred at the beginning of the following month, August, when the festival was over. Looking more carefully into the

---

[1] The Roman Calendar year, said to have been introduced by Romulus, consisted of ten months—1, Martius ; 2, Aprilis ; 3, Maius ; 4, Junius ; 5, Quintilis (afterwards Julius, in honour of Julius Cæsar) ; 6, Sextilis (afterwards Augustus, from Octavianus Augustus) ; 7, September ; 8, October ; 9, November ; 10, December.   The year so reckoned agreed neither with the solar period of the earth's rotation, nor with the lunar course ; so Numa Pompilius is said to have added the two months that head the present calendar—Januarius and Februarius. It was Julius Cæsar who fixed the calendar, named after him ' Julian,' on an astronomical basis.

details, it is necessary to note that the drought is described as being extreme before, but at the festival water
is easily found; there must then have been partial rain-
falls during the month of July—the days when the feast was
kept; while the heavy downfall, which sweeps the roads
and paved enclosures so clean as to leave no speck of
dust or dirt behind, came in the beginning of August.
Can this description of abundance of water supply, and
of partial and torrential rains in July and August fit the
case of Edessa? We say decidedly no; for that precisely
is the driest and most parched season of the year in Syria
and Mesopotamia. The reader should bear in mind that
the Mesopotamia of the Romans embraced the city of
Edessa, and it is to this we refer. Lately, while on
a visit to Rome, we had a special opportunity to test
the accuracy of our earlier information on this subject
regarding the climate at Urfa—the name by which the
old city of Edessa is designated by the Arabs. Having
met with natives of the place, we had the opportunity of
personally questioning them on the subject. We elicited
that the season of the rains occurs in the months January
to March inclusive; during the whole period of summer
it does not rain, and the greatest heats prevail in July
and August, when the land is quite parched. The Syrian
fifth month corresponds to January, the year commencing in September; the depth of wells at Urfa averages
twenty feet. All this clearly shows that the description
of the festival of Saint Thomas given by the Bishop
of Tours and held in July cannot be that celebrated at
Edessa. Further, the July festival in honour of the
Apostle can be no other than that shown in the Church
service-books, fixed for the 3rd of that month, and celebrated alike at Edessa and in India. If, then, climatic
circumstances force us to the conclusion that this festival
cannot be taken for a celebration at Edessa, can it be
applicable to the celebration in India at the Shrine?

Let us look at the details given of the fair held during the festival. The custom is noted that during this fair the fees or charges usually levied at fairs were not exacted. Now this is a peculiarly Indian custom, yet surviving in places where Western usages have not superseded those of native origin, and indicates that the narrative is in touch with India. At certain large and special fairs—often connected with religious festivals—in order also to attract people from surrounding districts, as also when the object is to establish an annual fair at some new centre, or to open a new market on a private property, the remission of customary rent charges, for a time, is rather the rule than the exception, whereas at the former, viz. the religious fairs, usually no charges are made.

What are the climatic influences prevailing at the Indian Shrine of the Apostle at Mylapore during the months of July and August ? The east or Coromandel coast has the benefit of two monsoons or rainy seasons ; one, the north-east monsoon, during October and November, the rainfall in the latter month being the heaviest in the year ; the other, the south-west monsoon, which coming across the peninsula from the Malabar coast prevails from July to some time in September. The rains during this monsoon are not heavy. Yet there are occasionally heavy downpours, like that described in the text, occurring when accompanied by thunder storms, as the writer himself has witnessed, in August. One such heavy monsoon-fall in early August is all that is required to explain the altered scene described in the text. To those who witness a monsoon out-burst for the first time, the scene is singularly impressive for the cooling change it effects in the atmosphere, the removal of all dirt and filth from the surface of the land, and the abundant supply of water it affords after a long and trying season of heat and drought. It is therefore not surprising to find one ignorant of the causes producing it, like Theodore, proclaim it a God-sent rain.

It is appropriate to note also that the earlier falls in July, when they do occur, mitigate the temporary water famine which otherwise would prevail; this evil was specially severe before the present reservoirs for the supply of Madras were formed ; even this feature of the land has not been overlooked in the narrative.

But might not the rainfall of the south-west monsoon have been much heavier on the Madras coast centuries ago than now? There can be little doubt that such was the case. Anybody who has paid attention to natural causes which increase, diminish, or bar altogether the downfall of rain from moisture-laden clouds traversing any tract of country, must know that it is regulated by the existence of forest lands on that tract. If there be an abundant or a sufficient supply of forests the rainfall will be abundant and ample from such passing clouds, but if the land be deforested by the improvident hand of man, the tract will receive next to no rain, except under peculiar atmospheric circumstances, combined with the amount of moisture prevailing in the air. For the present purpose it is sufficient to inform the reader that the whole of the hinterland of Madras has been entirely deforested almost as far back as the Nilgherries. The present data of rainfall, therefore, can afford no criterion of what it must have been during the prevalence of the south-west monsoon in ages back, before the denudation of the land had taken place. The oft-recurring *kad* or *kadu* (forest or jungle) in the names of villages and places in the hinterland of the peninsula, shows how different was the state of the land formerly. Ptolemy, in mentioning the early capital of the Sora, now styled the Chola, country, styles it *regia Arkati*, which, by common accord, is taken to designate Arkot. The Tamil form is Âr-kâd, which

means 'the six forests'; this town lies due west of
Madras, and may be taken as a sample of other names
that could be produced. These remarks are also borne
out by the fact that the south-west monsoon clouds may
now be seen fleeting over Madras and denying the
parched land the benefit of the moisture held in sus-
pense, which they subsequently discharge in the Bay of
Bengal under more favourable atmospheric conditions,
as captains of steamships are often known to remark.

These observations may be thought sufficient to justify
our view that St. Gregory wrongly attributed the scene
of the festival described as occurring at Edessa, whereas
it could only fit the surroundings of the Indian Shrine.
Even the error in giving the depth of the wells in that
neighbourhood, while not at all applicable to Edessa,
indicates that the narrator was a travelled Eastern who
had crossed the Syrian desert, and having but a slight
acquaintance of India, supplemented his remarks as to
the extent of drought with home ideas.

One further remark should be added on the details
of this pregnant narrative. While the monastery mentioned attached to the Shrine and Church suggests
Mesopotamian Ascetics and Monks and consequently
a Syrian Liturgy, Ritual, and Calendar—for the clergy
of every Rite invariably carry these with them wherever they go; the record that even in India the feast
of the 3rd of July was kept, shows that there, in
accordance with their Calendar, the clergy kept the
feast of the Translation of the Apostle's Relics to
Edessa. All this admirably fits in with, and confirms
the data previously given from the Hieronymian
Calendar. As to whether the taint of Nestorian error
had already sullied the purity of primitive faith, the
reader is referred to Chapter V., p. 199, note.[1]

---

[1] Gregorii Tvronensis *Opera*, ediderunt W. Arndt et Br. Krusch,
Hannoverae, 1884 (in two parts, and forms *tomus primus* of *Scriptores*

II.—KING ALFRED'S EMBASSY TO THE SHRINE, A.D. 883

The record of the next visit to the Apostle's tomb has come down to us with something like an interval of three hundred years. As the former went from the extreme East, so this goes from the extreme West. A venerable authority, the Anglo-Saxon Chronicle, relating the events of the early history of England, tells us that the greatest of her Anglo-Saxon kings who ruled over Southern England also venerated the memory of the Apostle of India and showed himself grateful

Rerum Merovingicarum, belonging to the series in 4to of *Monumenta Germaniae Historica*), part ii. pp. 507–508, *Liber in Gloria Martyrum*, cap. 31–32 :—

'Thomas apostolus secundum historiam passionis eius in India passus declaratur. Cujus beatum corpus post multum tempus adsumptum in civitatem quam Syri Aedissam vocant translatum est, ibique sepultum. Ergo in loco regionis Indiae, quo prius quievit, monasterium habetur et templum mirae magnitudinis diligenterque exornatum atque compositum. In hac igitur aede magnum miraculum Deus ostendit. Lignus etenim inibi positus, atque inluminatus, ante locum sepulturae ipsius perpetualiter die noctuque divino nutu resplendet, a nullo fomentum olei scirpique accipiens : neque vento extinguitur, neque casu dilabitur, neque ardendo minuitur ; habetque incrementum per Apostoli virtutem, quod nescitur ab homine, cognitum tamen habetur divinae potentiae. Hoc Theodorus qui ad ipsum locum accessit, nobis exposuit. In supra dicta igitur urbe, in qua beatos artus diximus tumulatos, adveniente festivitate, magnus adgregatur populorum coetus, ac de diversis regionibus cum votis negotiisque venientes vendendi, comparandique per triginta dies sine ulla thelonii exactione licentia datur. In his vero diebus qui in mense habentur quinto, magna et inusitata populis praebentur beneficia. Non scandalum surgit in plebe, non musca insedet mortificatae carni, non latex deest sitienti. Nam cum ibi reliquiis diebus plusquam centinûm pedum altitudine aqua hauriatur a puteis, nunc paululum fodias, affatim lymphas exuberantes invenies : quod non ambigitur virtute haec beati Apostoli impertiri. Decursis igitur festivitatis diebus, theloneum publico redditur, musca quae defuit adest, propinquitas aquae dehiscit. Dehinc emissa divinitus pluvia ita omne atrium templi a sordibus et diversis squaloribus qui per ipsa solemnia facti sunt, mundat, ut putes eum nec fuisse calcatum.

for benefits received by his intercession. While King Alfred was defending the city of London, besieged by the heathen Danes, he made a vow; but the date when this occurred is not known.[1] It was in fulfilment of this vow that King Alfred sent an Embassy with gifts to Rome, and to India to the Shrine of the Apostle: 'The year 883 [884]. In this year the army went up the Scheldt to Condé, and they sat down one year. And Marinus, the Pope, then sent *lignum Domini* [a relic of the Cross] to King Alfred. And in the same year Sighelm and Aethâlstan conveyed to Rome the alms which the king had vowed [to send] thither, and also to India to Saint Thomas and Saint Bartholomew, when they sat down against the army at London; and there, God be thanked, their prayer was very successful, after that vow.'[2]

It will be as well to see what some of the best modern writers of English history have to say in regard to this mission sent to India, whether they consider it an ascertained fact in history, or treat it as legendary. Dr. Lingard, the Catholic historian, an esteemed authority (*Hist. of Engl.*, vol. i. chap. iv., 6th edit., London, 1854, p. 112), says of the king: 'Often he sent considerable presents to Rome; sometimes to the nations in the Mediterranean and to

---

[1] Dr. R. Pauli in his *Life of Alfred the Great* (translated from the German, London 1893, pp. 146–148) says it is uncertain when the Pagans were before London, 880 or even later.

[2] See *The Anglo-Saxon Chronicle according to the several Original Authorities*, edited with a translation by Benjamin Thorpe, London, 1861, vol. ii. p. 66. Vol. i. contains the Anglo-Saxon texts, seven in number, in parallel columns; vol. ii., the translation. Of this passage there are six Anglo-Saxon texts (vol. i. pp. 150–153); all are dated 883. Four of the texts are practically identical, and translate as above; a fifth makes no mention of Sighelm and Aethalstan, and ends at 'Bartholomew'; the remaining sixth omits everything after 'sat one year.'

F

Jerusalem; on one occasion to the Indian Christians at Meliapour. Swithelm, the bearer of the royal alms, brought back to the king several Oriental pearls and aromatic liquors.' Professor E. A. Freeman, a distinguished Protestant historian, has the following (*Old Engl. Hist.*, London, 1869, p. 131): 'King Alfred was very attentive to religious matters, and gave great alms to the poor, and gifts to the churches. . . . He also sent several embassies to Rome. . . . He also sent an embassy to Jerusalem, and had letters from Abel the Patriarch there. And what seems stranger than all, he sent an embassy all the way to India with alms for the Christians there, called the Christians of Saint Thomas and Saint Bartholomew.' The writer of the article 'St. Thomas' (*Dict. of Christ. Antiq.*) has the following entry: 'In the 9th century Sighelm and Aethalstan were sent by King Alfred with alms to Rome and thence to India to St. Thomas and St. Bartholomew.'

The sending of this embassy with gifts is supported by the early Chroniclers whose works have come down to us. The first of these is Florence of Worcester, who died 1117. In his Chronicle under the year 883 he says: 'Asser, Bishop of Sherborne, died[1] and was succeeded by Swithelm, who carried King Alfred's alms to St. Thomas in India and returned

---

[1] Forester appends the following note: 'Asser did not die till 910 (see *Saxon Chronicle*), and he continued his life of Alfred to the forty-fifth year of that prince's age, A.D. 893. Ethelward, not Swithelm, appears to have been Asser's successor as bishop of Sherborne. See the list of bishops at the end of this work.' The lists of bishops are considered to be by Florence of Worcester, as they are in all the MSS. In the Sherborne list (p. 421) Asser is No. 11, Ethelward No. 12, and Sighelm No. 15; no dates are given. Pauli wrote his *Life of Alfred* about 1850; on pp. 146–148, dealing with the mission of Sighelm and Aethalstan to Rome and India, he says, 'they were probably distinguished laymen. Except on one occasion (890) Alfred's ambassadors to Rome were always laymen, so far as we know.'

in safety.'[1] William of Malmesbury in an original work writes: [Alfred] 'very attentive on bestowing alms, he confirmed the privileges granted to the churches which his father had sanctioned. Beyond the sea, to Rome and to Saint Thomas in India he sent many gifts. The legate employed for this purpose was Sigelinus the bishop of Sherborne, who with great success arrived in India, at which every one at this age wonders. Returning thence he brought back exotic gems and aromatic liquors which the land there produces; besides also a present, excelling all else in value, a portion of the Lord's rood sent to the King by Pope Martin.'[2] The Pope's name is undoubtedly a mistake, whether original or introduced by some careless amanuensis; no Martin was Pope at the time, but Marinus, the name correctly given in the Anglo-Saxon Chronicle, was then Pope;[3] he held the see of Peter from 882 to some date in 884. There occurs another substantial difference between what William says regarding the relic of the Cross sent by the Pope and the statement of the Anglo-Saxon Chronicle. The

---

[1] See the Chronicle of Florence of Worcester, translated by Thos. Forester, London 1854, p. 73.

[2] *Willelmi Malmesbiriensis, de gestis regum Anglorum libri quinque,* edition of T. D. Hardy, London, 1840, vol. i. p. 187: [Elfredus] Eleemosiniis intentus privilegia ecclesiastica, sicut pater statuerat, roboravit; et trans mare Romam et ad Sanctum Thomam in India, multa munera misit. Legatus in hoc missus Sigelinus Scireburnensis episcopus, cum magna prosperitate, quod quivis hoc seculo miretur, Indiam penetravit; inde rediens, exoticos splendores gemmarum et liquores aromatum, quorum illa humus ferax est, reportavit. William of Malmesbury dedicated his history to Robert, Earl of Gloucester, who died in 1147. The book itself is supposed to have been written between 1114 and 1123, and subsequently much improved; the author died 1142–1143.

[3] We have since had occasion to ascertain that Pope Martin, elected in 1281, though only the second of that name, took the name of Martin IV., as the two Popes bearing the name of Marinus were enumerated in the list of Popes under the name of Martin.

latter says the relic was sent the same year and
seemingly before Sighelm or Sigelinus conveyed the
king's alms to Rome, whereas William makes Sigelinus, on his return from India, the bearer of the relic
to the king. The Saxon Chronicle should undoubtedly
carry the greater weight; it is, besides, a contemporary
document.

III.—Visited by Marco Polo, a.d. 1293

The honour of the third visit to the tomb, memory
of which has come down to us, is somewhat contested
between Marco Polo, the great Venetian traveller, and
Friar John of Monte Corvino, both Italians. The visit
of Polo on his return from China described in his
narrative falls in 1293,[1] and that of the future Archbishop of Pekin (Cambalec) probably between 1292–
1293; in other words, the travellers crossed each other's
path somewhere on the route between India and China.
But as there is good reason to hold, as will presently be
seen, that the Venetian had paid India an earlier visit,
precedence is given to him.

Colonel Yule's monumental edition of Marco Polo's
Book of Travels will supply all we want, and we shall
also find Yule a most useful guide in dealing subsequently with the recorded visits of other travellers to
the Shrine.

'The Body of Messer Saint Thomas the Apostle,'
he says (vol. ii. chap. xviii. p. 338), 'lies in this province
of Maabar at a certain little town having no great
population; 'tis a place where few traders go, because

[1] Colonel Yule (*The Book of Ser Marco Polo*, 2nd edition, London,
1875, vol. i., Introduction, p. 22) says in the text that the party sailed
from the port of Zayton (Southern China) in the beginning of 1292;
according to Persian history, as given in the note, the Princess
Kokachin and party arrived in the north of Persia in the winter of
1293–1294; that would fix the date of their passage through Southern
India c. 1293.

there is very little merchandise to be got there, and it is a place not very accessible. Both Christians and Saracens, however, greatly frequent it in pilgrimage. For the Saracens also do hold the Saint in great reverence, and say that he was one of their own Saracens and a great prophet, giving him the title of *Avarian*, which is as much to say "Holy Man." The Christians who go thither in pilgrimage take of the earth from the place where the Saint was killed, and give a portion thereof to any one who is sick of a quartan or a tertian fever; and by the power of God and of Saint Thomas the sick man is incontinently cured. The earth I should tell you is red. A very fine miracle occurred there in the year of Christ, 1288, as I will now relate.' His earlier visit to India, of which mention is made above, probably occurred about that year.[1]   'The

[1] Yule (*ibid.*, p. 21), giving the personal history of Marco Polo, says: 'At one time we know that he held for three years the government of the great city of Yangchou, &c.; on another occasion we find him with his uncle Maffeo passing a year at Kanchau in Tangut; again, it would appear, visiting Kara Korum, the old capital of the Kaans in Mongolia; on another occasion in Champa, or Southern Cochin China; and again, or perhaps as part of the last expedition, on a mission to the Indian Seas, when he appears to have visited several of the southern states of India.' The party, with the Princess, left China in 1292; the occurrence mentioned above in the text is definitely fixed by Marco Polo at 1288, of which he seems to have personal knowledge of some sort; hence it is about that year the earlier visit to India may be placed. Polo probably did not visit Mylapore when travelling in the suite of the Princess, but must have seen the place on some previous occasion. The whole tenor of what he writes and the minute details given imply it. These details are such as to bespeak personal knowledge: 'the body lies at a certain little town having no great population'; 'it is a place not very accessible'; the mention of the practice of 'taking of the earth,' and the important detail, 'the earth, I should tell you, is red,' an observation that would not occur to one who had not visited the locality. Then again his statement, 'a very fine miracle occurred there in the year of Christ 1288, as I will now relate,' the emphatic manner in fixing the date, and the interest he takes in narrating what occurred, still further prove a personal acquaintance with these facts.

Christians,' he resumes a little further on, ' who have
charge of the Church have a great number of the
Indian nut trees whereby they get their living; and
they pay to one of those brother Kings six groats for
each tree every month.' [1]

In this narrative though the Shrine is located, the
church kept by the Christians mentioned, the pilgrimage
of Christians and Saracens not overlooked, and the
province called by its Mahomedan appellation, the
name of the 'little town,' however, is omitted. Nevertheless no reasonable person will refuse credence
to the statement that the little town where the body
lay was Mylapore, subsequently named San Thomé by
the Portuguese, now a suburb, lying to the south, of
the city of Madras. Similarly in the preceding narrative
of Theodore, which has come down to us through
St. Gregory of Tours, mention is made of a place, and
India is indicated, 'in loco regionis Indiae quo prius
quievit.' A church enclosing the Shrine, and pilgrims
flocking to it are similarly mentioned. Theodore also
takes note of a monastery then existing; of this Marco
Polo says nothing, so it may then have been destroyed
to be rebuilt at a later age. Polo speaks of the body
being there; St. Gregory with greater accuracy had
recorded 'in that part of India where it first rested,'
and 'after a long interval of time was removed to the
city of Edessa.' The omission of any mention of the
province is easily accounted for in the story narrated
by a pilgrim traveller, who was not in the habit of
taking geographical notes, but such an omission would
not occur in the Venetian's account. If, then, the state-

---

[1] In Native States in Southern India the tax on cocoanut and
other fruit trees is fixed at so much per tree per annum according
to age and yield ; and valuation of groves is based on the same data ;
these are ancestral usages. The text here appears faulty ; we should
substitute ' year' for month.

ment of Marco Polo carries conviction with it, by what criterion of historical criticism can the intelligent reader refuse it to the narrative of the pilgrim Theodore, who, seven hundred years earlier, had visited the tomb of the Apostle in India, and described it in similar terms?

As this chapter deals with the Shrine and its surroundings, we reserve for treatment elsewhere what Polo reports of indigenous traditions regarding the Saint's martyrdom.

IV.—VISITED BY FRIAR JOHN OF MONTE CORVINO, A.D. 1292–1293

John of Monte Corvino, a Franciscan Friar, is justly called the founder of the First Catholic Mission in China. He had been engaged for many years in mission work prior to being sent out to China.[1] From mention made of his age in the first of his three letters published by Colonel Yule (*Cathay and the Way Thither*, Hakluyt Society, London, 1866, vol. i.), it is inferred he was born *c.* 1247, but it is not known in what year he

[1] M. Henri Cordier, whom we had the pleasure of meeting at Paris, and of discussing with him the date of Friar John's visit to China, told us he held to the view he had expressed in a previous work, that the year could not be definitely fixed. We here reproduce the opinion expressed by this learned Chinese scholar in his edition of *Oderic de Pordenone*, Paris, 1891, Introduction, p. xviii. : 'We learn from a letter of Monte Corvino, dated from that city (Khan-bâliq) in 1305, that he had been alone in China for eleven years; and that two years before that letter a lay-brother named Arnold of Cologne had come and joined him : he would thus have arrived in China in 1292; that is to·say, during the lifetime of Kubilai.' 'These figures,' M. Cordier observes, 'do not quite agree with the rest of his letter; for he tells us that he had left Tauris in 1291, that he stayed thirteen months in India at the church of Saint Thomas (Mylapore), where he lost his travelling companion, the Dominican, Nicholas of Pistoia.' We would suggest the date of arrival as being between 1292 and 1293; it might even have been the beginning of 1294 when he entered China.

entered on his missionary labours. The earliest mention
of him dates from the year 1272, when he was sent by
the Emperor Michael Palaeologus on a mission to
Pope Gregory X., who reigned 1271–1276. John soon
returned to the East with several companions, and remained there till 1289. Once more he returned to the
Papal court with glad tidings of the desire of the peoples
in Armenia and Northern Persia to receive the faith, of
extensive conversions, and of the favourable disposition
of Arghun,[1] the reigning Khan of the House of Hulagu
(reigned 1284–1291). The Pope rejoiced at the good
news, and sent him back; this was his fourth trip, at the
head of a second band of helpers. Gregory X. at the
same time entrusted him with letters to Prince Arghun,
the King and Queen of Lesser Armenia, and, among
others, also to the great Khan Kublai, reigning in China.
'John remained at Tabriz,' says Yule, *ibid.*, p. 166, 'till
1291, and then proceeded to the Far East in order to
fulfil his mission to Kublai, travelling by the way of
India. It is not likely that he reached Cambalec in the
lifetime of the old Khan, who died in the beginning of
1294, for voyages were slow, and he stayed long at St.
Thomas and other places on the coast of Malabar or
Coromandel.' He was created Archbishop of Cambalec in 1307 with the full powers of a Patriarch, and
seven suffragan sees were created to be placed under
him, for which seven friars of his Order were sent out

---

[1] This is the Prince, the Khan of Persia and Kublai's grand-
nephew, who in 1286 lost his favourite wife, the Khatun Bulughan,
who left him her dying injunction 'that her place should be filled
only by a lady of her own kin.' Hence ambassadors were sent to
the court of Kaanbaligh (the Cambalec of our Italian travellers) to
seek such a bride. 'The message was courteously received, and the
choice fell on Lady Kokachin, a maiden of seventeen *moult bele dame
et avenant*,' as Marco says; in whose suite, on her way to meet
Prince Arghun, Marco and his uncles left China (Yule's *Marco
Polo*, vol. i., Introduction, p. 21).

consecrated bishops from Rome. Of this large body of bishops only three reached their destination, three others succumbed on their journey to the effects of the Indian climate, while the seventh either did not start or returned after going a part of the way, and sixteen years later was the occupant of a see in Corsica, but died Bishop of Trieste.

'I, John of Monte Corvino (he writes in his first letter, *ibid.*, p. 197), from the city of Cambalec in the Kingdom of Cathay, in the year of the Lord 1305, and on the 8th day of January, of the Order of Minor Friars, departed from Tauris, a city of the Persians, in the year of the Lord 1291, and proceeded to India. And I remained in the country of India, wherein stands the Church of St. Thomas the Apostle, for thirteen months, and in that region baptised in different places about one hundred persons. The companion of my journey was Friar Nicholas of Pistoia, of the Order of Preachers, who died there, and was buried in the church aforesaid.'

In his second letter, also 'dated from Cambalec a city of Cathay,' and in the 'year 1306, on Quinquagesima Sunday in the month of February,' he gives the heads of his first letter, which show that it has come down to us entire. The second, however, did not fare as well; it got separated into two sections; of these the latter was lost, but the substance incorporated by Wadding in his *Annales Minorum*, tom. vi. pp. 71-72, has been preserved. Yule shows that the two sections form one complete letter. The date given above, 1306, is borne by the once lost section; the other bears no date, but the two fit in aptly as to time. The letter contains only a short paragraph referring to India in the first section, but not bearing on our subject; the second portion will be quoted in Chapter V. The third letter, which is actually the first in date and written from India,

it is unnecessary to quote.[1]   Archbishop John, aged
upwards of eighty years, died at Cambalec in 1328.[2]

V.—MENTIONED BY BLESSED ODERIC,
A.D. 1324–1325

Blessed Oderic of Pordenone in the district of
Friuli, Italy, was born 1286 (see Yule's *Cathay*, vol. i.
pp. 4 and 6); at an early age he took the vows of
a Franciscan, and acquired a reputation for holiness
of life.   From a statement he makes at the beginning of his book it is inferred that he left his convent
for foreign missions in the year 1315–1316, being

---

[1] This letter was sent from the Coromandel coast by a bearer,
no doubt a European and probably an Italian traveller who met
John and his companion Nicholas at the tomb of the Apostle, and in
whose arms the latter is said to have expired (see Friar Menentillus'
covering letter, *Cathay*, vol. ii. p. 210).   As no mention of this
death occurs in this letter, and as it seems to be entire, it may have
been written prior to the occurrence : it is therefore legitimate to
infer that another letter, which has not come down to us, must have
contained the announcement of his companion's death.   Besides
this homeward-bound traveller, John mentions in his second letter a
'gentleman of Lucolongo, a faithful Christian man and great
merchant,' who was the companion of his journey from Tauris, who
'bought the ground for an establishment, and gave it to him for the
love of God,' whereon he built a church separated only by a street
from the great Khan's palace.   All this goes to show that, during the
thirteenth and beginning of the fourteenth century, intercourse
between India and even China and Europe was not of such rare
occurrence as people are sometimes led to suppose ; and that
besides the Polo family, a not inconsiderable number of Europeans
journeyed to and fro between Europe and the Far East, though
their letters and correspondence are only forthcoming in a few
cases. See Angelo De Gubernatis : *Storia dei Viaggiatori Italiani
nelle Indie Orientali*, Livorno, 1875 ; also his earlier *Memoria
intorno ai Viaggiatori Italiani nelle Indie Orientali dal Secolo XIII.
al XVI.*, Firenze, 1867.

[2] This date is obtained from the letter of the Christian princes
at the great Khan's court addressed to the Pope, asking for a
successor to their late lamented archbishop, whom they describe as
'a man of weighty, capable, and holy character.' See their letter,
dated about July 1336, in Yule's *Cathay*, vol. ii. p. 314.

then thirty years of age.   After spending some years
as a missionary in Armenia and Persia, he landed at
Tana,[1] to recover the bones of the four brethren of his
Order who had suffered martyrdom there in the spring
of 1321.[2]   This removal which, with even the heavy

[1] From the island of Ormuz he passes to Tana in twenty-eight
days (Yule's *Cathay*, vol. i. p. 57), where the four friars had suffered
martyrdom. 'The land (of Tana) is under the dominion of the
Saracens, who have taken it by force of arms, and they are now
subject to the Empire of Dile' (Delhi), *ibid.*, vol. i. p. 58.   The Kiji
kings of Delhi overran the West Coast and the Deccan in the early
years of the fourteenth century, and these were more or less subject
to that empire at this period.   The Sultan of Delhi at the time must
have been Gheiass-Uddin Toghlak, who ascended the throne in 1320
according to the best chronology (Yule).

[2] The Holy See sanctioned the *cultus* of the Martyrs of Tana
by a decree of July 10, 1894; by another, of August 14, 1894, the
Congregation of Rites granted the recital of an approved Office and
Mass for the feast of Blessed Thomas of Tolentino.   The addition
authorised for insertion in the *Martyrologium Romano-Seraphicum
Sanctorum et Beatorum trium Ordinum S. P. N. Francisci* is the
following :—

Aprili 6.—Tanae in India beati Thomae a Tolentino Ordinis
Minorum, qui cum tribus sociis ejusdem ordinis glorioso pro fide
Christi martyrio coronatus est.

From the Lesson of the Breviary, which we subjoin, the date on
which the martyrdom took place was the 2nd of April 1321 :—

Ayton rex Armenorum sacerdotes aliquot a Ministro General
Ordinis Minorum expostulavit, qui in ipsius regno catholicam re-
ligionem propagarent ac tuerentur.   Thomas igitur quatuor addictis
sodalibus, illuc est missus ; exceptique a populo summa veneratione
innumeros schismaticos ad Ecclesiae unitatem reduxerunt, et in-
fidelibus quamplurimis persuasere ut christiana dogmata profiterentur.
Accidit autem ut Ayton ab armis Saracenorum premeretur ; quamob-
rem Thomas cum binis sociis ad Nicolaum quartum Romanum
Pontificem et ad reges Gallorum et Angliae ab eo legatus auxilia
petiturus venit ; qua legatione perfunctus in Armeniam reversus est,
abductis secum duodecim religiosis viris ex eodem Franciscalium
ordine in aeternam earum gentium utilitatem.   In Persiam trans-
gressus, inde iterum a sodalibus suis in Europam mittitur docturus
Pontificem de christianae religionis provectu in Tartarorum imperio.
Erat is Clemens eo nomine quintus ; qui Thomae nuntiis usque adeo
delectatus est, ut Joannem a Monte Corvino illic strenue operantem,
Archiepiscopum Cambalicensem primumque Sedis Apostolicae Le-

monsoon rains in India, would have to be placed at least two years after the burial, could only have been effected *c.* 1323. Thence he proceeded to Quilon, which he calls Palumbum. There he took passage on board a ship—a junk—to a 'certain city called Zayton, in which our Friars have two houses, in order there to deposit these sacred relics. On board that ship there were quite 700 souls, what with sailors and merchants.' This shows he took passage on board a Chinese junk he found at Quilon homeward-bound. After discussing Malabar, which he calls ' Minibar' : ' From this realm,' he continues, p. 80, ''tis a journey of ten days to another realm which is called Mobar, and this is very great, and hath in it many cities and towns. And in this realm is laid the body of the Blessed Thomas the Apostle. His church is filled with idols, and beside it are some fifteen houses of the Nestorians; that is to say, Christians, but vile and pestilent heretics.' [1]

gatum apud Orientalium gentes creaverit eique Franciscales septenos addiderit suffraganeos Episcopos, quibus ecclesiastica hierarchia constitueretur. Thomas his feliciter gestis in Orientem tertio redit. Dum vero novam apud Tartaros et Indos expeditionem cogitans Colam contendit, adversa navigatione Tanam deducitur, ubi gloriosum cum tribus suis sociis martyrium fecit. Nam a Saracenis comprehensus ac de religione multa interrogatus, fidei catholicae veritatem praedicans, Mahumetis falsitatem libero sermone corripuit. Vinculis propterea, conviciis ac verberibus affectus, tum soli ardentissimo diu objectus, denique quarto nonas Aprilis millesimi trecentesimi vigesimi primi truncato capite vitam finivit. Eius sacrum corpus a beato Oderico in templum Fratrum Minorum civitatis Zaitonensis elatum est ; abscissum vero caput Tolentinum delatum, magna ibidem pietate colitur. Cultum autem beato Thomae ab immemorabili tempore praestitum Leo decimus tertius Pontifex Maximus ex Sacrorum Rituum Congregationis consulto ratum habuit et confirmavit.

[1] Blessed Oderic went on to China with his treasure and landed at Zayton : he stayed three years with Archbishop John of Cambalec, and returned home, Yule says, *viâ* Tibet through Lhassa, Khorassan, and by the south of the Caspian to Tabriz and thence to Venice. In the month of May 1330, while attached to the Convent of St. Anthony of Padua, in compliance with the request of Friar Guidotto,

VI.—Visited by Bishop John de Marignolli, A.D. 1349

The history of Bishop John's narrative is quite romantic. 'The notices of Eastern travel,' says Yule (*Cathay*, vol. ii. p. 311), 'are found like unexpected fossils in a mud-bank imbedded in a Chronicle of Bohemia,' which the bishop—then attached to the court of the Emperor Charles IV. at Prague, whom he had met in Italy when Charles went to be crowned by the Pope in 1354, and whom he accompanied to Germany—wrote at the request of the said Emperor. 'Charles,' the English editor remarks, 'would have shown a great deal more sense if he had directed his chaplain to write a detailed narrative of his own Eastern experiences.' The task imposed on the bishop appears to have been most uncongenial to him, so to relieve himself somewhat of its tediousness, he interpolates his work by inserting in odd places scraps of his travels.

Some slight details regarding John of Florence are found in Wadding's *Annales Minorum*, and but for the above discovery the identity of the two Johns would have remained undetected. John was a native of Florence, and belonged to the noble family of the Marignolli of San Lorenzo, who derived their name from a village named Marignolle in the valley of the Arno. In 1338, after the death of Archbishop John of Cambalec, there arrived at Avignon an embassy from the great Khan of Cathay, bringing a letter from the Khan himself and another from the Christian princes at his court to the

the minister of the Province, he related his story, which was taken down, or turned into homely Latin, by William of Solagna of his Order. On his way to the Papal court at Avignon he fell sick and was taken back to his province of Udine, where he died on the 14th of January 1331. He was abroad fourteen and a half years. The decree of his beatification was issued by Clement XIII. in 1755.

Pope. The embassy was graciously received by Pope Benedict XII., who reigned 1334-1342; replies to the letters were duly sent by the Khan's messengers, and the Pope expressed his intention of speedily sending envoys to the Court. On 31st October 1338 he nominated the four following envoys: Nicholas Boneti, Nicholas of Molano, John of Florence, and Gregory of Hungary. The first, Yule says, either never started or returned after going part of the way, and is found in 1347 as bishop of Malta. The party left Avignon in December 1338, and journeying across Asia did not probably arrive at Pekin much before the middle of 1342. After a stay of three or four years at the capital, Marignolli proceeded to the houses of his Order at Zayton, and thence sailed for India on the 26th of December (probably) 1347. He mentions his arrival at Columbum (Quilon) just before the following Easter, where he tarried with the Christians for upwards of a year; during the monsoon of 1349 he set sail to visit the Shrine of the Apostle.

He says of the Shrine (p. 374): 'The third province of India is called Maabar, and the Church of St. Thomas, which he built with his own hands, is there, besides another which he built by the agency of workmen.' Regarding a local tradition of the Apostle's presence on the island of Ceylon, he reports the Saint ordering the trunk of a tree that had been cut down on the island: 'Go and tarry for us at the haven of the city of Mirapolis'; which, as Yule observes, is a Graecized form of the name of Mylapore. The local traditions of the Apostle's martyrdom and others, which he relates, will be noticed in Chapter IV.

VII.—VISITED BY NICOLÒ DE' CONTI, A.D. 1425–1430

Nicolò de' Conti left Italy while young, traded at Damascus for many years as a merchant, thence proceeded further east through Persia, sailing by the coast of Malabar onwards; he visited some parts of the interior of Hindustan, Burmah, and Bengal; also the islands of Ceylon, Sumatra, and Java; and also went to Southern China. On his way homeward he sailed up the Red Sea, crossed the desert to Cairo, and eventually returned to Venice after an absence of twenty-five years. Of his visit to Mylapore, after rounding the peninsula, he says: 'Proceeding onwards the said Nicolò arrived at a maritime city, which is named Malepur [should be Malpuria], situated in the second gulf beyond the Indus (the Bay of Bengal). Here the body of Saint Thomas lies honourably buried in a large and beautiful church; it is worshipped [venerated] by heretics, who are called Nestorians, and inhabit this city to the number of a thousand. These Nestorians are scattered over all India, as the Jews among us.'[1]

On his return to Italy, Conti sought absolution from Pope Eugenius IV., then at Florence, for having denied

[1] The quotation given above is from R. H. Major's *India in the Fifteenth Century*, Hakluyt Society, London, 1857, p. 7 of text. While at Paris we were able to see, through M. Cordier's kindness, the primitive Latin text published long after the narrative had been taken down in writing by Poggio. It is to be found in *Poggii Bracciolani, Historiae de varietate fortunae, libri quatuor*, published at Paris, 1723, by one 'Joanne Oliva (Rhodigiano)'; the travels form the fourth book of the 'Historiae,' and occupy pp. 126–153, but bear no separate heading to indicate what they are. We reproduce the text of the passage above quoted from the Latin original, p. 129:—

Malpuria deinde maritima civitas in secundo sinu ultra Indiam sita, Nicolaum excepit. Hic corpus Sancti Thomae honorifice sepultum est in amplissima, ornatissimaque basilica, colitur a haereticis. Hi Nestoritae appellantur qui ad mille hominum in ea urbe habitant: hi per omnem Indiam tanquam Iudaei inter nos sunt dispersi.

his faith during his travels in the East. The Pope imposed on him as penance to dictate an account of his travels. The Pope's secretary, Poggio, took down the narrative in Latin, but this remained unpublished at the time, while an Italian translation was put in circulation. M. Henri Cordier informed us that the interview between Pope Eugenius and Conti at Florence took place in the year 1438, which was the only time the Pope was there. It is from this date that Conti's return to Italy can be fixed.   Supposing Conti had returned two or three years earlier, we come to 1435, and his evidence bearing on the Shrine at Mylapore might be of a date even ten years earlier ; thus we come to *c.* 1425 : it will not be unsafe to fix the date somewhere between 1425–1430.

VIII.—WHAT AMR', SON OF MATTHEW, SAYS, A.D. 1340

Amr', son of Matthew, a Nestorian writer, who flourished about 1340 (Assemani, *Bibl. Oriental.*, tom. iii. p. 580), hands down the Nestorian tradition (*ibid.*, tom. iv. p. 34) regarding Saint Thomas in India : ' His tomb stands on the peninsula Meilan in India, to the right of the altar in the monastery bearing his name.'   The topographical details would denote information brought back by a pilgrim or merchant who had seen the place. Correctly enough, mention is not made of the body, but only of the tomb ; the church is implied while the altar and monastery are mentioned ; the position is fixed on the seaboard ; and a corrupt form of the name of Mylapore is given.

IX.—WHAT THE NESTORIAN BISHOPS SAY, A.D. 1504

The letter written in 1504 from the Malabar coast to the Catholicus of the East, the head of the Nestorian Church, by the four Nestorian bishops, who had

recently arrived there, brings the record of the Indian
Shrine of the Apostle down to the arrival of the
Portuguese in India. After describing the religious
activity awakened by their coming, they say (Assemani,
Bibl. Oriental., tom. iii. p. 594 f.) : ' The houses as well
of Saint Thomas the Apostle have commenced to be
occupied by some Christians ;who are looking after the
repairs ; they are situated at a distance from our aforesaid Christians (of Malabar) of about twenty-five days,[1]
and stand in a city on the sea named Meliapor, in the
province of Silan, which is one of the provinces of
India.' It should cause no surprise to find the new
arrivals mixing up Ceylon and India, and locating
Mylapore in the former. The Shrine would seem to
have fallen sadly into neglect during the lapse of the
preceding half century between the visit of Nicolò de'
Conti and this account sent to Bagdad. An express
mention of the tomb of the Apostle on the site of
the ' houses of Saint Thomas ' was not necessary, as its
existence was too well known to require any ; and, for
all we know, the expression may be meant to cover all
the buildings there—so the bishops confine themselves
to writing of their restoration, which would ensure the
return of a resident native colony of caretakers.

This letter mentions also the arrival of the Portuguese on the coast; we reproduce the passage : ' Our
Fathers should also know that powerful ships have been
sent out from the West by our brethren the Franks to

---

[1] The length of the journey from Malabar to Mylapore, fixed at
twenty-five days, denotes the time it took travellers on foot to go across
the hills from Malabar to the Coromandel coast. Indians did not make
the journey by sea owing to danger, delays, and cost ; and up to recent
years the pilgrimage to Saint Thomas's Shrine used to be made on
foot by the Saint Thomas Christians. But on the extension of railways
they may also, like their fellow-pilgrims in Europe, journey by rail in
future. See Paulinus à Sto. Bartholomeo, *India Oriental.*, pp. 240–
241, on land journeys in India.

these Indian shores.   The voyage occupies a whole
year ; sailing first due south they pass the land of Khus,
that is Aethiopia ; thence they come to these lands of
India ; and after purchasing pepper and other merchandise they return home.   By this route, now opened
and thoroughly explored, the above King, whom may
God preserve, sent six other enormous ships, which
arrived after a six months' sail at the city of Calicut.
They are most expert sailors.'

Since the above was written, an interesting paper on
'The Connection of St. Thomas with India,' by W. R.
Philipps, has appeared in the *Indian Antiquary*, vol.
xxxii., 1903.   We feel bound to refer to it here because
of vague hints thrown out and 'speculation' indulged in
that 'Carmana,' our modern Karmān in Southern Persia,
might represent Calamina, where some writers have said
the Apostle Thomas suffered martyrdom and was buried.
The writer holds that, 'from a geographical, an ethnical,
and indeed, as it seems to me, from every point of view'
(p. 149), the site of the Apostle's tomb ought to be looked
for in that quarter rather than in Southern India.

The question of 'Calamina' will be treated by us
at the close of the following chapter, and what strictly
appertains to it need not be discussed here ; but now
we need only say Calamina does not exist, and never
had a geographical existence.   The question, however,
regarding the Indian tomb of the Apostle is quite
a different subject.   It is, of course, and it ought to
be, quite immaterial to the scholar where the tomb
is located.   He will, however, feel bound to follow
the evidence given by history for its identification.   If
India is the country, as we have found to be the
case on the evidence adduced, where we should
look for it, what place is there in India, other than
Mylapore, which has ever set forth a claim to it ?

Decidedly none : not only in no other part of India,
nor elsewhere, has such a claim been raised—that
of Edessa was for a second tomb where the sacred
remains rested after removal from India, as has been
seen and will again be discussed in the next chapter.
Why then should there be any objection to its being
placed in Southern India, and topographically at Mylapore ?   The writer admits indeed 'there is nothing
inherently improbable in such a supposition.'   As to
'Carmana' or Carmania of old, now Karmān, the Nestorians, who had churches, priests, and Christians in that
part of Persia down to past the middle of the seventh
century, must certainly have known if at any time it
held the Apostle's tomb.   A claim so much nearer home
would not have been overlooked by them ; they certainly would not have come to India to search for it.
We give below two quotations that show how groundless
is the suggestion now put forward in the paper under
discussion.   Assemani (*Bibl. Oriental.*, tom. iii.) publishes several letters of the Nestorian patriarch, Jesuab,
A.D. 650–660 ; the extracts are taken from letter No. 14
(p. 130), addressed to Simeon, bishop of Revardshir, the
Metropolitan of Persia at the time ; the first refers to
the Christians at Merv, the second to those at Carmania :—

Ubinam ingens Maruanitarum (civitatis Maru [Merv])
populus qui quum neque gladium neque ignem aut
tormenta vidissent, solo medietatis bonorum suorum
amore capti, velut amentes, e vestigio in barathrum
perfidiae, hoc est, in aeternam perniciem ruerunt.   The
writer goes on to say all denied the faith, except two
priests, who, as he remarks—instar perustarum titionum
ex flamma impietatis evadentibus, &c.

Ubinam etiam sunt Caramaniae totiusque Persidis
sanctuaria ? quae non per adventum satanae, aut jussu
regum terrae, aut mandatis praesidis provinciarum,

excisa corruerunt, sed exigui unius vilissimi daemonis flatu, &c.

There were, then, Nestorians in the town and province of Karmān; if they never left any intimation to posterity that the Apostle's tomb was in their midst, it is unlikely any later suggestion will induce a scholar to place it there.

We owe it in fairness to the writer of the paper to add that having received from us a copy of the above passages, he reproduced them by way of rectification in a note published in the *Indian Antiquary*, 1904, p. 31, under the heading *Miscellanea*. This phase of the question may now be considered closed.

CHAPTER IV

FURTHER HISTORICAL AND TRADITIONAL
RECORDS OF THE APOSTLE

1. THE APOSTLE'S RELICS AT EDESSA AND SUBSEQUENT
REMOVAL

THE Syriac text of the *Acts of Judas Thomas*, edited by
Wright (*ut supr.*), as also P. Bedjan's edition of the
same in *Acta Martyrum et Sanctorum*, Paris, vol. iii.,
state that the Bones of the Apostle were removed from
India during the lifetime of the king under whom
Thomas suffered martyrdom: the quotation is from
Wright's translation, 'for one of the brethren had taken
them away secretly and conveyed them to the West.'
The Greek version recites : εἰς τῶν ἀδελφῶν κλέψας αὐτὸν
εἰς Μεσοποταμίαν ἀπήγαγεν—for one of the brethren
having stolen him [the Apostle's remains] had removed
him to Mesopotamia. The Latin, *De Miraculis*, says :
Misdeus, reserato sepulchro, ossa invenire non potuit,
quoniam reliquias sancti apostoli quidam de fratribus
rapuerunt, et in urbe Edissa a nostris sepultus est.
St. Gregory of Tours (*l.c.*) says : Thomas apostolus
secundum historiam passionis ejus in Indiam passus
declaratur. Cujus beatum corpus post multum tempus
adsumptum in civitatem, quam Syri Aedissam vocant,
translatum est ibique sepultum. The older Latin, *Passio*,
recites : Syri ab Alexandro imperatore romano veniente
victore de Persidis praelio, Xerse rege devicto, impetra-
runt hoc ut mitteret ad regulos Indorum ut redderent
defunctum civibus ; sicque factum ut translatum esset

de India corpus apostoli et positum in civitate Edissa in locello argenteo quod pendet ex catenis argenteis. The date of the war waged against the Persians by the Emperor Alexander brings us to A.D. 233 (Gibbon's *Decline and Fall of the Roman Empire*, chap. viii.), and the mention of the silver casket holding the Relics, to the year 442 (*Chronicon Edessen.*, Guidi's ed., *infr.*, p. 7).

St. Ephraem gave us no hint when the Bones of the Apostle were removed to Edessa by the merchant, whose name also he omitted to mention. There are thus two traditions—one that the Relics or Bones (not the whole and entire body as some have supposed, importing European ideas into Eastern questions, and these have based thereon the inference that the Apostle's body could not have been in India if it were buried at Edessa) were removed from India in the Apostolic age. The other that the removal took place at a much later date. The Alexandrian date—towards the middle of the third century—on general grounds does appear the more probable of the two, not because of the supposed interposition of the emperor, but because it fits in better with surrounding data, and with the reopening of the trade route to India *viâ* the Euphrates; by the successful termination of the war, the way would be paved for such removal.

The Relics of the Apostle, while at Edessa, underwent a local translation from one church to another. In the short life of St. Ephraem, from which Assemani has published extracts (*Bibl. Oriental.*, i. p. 49), the following event is narrated: 'About this time a paralytic lay at the door of the church of Saint Thomas in the same city [Edessa]: on seeing the Saint, according to his custom, he begged alms. Ephraem replied, gold and silver I have not, but of what I have I will give to thee. Wilt thou be healed? Certainly! answered the paralytic. If thou canst do aught, for the Lord's sake

help me. Ephraem then taking him by the hand said,
In the name of our Lord Jesus Christ, arise. Immediately the man suffering from paralysis was healed,
and he who was lame stood upright on his feet,' &c.
The reader will remark the strong resemblance this
narrative bears to that mentioned in the *Acts of the
Apostles* (chap. iii. 6–8) of the cure of the lame man by
the Apostles Peter and John. We are not here vouch-
ing for the authenticity of the cure and its details; it is
unnecessary for our present purpose; but the narrative
discloses a local circumstance we feel bound to accept—
that during the life of Ephraem there existed at Edessa
a church named after the Apostle, holding the Relics of
which Ephraem speaks in the hymns quoted in a preceding chapter.

Some years later another and a larger church in
the same city was completed in honour of the Apostle,
described as the 'Great Church,' or the 'Basilica'; and
to this the Relics were removed with great pomp and
ceremony. The *Edessan Chronicle*, which is an excerpt
from the city archives made by an anonymous (published
first by Assemani), No. xxxviii., recites[1]: Anno 705, mense
ab (augusto), die 22 advexerunt arcam Mar Thomae
apostoli, in templum magnum eidem dicatum, diebus Mar
Cyri episcopi. 'In the Seleucian year 705 = A.D. 394,
on the 22nd of August, when Cyrus was bishop, the
casket [containing the Relics] of the Apostle Thomas
was removed to the great church erected in his honour.'
A further entry, No. lxi., recites: Anno 753 Anatolius
Stratelates (militiae praefectus) fecit argenteam capsam
in honorem ossium sancti Thomae apostoli. 'In the
year 442–443 Anatolius the General (in command of the
troops) made an offering of a silver casket to hold the

---

[1] *Bibl. Oriental.*, vol. i. p. 388 ff.; re-edited by Guidi, *Chronica
Minora*, tom. iv. of third series of 'Corpus Scriptorum Christianorum
Orientalium,' 1903, versio, p. 6, No. xxxviii.

Bones of the Apostle Saint Thomas.' This was sus-
pended, as we have seen, by silver chains from the
roof.

Some writers have confused the second removal men-
tioned here with the first arrival of the Relics at Edessa.
Barhebraeus (*Chronicon Ecclesiast.*, ed. of Abbeloos, and
Lamy, tom. i., col. 66) says: 'Eulogius was made Bishop of
Edessa, and he built the Church of Mar Daniel, which is also
styled of Mar Domitius. During his episcopate the casket
of Mar Thomas the Apostle was brought from India to
Edessa, and was placed in the Church of Mar Thomas.'
The learned writer is here mistaken. The *Edessan
Chronicle*, No. xxxiv., has the following entry, ' Per idem
tempus' [that is, A. Seleuc. 689=A.D. 378–379], 'Mar
Eulogius became bishop,' &c.; he died A. Seleuc. 698=
A.D. 387–388, as is stated in No. xxxvii. If Barhebraeus'
statement were true, the Relics would have entered
Edessa several years after the death of St. Ephraem;
this of course cannot be admitted.

Ephraem, who was born at Nisibis and had lived
there up to the year 363, quitted it before the entry of
the Persians, when that city, after Julian's defeat and
death, was by Jovian, under the conditions of peace
forced upon him by Sapor, King of Persia, surrendered
to the Persians, and removed to Edessa. He lived
there until his death, which occurred on the 9th of
June 373 (see *Chronicon Edessen.*, No. xxx.; also Lamy,
St. Ephr., Hymni et Serm., tom. iv., praef., p. xxviii.,
and tom. ii. pp. 89–97). It was during this period of ten
years that he wrote his hymns on Saint Thomas. It
becomes thus perfectly clear that the Relics had been
at Edessa long before the time assigned by Barhebraeus
for their arrival from India. From the manner in which
Ephraem speaks of their presence among the citizens
and of the influence they exercised on them, the
reader can realise for himself that a sufficiently lengthy

period must have elapsed since their first arrival at Edessa.

The writer of the article 'Saint Thomas' in the *Dictionary of Christian Antiquity* makes the error of confusing the older with the new church, and supposes that the cure of the leper mentioned above occurred at the door of the great church. This second church was completed after Ephraem's death, and the Relics removed thereto in the year 394, as shown above.

Both the Church historians, Socrates and Sozomen, record the erection of the new church, but not in the sense of the writer of the above article, who states that 'St. Thomas was interred at Edessa, [as] may be inferred from Socrates and Sozomen.' They say nothing to imply a burial of the Apostle in the church. After having detailed in previous chapters the persecution waged by the Emperor Valens against the Catholics, they pass to his attempt to impose the Arian belief on the city of Edessa.[1] Socrates (*Hist. Eccl.*, lib. iv. cap. xviii.; Migne, *P. Gr.-L.*, tom. lxvii.) says : 'I think it unworthy to pass over in silence what had been done in Edessa of Mesopotamia. In that city there is a renowned and splendid basilica (μαρτύριον) dedicated to Thomas the Apostle, &c., which the emperor [Valens] was desirous to see,' &c.[2] And Sozomen (*Hist. Eccl.*, lib. vi. cap. xviii.;

---

[1] The Edessan Chronicle supplies the following data in support of the persecution of Catholics (Guidi, *Chronica Minora*, Scriptores Syri, series 3a, tom. iv., Parisiis, 1903, *versio*, p. 5 *seq.*). After mentioning, No. xxx., the death of St. Ephraem, which occurred on the 9th of June, A. Seleuc. 684–311＝A.D. 373, in the following entry, No. xxxi., it recites : 'In the month of Sept. of the same year the church of Edessa because of the Arian intrusion had to be surrendered by the people.' The entry of the Arians thus took place three months after the death of the Saint ; at No. xxxiii., 'the same year,' that is, the year A. Sel., given previously, 689–311＝A.D. 378–79, 'on the 27 of *Kanun* (December) the Catholics re-entered and occupied the church of Edessa.'

[2] It must be taken for granted that the church was not com-

Migne, *P. Gr.-L.*, tom. lxvii.) : ' Having heard that in the city of Edessa there was a noble church (εὐκτήριον), dedicated to Thomas the Apostle, he went there to see it. He [Valens] found the people of the Catholic church holding their assemblies in a field near the city—for there also the Catholic churches were taken from them. He violently reproached the prefect, and even struck him on the cheek,' &c. Neither passage, as may be seen, can be construed to support the theory put forth that the Apostle had been buried in that church, implying a burial after death. Rufinus (born about 345, died 410), who visited the city of Edessa some time afterwards, says much the same as what the two above quotations contain (*Hist. Eccl.*, lib. ii. cap. v., Migne, *P. L.*, tom. xxi. col. 513): Edessa namque Mesopotamiae urbs fidelium populorum est, Thomae Apostoli Reliquiis decorata. Ubi cum per se imperator populos vidisset ecclesiis ejectos in campo habere conventiculum, tanta, dicitur, iracundia accensus est, &c. Here we find mention made of the Relics, not of a burial ; and indeed it would have been surprising had Rufinus expressed himself differently, since he had ample opportunity to acquaint himself personally with ، the local traditions of Edessa and the history of the Relics, when he visited the city.[1]

At this church great annual festivals used to be held. A sermon preached at one of these celebrations has come down to us. This, from internal evidence, Tillemont holds (*Mémoir. Hist. Eccl.*, vol. i. p. 358) to have

---

pleted at the time of the emperor's visit, and certainly did not then hold the relics of the Apostle. The reader is referred to the date given above of their transfer to this new church, A.D. 394.

[1] His visit is mentioned in the eighth chapter. After describing what he had seen of the disciples of St. Anthony in Egypt, he adds what he had himself seen in the neighbourhood of Edessa (*ibid.*, col. 517): Habuit autem per idem tempus Mesopotamia viros nobiles iisdem studiis pollentes. Quorum aliquantos per nos apud Edessam et in Carcarum partibus vidimus ; plures autem auditione didicimus.

been delivered in the year 402. The homily had been wrongly attributed to St. John Chrysostom.[1] What is peculiar about it is, that the homily should have been cited under the name of this Doctor by the Lateran Council held by Pope Martin I., A.D. 649, and by the Sixth Ecumenical Council held at Constantinople, A.D. 680. Tillemont (*ibid.*, vol. xi. p. 392) suggests three grounds for rejecting it as not the composition of the Doctor of the Church—difference of style, thoughts expressed therein not held worthy of him—and since the context shows the sermon to have been delivered at Edessa and before the Shrine of the Apostle in the year aforesaid, there is no reason to suppose that he (Chrysostom) had then visited the city. He concludes with the remark that even in the lifetime of this great preacher homilies came to be attributed to him not the product of his genius. The sermon is based on the text from St. John xx. 28, containing Thomas's avowal of Christ's divinity, ' My Lord and my God !' and was preached against the Arian denial. The opening section contains language grossly exaggerated, but the latter portion is a fine piece of eloquence, not unlike what may be found in some of Chrysostom's homilies.

Tillemont is, however, wrong in an inference he bases on the composition, that 'the homily clearly states that the body of the Apostle was all entire in one place, and that, where the preacher delivered the homily' (vol. i. pp. 358–359). We reproduce the passage which occurs at the opening of the address : 'Shall I speak of Thomas as a man ? But his tomb (τάφος) proclaims his death ? But then I shall be reproached by the very events (we witness). He is dead and he is immortal ; he as a man died, but he dazzled the world as an angel.

---

[1] *Oper. S. Joan. Chrysost.*, tom. viii., *Sermo in sanctum Thomam apostolum*, col. 497–500, Migne, *P. Gr.-L.*, tom. lix. ; ed. Montfaucon, Parisiis, 1836, tom. viii. p. 625.

He suffered martyrdom (*passionem excepit*), and he struggles in his sufferings. He lies here below and is in glory above. Nothing can conceal him; he has spread his light over the whole world. He has been buried, but he shines forth everywhere as the sun. The relics of the just have gone round the world, &c. Every corner of the earth holds a part of Thomas; he has filled every place, and in each place he subsists entire, &c. The barbarians honour Thomas, all people celebrate his feast this day, and make an offering of his words as a gift to the Lord, "My Lord and my God!"' The presence of the Apostle spoken of is his spiritual and moral presence and influence. The passage, 'he lies here below,' is easily understood of the body being on earth while the spirit soars aloft; but in this case it may have also a reference to the presence of his Relics in the church. But it is not justifiable to take this passage in an isolated form and apart from the historical connections of these Relics, known to the people present at the sermon.

Frequent mention of the continued presence of the Relics at Edessa could be adduced from different writers down to the period of the Crusades. The last witness who makes mention of them, Archbishop William of Tyre, will be found quoted later. But, while it will not be necessary to extend this investigation further, we will not deprive the reader of the beautiful narrative left us by a lady pilgrim who visited the Shrine early in the last quarter of the fourth century. For, apart from the fact of her narrative confirming the general tradition, she gives us a glimpse of what took place at the Shrine within a few years of the death of St. Ephraem. We are indebted to Professor Gamurrini for having brought to light this early 'Peregrinatio ad Loca Sancta' from the one MS known to exist, which fortunately fell into

his hands : for details of text, discovery, and history of
the same, the reader should consult his two papers in
the Roman publication, *Studi e Documenti di Storia*,
1884–1885—the vol. ix. of 1888 contains the first edition
of the 'Peregrinatio'; see also *Bibl. dell' Academia
Storico-Giuridica*, Roma, vol. iv., 1887, pp. xxvii. ff. The
book was published apart with notes, *S. Silviae Aquitanae
Peregrinatio ad Loca Sancta*, altera editio, Romae, typis
Vaticanis, 1888, in 4to ; we quote from the latter edition,
pp. 33–34 :—

'Pervenimus in nomine Christi Dei nostri Edessam :
ubi cum pervenissemus, statim perreximus ad ecclesiam
et ad martyrium sancti Thomae. Itaque ergo juxta consuetudinem factis orationibus, et caetera quae consuetudo
erat fieri in locis sanctis ; nec non etiam et aliquanta
ipsius sancti Thomae ibi legimus.

'Ecclesia autem ibi, quae est ingens et valde pulchra
et nova dispositione, et vere digna est esse domus Dei ;
et quoniam multa erant, quae ibi desiderabam videre,
necesse me fuit ibi stativa triduana facere. Ac sic ergo
vidi in eādem civitate martyria plurima ; nec non
et sanctos monachos commanentes, alios per martyria,
alios longius de civitate in secretioribus locis habentes
monasteria. Et quoniam sanctus episcopus ipsius
civitatis, vir vere religiosus et monachus et confessor,
suscipiens me libenter ait mihi, quoniam video te, filia,
gratia religionis tam magnum laborem tibi imposuisse,
ut de extremis porro terris venires ad haec loca : itaque
ergo, si libenter habes, quaecumque loca sunt hic grata
ad videndum christianis, ostendimus tibi. Tunc ergo
gratias agens Deo primum, et sic ipsum rogavi pluri-
mum, ut dignaretur facere quod dicebat. Itaque ergo
duxit me primum ad palatium Aggari regis,' &c.

We append a translation :—

'In the name of Christ our God we arrived safely at
Edessa. On arriving there we visited without delay the

church and the martyrium of Saint Thomas [the Apostle].
In accordance with our usage we there performed our
devotions and what else we are accustomed to do when
visiting holy places. We also read portions of the Acts
of Saint Thomas [at his Shrine]. The church is indeed
a large and handsome edifice of a new design, and
it is really worthy to be the House of God. As
the city held many sites which I desired to visit, I
stayed there for three days. And so I was able to see
many shrines of martyrs, as also holy monks dwelling,
some at the shrines, others in monasteries situated in
isolated places far from the city. The holy bishop of
the place, a truly religious man, a monk, and a confessor
of the faith, received me most kindly. He said to me,
Since thou, my daughter, for the sake of devotion hast
undertaken so great a task as to journey so far from the
extreme end of the world, if it be pleasing to thee, I
shall with pleasure take and show thee all the sites
which are of interest to us Christians. First thanking
God [for this favour], I begged of him to do what he
had offered. So he guided me first to the palace of
King Aggar ' [Abgar], &c.

The date of this pilgrimage is fixed by the learned editor
between the years 385 and 388, and this partly from
internal evidence. The writer herself he took to be one
Silvia, whose brother at the time held the highest office
at the imperial court of Constantinople ; he supposed
she came on this pilgrimage from Aquitania in France.
The account has been written by her for the benefit of
religious ladies living in a convent, to whom she shows
herself greatly attached. Proof for much of all this is
forthcoming from the context of the book. But the
opinion that the writer was Silvia was not accepted as
decisive, but as one that may be retained until further
discoveries on the subject were made. From the quotation given the reader is able to see the familiar tone in

city and it had passed under Arab or Saracen sway.
When the Crusaders first obtained possession of the city
and surrounding country, and it had become a county
of the new Kingdom of Baldwin, they were known to be
still there. The latest mention we find of them is, as
we said before, by Archbishop William of Tyre in his
Historia Rerum in partibus Transmarinis gestarum
(Migne, *P. L.*, tom. cci.). In book xvi. chap. iii. the
year of the events narrated is given 'anno 1142'; at
the beginning of chap. iv. William narrates what occurred ' eodem anno' [viz. 1142]; at col. 642 he says:
'Sanguinus [Zenghi] imperator Turcarum e civitate
Musula [Mosul] obsedit urbem Edessam'; and at
chap. v. col. 644: destructo ex magna parte muro
civitatis hostis ingreditur, cives gladio perierunt nullo
parcens sive aetati sive sexui; and towards the end
(col. 645): Urbs antiquissima et nomini christiano e
temporibus Apostolorum devota, verbo et praedicatione
Apostoli Thaddaei ab infidelium superstitione eruta,
indebitae jugum passa est servitutis. Dicitur in eadem
urbe et corpus beati Thomae apostoli, una cum prae-
dicti apostoli, et beati Abgari regis corporibus esse
sepultum, &c. All this goes to establish the fact that
when Zenghi, the Emir of Mosul, captured the city in
1142, the Remains of the Apostle Thomas were known to
be yet there. Pagi (*apud* Baron. *Annales*, 1144, cap. xiv.)
assigns the capture of Edessa to the year 1144, and
Mansi holds it to have taken place in 1143; Baronius
himself in his Annals does not mention the capture of
the city by the Saracens. Would not William of Tyre,
being practically on the spot, be in a better position to
know more accurately the exact date than writers in
Europe who would receive the news a year or two later,
and perhaps with no fixed date ?

The city was captured by Zenghi from the Christian
knights after a siege of twenty-eight days. A year later,

the Saracen hold becoming weaker, the citizens invited
Count Joscelin, the holder of the county, to return. He
re-entered the city and held it with his knights, but the
fortress remained in the hands of the Mussulmans.
Noradin, the son of Zenghi deceased, who had been
engaged in asserting his claim to the throne, on learning what had happened, hastily recruited an army and
arrived suddenly before the city, which he promptly re-
captured ; he sacked the place, slaughtered the inhabitants, and destroyed the city.   A full account of these
events will also be found in Michaud's *Histoire des Crusades*, Paris, 1849, vol. i. pp. 350–357, with details from
Mahommedan sources as well ; see also Rubens Duval's
Histoire politique, religeuse, et littéraire d'Edesse, Paris,
1892, chap. xiii., p. 252 ff.   Pagi (*l.c.*) quotes the
Annales of one Signantius, abbot, who, writing of the
destruction of churches that had occurred, mentions
also that of the Apostle—'in qua Thomaei Apostoli
corpus reconditum est.'

It is taken for granted that it was after this second
sack and destruction of Edessa that some of the surviving Christian inhabitants recovered the Relics of the
Apostle from the ruins of the church.   As the whole
of Asia Minor was liable to be overrun by the rising
Mahommedan power, these were transferred for safety
to an island off the coast—that of Chios.   No details are
now likely to be found as to how and when the transfer
to Chios took place ; there is, however, ample evidence
that they were there held to be the genuine Relics of the
Apostle, as the stone—for they appear to have been
placed in some sort of a tomb—which covered the remains bore his name and bust engraved, of which an
illustration is reproduced.
Of their subsequent history we are put in possession
of ample details through the kindness of Archdeacon

H

Perenich of Ortona, who is also the Vicar-General of
that diocese, jointly administered *in perpetuum*, together
with his own, by the Archbishop of Lanciano. Ughelli
gives an account of the removal from Chios to Ortona
à Mare, but by some strange fatuity and ignorance of
elementary geography he describes the removal as
having taken place by sea from Edessa. Nicholas
Coleti, in the second edition of Ughelli's work, corrects
the mistake, saying the island of Chios should stand in
the place of Edessa, but leaves the text unaltered. The
following details are taken from this second edition.[1]
The cathedral, which was formerly dedicated to our
Lady, is now dedicated to the Apostle Thomas, and
holds his Relics in a chapel. An inscription in the
church attests that the first dedication was made on the
10th November 1127 ; the Relics rest there since 1258.
A local document is reproduced by Ughelli in the text
which gives an account of the transfer from Chios (see
cols. 774-776). The local story recites that on the 17th
of June 1258, by order of Manfred, Prince of Taranto,
a fleet under Philip Leonard, the admiral of the prince.
had sailed under the orders of a certain Stolio ; the
ships eventually reached Chios. On the approach of
the fleet the inhabitants fled the town, and a landing
being effected, it came to be known, through a monk
found in the church, that the Relics of the Apostle
Thomas reposed under a slab bearing an inscription
and the figure of a bust. The Relics, together with
the covering stone, were removed to the ship of Leo
Acciaiuoli of Ortona, and the ship in company with
two others set sail for Ortona, which was reached Friday
the sixth of September. The Relics were removed in
solemn pomp to the cathedral. A monument recording

---

[1] *Italia Sacra, Ferdinandi Ughelli, Abbatis SS. Vincentii et
Anastasii ad aquas Salvias ;* editio secunda cura Nicolai Coleti,
Venetiis, 1720, tom. vi. col. 773 *seq.*

the event was placed in the church at a later date, bearing the following inscription :—

D. O. M.

LEONI DUCI ET CIVI ORTONENSI
CLASSIS PRAEFECTO
QUO SUB MANFREDO A CHIO INSULA
ANNO DOMINI MCCLVIII
OSSA BEATI THOMAE APOSTOLI
CAELITUS ADMONITUS
AD ORTONAM PATRIAM
TRANSPORTAVIT
CIVES ORTONENSES OB TAM PRAECLARUM
FACINUS GRATI ANIMI ERGO
MONUMENTUM AETERNUM
POSUERE
ANNO DOMINI MDCIII.

And outside the church, the following :—

Magne Leo in patriam spoliis Orientis onustus
    Dum remeas, Thomae huc ossa beata refers.
Thomae ossa infidi, tetigit qui vulnera Christi,
    Tartara ex latebra quem rediisse negat.
Plus tibi debemus cives pro munere tanto,
    Quam si adducta tibi huc India tota foret.

While at Ortona the Relics underwent another vicissitude. A Turkish fleet under Ali Pasha captured the town on Thursday, 1st August 1566; the town was sacked by the enemy, who burnt and destroyed the churches, including that of the Apostle. Finding the altar of the Saint protected by heavy iron railings, and their efforts to burst open the Shrine failing, they employed gunpowder, and caused an explosion which burst up the stone forming the altar slab and fractured also that of chalcedony brought from Chios, mentioned in the footnote. It would seem that they expected to find great treasure there. On the departure of the Turkish fleet, when the inhabitants were able once more to return to the city and ascertain the extent and nature of the damage sustained, they found, at the bottom of the accumulated debris and cinders, the sacred bones of the Apostle, which had reposed under the altar with the relics of other saints, most providentially preserved intact. But they missed his head; after further search it was found crushed under the weight of a portion of the fractured altar-stone; they reverently picked it up, and were afterwards able, to their great joy and satisfaction, to reconstruct the skull so thoroughly that no part was found missing. A Notarial Act of what had occurred was drawn up by those present, attested and signed by the Bishop, John Domenic Rebiba; the Judge, John Vincent de Renaldo; the Syndic, Pompeius Panza; Joseph Massarius, Public Notary, and many others. This 'Deed of the Verification of the Relics' bears the date of 16th November 1566. A copy of this document has been kindly furnished by the Archdeacon, Vicar-General of Ortona.[1]

[1] The principal sections of the deed are as follows :—

'Deposuerunt, declaraverunt, et confessi et testificati fuerunt cum juramento in vulgari sermone :

'Che al primo del mese di Agosto dell' anno di N. S. 1566, giorno di Giovedi, essendo brugiata la detta Venerab. Chiesa di S. Tommaso Apostolo nella detta città di Ortona dall' armata Turchesca, essi D. Bartolomeo, &c., &c., ed andando per vedere il danno di detta Chiesa, la ritrovarono tutta brugiata, e rivoltandosi verso il sacrato Altare, ove riposavano l' Ossa del Glorioso Apostolo Tommaso, lo ritrovarono tutto in terra spezzato, e la gran feriata riversata sotto sopra, ed entro, dove era la casetta delle Sante Reliquie, uno grandissimo fuoco, e carboni accesi, &c., &c. Con alcuni legni incominciarono a levare il fuoco da detto Altare, e incominciarono a ritrovare le sante Ossa immacolate e intatte, come se non state fossero nel fuoco, e lustravan come vetro; il che vedendo essi Don Bartolomeo e Luca in presenza di essi Giovanni, Bernardino, Leonardo, Bernardo, Sebastiano ed altri, cominciarono a pigliare dette sante Ossa, e porle in una tovaglia, e in alcuni fazzoletti, non senza grandissima effusione di lagrime di tutti, e cosi

The slab of chalcedony marble, which was brought over from Chios, is preserved in the church, and, as said above, it was fractured by the Turks. It has the bust of the Apostle engraved on it, and on either side of the head are engraved the Greek words Ἄγιος Θῶμας, 'Saint Thomas.' Owing to the stone being fractured by the explosion, it is now affixed to the wall of the chapel where the Apostle's Relics were replaced, and the following inscription is placed below it :—

MARMOR CALCEDONIUM
PARVA DIVI THOMAE APLI IMAGINE
AC NOMINE GRECE INSCULPTO
DECORUM
SARACENORUM BARBARIE
SACRA OMNIA ANNO MDLXVI
INCENDIO VASTANTIUM
INFRACTUM
NATIVOQUE OB IGNEM COLORE DESERTUM
URNAE EJUS APLI EX AERE
EXTERNAE DEAURATAE
SUB ALTARI CONDITAE
ELEGANTIUS NUPER ERECTO
ADPOSITUM
AD SACRAE POSTERITATIS MEMORIAM
ORDO POPULUSQUE ORTONENSIS
HIC COLLOCANDUM CURAVIT
ANNO MDCCLXXIV

ne ricuperaron una gran quantità, facendo il simile esso Don Bartolomeo e Luca il sabato sequente in presenza di detti D. Giov. Aloisio, Giov. Bernardino, Giov. Leonardo, ed altri. Poscia la Domenica sequente, quarto di detto mese di Agosto 1566 detto Giov. Antonio con detto Luca ed altri ritornarono in detto luogo e compitamente ricuperarono tutte le sante Reliquie di detto Apostolo dalli carboni e sassi, &c., poi non potendo ritrovare il Glorioso capo d'esso Apostolo, detti D. Giovanni Ant°, Luca ed altri sudetti stavano malinconici, e piangendo, sempre pregando Nostro Signore G. C. loro volesse ispirare dove stava detto capo, e così cominciarono tutti con gran fatica a muovere detta feriata ; e Iddio lodato, ritrovarono la testa di detto Glorioso Apostolo di Cristo sotto alcune pietre di detto santo Altare, rimasta sotto detta feriata illesa dal

The sacred Relics now repose in a bronze urn placed beneath a marble altar. The head of the Apostle is placed in a silver bust (see illustration), and is exposed to public veneration on the celebration of the feast.[1]

Ughelli cites a book written by De Lectis on the transfer of the Apostle's Relics to Ortona. This, the latter says, took place on the date above mentioned, sixth September 1258; the Archdeacon has kindly informed us that the book, of which we could find no copy, was printed at Fermo at the press of Astolfo de' Grandi in 1577, and bears the title: *Vita del glorioso Apostolo di Cristo Tommaso, con la traslazione e miracoli in esso per virtù di Dio operati*, &c.

II.—THE APOSTLE'S MARTYRDOM UPHELD

Tillemont, in his remarks on the Apostle's history, makes a reference to Heracleon's statement that Thomas did not suffer a martyr's death, only to reject it. He points

fuoco, ma però rotta per il peso che l' era caduta sopra ; e così divotamente con lagrime pigliarono la detta testa e, fù ricomposta per le mani di essi D. Bartolomeo, D. Giovanni, ed alcuni altri sacerdoti, con l' intervento del quondam D. Muzio de Sanctis allora Vicario di detta Chiesa, in presenza del Magnifico Giovan Battista de Lectis Fisico [*anglice*, Physician] e detti Giov. Tommaso de Summa e Giuseppe Masca ed altri, ricomponendola di modo come se mai rotta stata fosse, con tutto il martirio, senza mancarvi pur un minimo osso, &c., &c., e di pui li sopradetti dichiarano che ivi erano conservate altre sante reliquie, ed essi tutti dicono ed affermano che l' Ossa del Glorioso Apostolo Tommaso riconobbero da quelle altre dallo splendore e lucidezza che avvevano quell' Ossa, le quali erano negre come ebano, l' altre erano bianche.'

[1] The Archdeacon writes : 'Thrice in the year feasts are kept in honour of the Apostle. On the first Sunday of May, the day fixed for the celebration of the solemn transfer to Ortona ; the 6th of September, the day of the arrival of the Relics at Ortona ; and on the 21st of December, the day of the Apostle's martyrdom. The feast day in May is the occasion when [the Head of the glorious Apostle, enshrined in a rich silver bust, is exposed to public veneration, and is carried in solemn procession through the city. This is not done at the other festivals. The May festival is kept up for three days.

out that Theodoret numbers him among the martyrs, and observes that this passage can hardly be applied to any other but the Apostle. The passage occurs in the work entitled 'Graecorum Affectionum Curatio' (Migne, *P. Gr.-L.*, vol. lxxxiii., of Theodoret's works, vol. iv., *Sermo viii. de Martyribus*): Pro aliis festis vestris [videlicet gentilium] Petri et Pauli et Thomae et Sergii et Marcelli et Leontii et Panteleemonis et Antonini et Mauricii aliorumque martyrum solemnitates peraguntur.[1] He opposes the Christian festivals in honour of the martyrs to those kept by the pagans in honour of their divinities in Syria. The name of Thomas occurring after those of Peter and Paul cannot but be that of the Apostle Thomas, there being besides no prominent martyr of that name; and if a reason be sought why Thomas is named in preference to any other Apostle, it will occur that it arose from the circumstance that in the country, and around, where Theodoret resided, no martyr was held in greater honour, or no festival was celebrated with greater pomp and affluence of people, than that of Thomas in the chief town of the neighbourhood, Edessa.

Tillemont also makes mention of St. Gaudentius, who expressly states that the Apostle was killed by infidels; the quotation was given in Chapter II. p. 45.

There is also the evidence of St. Asterius, Metropolitan of Amasia in Pontus, who died at the end of the fifth century, 499 (Migne, *P. Gr.-L.*, tom. xl. col. 326—*In praise of the Martyrs*): 'Consider how many you slight by one wrong: John the Baptist, James, named the brother of the Lord, Peter, Paul, Thomas. These I call leaders

---

[1] Theodoret, born 387-396, was made bishop of Cyrus near the Euphrates in 423, died *c.* 458 (Bardenhewer's *Les Pères de l'Eglise*). The passage of Theodoret given above is quoted by Card. Baronius in his essay prefacing the *Martyrologium Romanum*, and by Ruinart in the general introduction to his *Acta Sincera Martyrum*.

of Martyrs.' St. Nilus of Constantinople, who died in 430, is equally clear on the subject; he retired from the court with his son Theodulus to the monastery of Mount Sinai (*apud* Photium in *Bibliotheca*, Codex 276, homil. secunda—*De Christi Ascensione*) : 'Stephen, like a branch, is lopped off from the Church, and another palm fruitful of martyrs springs up. James and Peter are cut off ; another martyr arises, and when he is struck off, another fruitful palm sprouts. The vintage removes Paul, and, another shoot maturing, Thomas appears,' &c.

There have not been wanting, however, writers of modern date [1] who do not hesitate to put forth this old fable, first prompted by Valentinian envy at the glory derived by the Church from the number of her martyrs, to rob the Apostle Thomas and others of the glory of having attested the truth of their preachings by the seal of martyrdom. Heracleon's passage referred to occurs in Clement of Alexandria's *Stromat.*, lib. iv. cap. ix. : ' For not all that were saved made the confession in words [before tribunals and magistrates] and so died [by suffering martyrdom] ; of this number were Matthew, Philip, Thomas, Levi,[2] and many others.' Dr. Murdock comments that Clement allows the statement to pass unchallenged ; this he takes as a proof that he had nothing to allege against it. Heracleon denies the martyrdom not of one but of several of the Twelve Apostles ; and it is not a little surprising that, in the light of present-day ecclesiastical literature, writers are found to appeal to such an authority in opposition to the common belief of Christendom. The first question

---

[1] Among modern writers who contest the martyrdom of the Apostle Thomas are Dr. James Murdock in his *Notes* to Mosheim's *Ecclesiastical History*, 11th ed., London, 1878, p. 21 ; R. A. Lipsius, *Dict. of Christian Biography*, art. 'Acts of the Apostles (Apocryphal),' pp. 26–32, &c.

[2] In the Gospels Levi is Matthew ; compare Luke v. 27 and Mark ii. 14 with Matthew ix. 9.

to be asked is, Does Clement's silence imply his avowal of the truth of Heracleon's assertion ? Those who have had occasion to study this work of Clement cannot but be aware how great is the difficulty of ascertaining what the writer accepts and what he merely adduces by way of erudition and a show of general knowledge. Let us turn to the author himself and see if he offers a key to the solution of this difficulty. There are certain passages in which he explains his method of treating the subjects he brings forward. In one place he says (*Stromat.*, lib. vii. cap. xviii.; Migne., *P.Gr.-L.*, tom. ix. col. 556) : ' The Stromates may not be compared to a cared-for garden, planted on symmetrical lines to please the eye, but rather to a mountain all covered with (wild) trees of cypress, plane, laurel with (creeping) ivy, as well as with apple, olive, and fig trees in such manner that of set purpose the fruit-bearing and the wild trees are intermixed.' And again, ' The Stromates thus disregard connection, and style, as the pagans themselves renounce all flower of language and sow their dogmas secretly and without method, wishing the reader to take pains and endeavour to detect them.' And once more (lib. vi. cap. i.) : ' The flowers on the lawn and the fruit-bearing trees in the orchards are not ranged separately according to species, &c. ; so in like manner all the different thoughts that have passed in our mind—without any effort of style and order but of set purpose— are jotted down pell-mell, and like unto a variegated meadow our varied work of the Stromates has been composed.' [1] After this open avowal by the author that he has purposely jotted down indiscriminately ideas of all sorts that have floated through his mind, it would seem useless to inquire why Clement did not correct the Valentinian's assertion if he disapproved of it.

[1] These passages are quoted from Bardenhewer's *Les Pères de l'Eglise*, vol. i. p. 241, Paris, 1898.

Additional evidence for the Apostle's martyrdom was given in Chapter II., and will be found elsewhere.

III.—DIFFERENT VERSIONS OF THE MARTYRDOM

It will be part of our task to set forth successively the different versions of the Martyrdom.

The Acts of Thomas :—

The Syriac text, Wright's translation, p. 293 f. : On the King having decided on the Apostle's death, he hesitated as to what orders he should issue, 'because he was afraid of the great multitude that was there present, and because many believed in the Lord even of the King's nobles.' The King therefore decided on taking Thomas away from the crowd. He made him accompany him under a guard to a distance of about half a mile beyond the town, and then said to them, 'Go up on the mountain and stab him.' On their reaching the top of the hill Thomas asked to be allowed to pray, and having done so, he bid the soldiers execute the order they had received : 'the soldiers then came and struck him all together.'[1]

---

[1] There are two Mounts St. Thomas in the vicinity of Mylapore, the 'great' and the 'little' mount. The former is the one generally designated as Mount St. Thomas. The following topographical details will enable the reader to form a clear idea of the localities reputed to be connected with the memory of the Apostle at Mylapore (consult Map of Mylapore and its Environs, and Illustrations) :—

1. *Mount St. Thomas* ('the Great').—The church which now crowns the summit was erected by the Portuguese ; there had been one probably before. When the writer visited the place, on climbing the hill, he was struck by noticing, halfway up the hill, an artificially levelled spot—the hill itself is an abrupt, insulated hill of protruding granite. On inquiry he was informed that in former ages the Nestorians had a bishop's residence on the spot. He has since learned that there exists an old record in the archives of the diocese of Mylapore—undated and unsigned—stating that at the time the Portuguese arrived at Mylapore (subsequently named *San Thomé*) the Mount St. Thomas was wooded, and was the resort of Nestorian

The Greek version reads : 'He handed him to four soldiers in command of an officer, ordering them to take him up on the mountain and there to pierce him with their lances, and then return to town, &c.   Having ascended the mount and reaching the spot of execution, Uzanes persuaded the soldiers to allow him to pray, and having prayed, (he said), Arise, complete the orders of him who sent you—the four coming forward pierced him with their lances, and falling he died,' &c.

The Latin *De Miraculis* has the same story, and

hermits [say, monks]; the church and monastery that had stood on the mount had crumbled and was in ruins.   The mount is about six miles from Mylapore, and is traditionally reputed to be the site of the Apostle's martyrdom.   It stands out conspicuously by its towering height in a flat country.

2. *The Little mount* is only two miles from the town of San Thomé ; it is an outcrop of granite some eighty feet high.   Local tradition points to it, not as the site of the martyrdom—it is made the centre of the peacock legend—but as the place where the Apostle sought refuge from his persecutors, and probably it was the place he would resort to for prayer and contemplation ; it has a small cave at the summit, now enclosed in the church crowning the knoll.   The Jewish custom should here be remembered, practised by our Lord as well, of resorting to hill tops for prayer and seclusion (Luke vi. 12 ; xxii. 39, &c.) ; further, all the shrines of Israel were situated on hill tops.   The most prominent hill on the Malabar coast, a table-top mountain in appearance, named Maleatur, is also traditionally connected with the Apostle.   Near the summit of the granite outcrop of the 'little' mount, there is a cleft in the rock which always holds some water, though it is difficult to say whence it comes.

3. *The Apostle's Tomb.*—This traditional site, now adjacent to the seashore, has recently come to be enclosed in the crypt of the new Cathedral of San Thomé.   We have said 'now adjacent,' because there is an old tradition that the sea was at one time some miles, say two or three, farther to the east, that extent of foreshore having been gradually cut away—even now on a calm day portions of older Mylapore can be seen lying in the bed of the sea ; and further there is evidence that when St. Francis Xavier visited the place and spent a month there, he lived with the Portuguese priest stationed there. Then there was a house and a garden to the east of the tomb ; the house has since disappeared, engulfed in the sea with what land once stood between it and the shore.   The erosion still continues.

mentions that he was put to death by the lance. The Latin *Passio* alters the account entirely. In this version the death of the Apostle occurs at a much earlier period. When at the Apostle's prayer and bidding the idol in the temple was destroyed (see *Critical Analysis*, &c., No. 32), 'The priest of the temple, raising a sword, transfixed the Apostle, saying, I will avenge the insult to my God.'

Liturgical Books and Martyrologies :—

The old Nestorian Calendar (quoted Chap. II. p. 23) says [Thomas] 'was pierced by a lance in India.'

The Jacobite Breviary: 'Pierced by a lance he gained a martyr's crown.'

The Nestorian Breviary : 'Who for the faith was by a lance pierced.'

The other entries omit to state how the Apostle was put to death.

The Latin Church :—

No entry of detail of death is found earlier than Florus' addition to St. Bede's Martyrology, of the year 830: 'Pierced by a lance he died.'

The Greek Church :—

Synaxaris (Bolland. SS., see Chap. II. p. 66, second quotation): 'Was killed, pierced by lances.'

The Menologium of the Emperor Basil, ninth century (*ut supr.*): 'Pierced by a lance he was killed.'

Local version of the martyrdom prevailing on the Coromandel coast, Mylapore :[1]—

Different reports of this tradition have come down to us. The earliest is recorded by Marco Polo, and

---

[1] The name signifies peacock town. The etymology given by Yule is Mayiláppur: *Mayila*, peafowl, and *pur*, the Indian suffix denoting place. Burnell gives a different derivation, and thinks it was probably *Malaippuram*, mount-town; but Mylapore lies on a

that of Bishop John de' Marignolli comes next. We reproduce them from Yule's *Marco Polo*, 2nd ed., and his *Cathay and the Way Thither*. Marco Polo (*ut supr.*, vol. ii. p. 340): 'Now I will tell you the manner in which the Christian brethren who keep the church relate the story of the Saint's death. They tell the Saint was in the wood outside his hermitage saying his prayers, and round about him were many peacocks, for these are more plentiful in that country than anywhere else. And one of the idolaters of that country being of the lineage of those called *Govi* that I told you of, having gone with his bow and arrows to shoot peafowl, not seeing the Saint, let fly an arrow at one of the peacocks; and this arrow struck the holy man on the right side, insomuch that he died of the wound, sweetly addressing himself to his Creator. Before he came to that place where he thus died, he had been in Nubia, where he converted much people to the faith of Jesus Christ.'

Marignolli's account (*Cathay*, vol. ii. p. 374 f.): 'The third province of India is called Maabar, and the church of Saint Thomas which he built with his own hands is there, besides another which he built by the agency of workmen. These he paid with certain great stones which I have seen there and with a log cut down at Adam's Mount in Seyllan, which he caused to be sawn up, and from the sawdust other trees were sown. Now that log, huge as it was, was cut down by two slaves of his and drawn to the seaside by the Saint's own girdle. When the log reached the sea he said to it, "Go now and tarry for us in the haven of the city of Mirapolis." It arrived there accordingly, whereupon the King of that

---

flat seashore. The mount mentioned in the Acts, as the spot where the Apostle was executed by the king's order, now called the Great Mount St. Thomas, never held a town. The Catalan map of 1375 gives the name *Mirapor*.

place with his whole army endeavoured to draw it ashore, but ten thousand men were not able to make it stir. Then Saint Thomas the Apostle himself came on the ground, riding on an ass, wearing a shirt, a stole, a mantle of peacock feathers, and attended by two great lions, just as he is painted, and called out, "Touch not the log, for it is mine." "How," quoth the King, "dost thou make it out to be thine?" So the Apostle, loosing the cord wherewith he was girt, ordered his slaves to tie to the log and draw it ashore. And this being accomplished with the greatest ease, the King was converted, and bestowed upon the Saint as much land as he could ride round upon his ass. So during the daytime he used to go on building his churches in the city, but at night he retired at a distance of three Italian miles, where there were numberless peacocks . . . and thus being shot in the side with an arrow, such as is called *freccia* (so that his wound was like that in the side of Christ into which he had thrust his hand), he lay there before his oratory from the hour of complins, continuing throughout the night to preach, whilst all his blessed blood was welling from his side ; and in the morning he gave up his soul to God. The priests gathered up the earth with which his blood had mingled and buried it with him.'

Both these early travellers, as well as Barbosa, were told substantially the same tale concerning the Apostle's death.

We will add a further recital given by Linschoten [1]: 'They say that when S. Thomas had long preached in the Kingdom of Narsinga, and but little profited, because the Bramenes, which are the ministers of the Pagodes,

[1] Vol. i. chap. xv. p. 85 f. of the edition by Dr. Arthur Coke Burnell, *Voyage of Linschoten to the East Indies*, Hakluyt Society, London, 1885, of A.D. 1584–1589. Burnell reproduces an early English translation, placing within brackets interpolations and redundancies. These have been omitted.

their false and devilish idols, sought all means to hinder
him. S. Thomas desired the King to grant him a place
where to build a chappell, wherein he might pray and
instruct the people, which was denied him, by the
means of the Bramenes and other Enchaunters, wherein
they put their trust: but it pleased God (as they say)
that a great tree or péece of wood fell into the mouth
of the haven of the towne of Meliapor, whereby neyther
shippe nor boate could pass out, nor come in, to the
King's great hinderance, and the losse of the daylie
trafique to the towne: whereupon the King assembled
to the number of three hundreth Elephantes, to draw
the tree or péece of wood by force out, but all in
vaine, for he could not do it: which he perceiving,
neither yet that all his Bramenes and Southsayers
could give him counsell, he promised great and large
rewards to him that could devise any meanes for the
helping thereof; whereupon the Apostle S. Thomas went
unto the King and told him that he alone (if it pleased
him) could pull it forth, desiring no other reward for his
paynes, but only the same péece of wood to make him a
chappell or house to pray in : which the King granted,
although both he and his Bramenes esteemed it for a jest,
and laughed thereat : wherewith S. Thomas took his
girdell, and binding about the péece of wood, without
any payne drew it out of the river upon the land, to the
great wonder of all beholders, specially of the King, that
presentlie gave him leave to make his chappell of the
same péece of wood : through which miracle divers of
them received Baptisme, and became Christians, whereby
the Bramenes fell into much lesse estimation with the
common people, in authoritie : so that they were great
enemies to S. Thomas, and by all meanes sought to bring
him to his death, which in the end they performed,
having thereunto persuaded some of the people, which
thrust him into the backe béeing on his knées in the

same chappell praying : which History as yet is found painted and set in manie places and churches of India for a memorie.'

When the writer visited Mylapore for the first time, he likewise was told the story of the peacock, and that the incident had happened at the Little Mount, where he then was, as also that the Apostle fled or was carried to the Great Mount, where he died. Yet this narrative did not conceal the impression that the people who were recounting the event held that the Apostle Thomas was killed for the faith. He would premise, from the long experience he has had in Malabar, that the inner characteristics of the Southern Indian are nowhere more prominent and more clearly marked now than in Malabar, and are more observable there than they are in the present-day dwellers of the eastern coast, where a greater and more constant contact with foreign races and manners has largely helped to round off, if not efface, such peculiarities. It should at the same time be clearly borne in mind that the inhabitants of both the southern coasts are of the same race, and, even in times not so very ancient, used the same language and the same writing on the western coast as on the eastern, even down to the days of our early missionaries ; the inscriptions that have survived in Malabar, and the early books printed, were produced in no other than the ancient form of Tamil letters. The writer, then, clearly realised that those at Mylapore did not intend to deny the martyrdom ; but under the plausible veil of the accidental flight of an arrow having for its object not the peacock but the person of the Apostle, he understood, they meant to avert by this device the slur, the shame, and the dishonour that would fall on their town and people did they openly avow to the stranger that the Apostle had been done to death by their forefathers. This view of the Mylapore legend may appear singular and fantastic to those not thoroughly acquainted with native character, thought, and ways in Southern India, but the writer has had more than one instance to convince him of the truth of the observation he here mentions.   In fact, it is nothing more nor less than an application of the principle of 'Saving-Face,' of which more than one instance has of late been offered by China in her intercourse with Western nations.

There are, besides, interesting variations and details in these narratives worth a closer inspection.   In the first narrative, that of Marco Polo, we have : ' I will now tell you the manner in which the Christian brethren who keep the church relate the story of the Saint's death'; but if we go back to what preceded this narrative, *i.e.* the section quoted in a preceding chapter, we have what appears to be a different view of the case : ' The Christians who go thither in pilgrimage take of the earth from the place where the Saint was killed, and give a portion thereof to any one who is sick of a quartan or tertian fever,' &c.   Marignolli says the same : ' When this earth is taken as a potion it cures diseases, and in this manner open miracles are wrought both among Christians and Tartars and Pagans.'   Now, this Christian practice applies to tombs of martyrs, and was not certainly in the early ages extended to the tombs of holy persons who had not died for the faith ; the practice, in other words, attests the Apostle's martyrdom. Ruinart (*Acta Sincera Martyr. in passione SS. Epiodii et Alexandri*) writes : Eorum sacra corpora tempore Gregorii Turonensis in crypta sancti Joannis sub altari cum beati Irenaei reliquiis collocata erant, *de quorum monumentis*, ut ait ille [S. Gregor. Turon.] 'de Gloria Martyrum,' cap. 50, *si pulverem cum fide colligitur extemplo medetur infirmis.*   St. Gregory Nyssen (Migne, *P. Gr.-L.*, tom. xlvi.; *Oper.*, tom. iii., col. 739), *Sermo in*

I

laudem Sancti et magni martyris Theodori, says : Si quis etiam pulverem quo conditorium, ubi martyris corpus quiescit, obsitum est, auferre permittat, pro munere pulvis accipitur et tanquam res magni pretii condenda terra colligitur.

It may be interesting to note that this St. Theodore—whose feast is kept on the 9th of November, and who was greatly venerated in the early ages, having churches erected in his honour in different countries, one even in the Forum at Rome—though bearing a Greek name, was by no means a Greek. The homily of Gregory quoted above gives a full account of his martyrdom and of the festival kept at the church which enclosed his sacred remains ; it had also mural paintings and pavement decorations illustrating his martyrdom and glorious triumph for the faith. The following details are given : he enrolled himself in one of the Roman legions, and suffered martyrdom as a Christian soldier at Amasia, the metropolis of Pontus, A.D. 306. As to the country of his birth, this is what Gregory reports : Patria praeclara et strenuo huic viro est ea regio quae ad solem spectat orientem, nam etiam hic, sicut Job, ex partibus orientalibus nobilis est. The name Theodore, God's gift, has its corresponding term in other languages as well, like *Deusdedit* and *Deodatus* in Latin, so also there is a Syriac equivalent, *Jaballah.* Theodore would appear to belong to the land beyond the Roman border, and may have been an Assyrian : he must certainly have been a Christian before his enlistment in the pagan legion of the empire.

But to return to our subject. While the two first narratives give internal evidence of the Apostle's martyrdom, the third version of the story is explicit on the subject : 'The Bramenes were great enemies to S. Thomas, and by all meanes sought to bring him to death, which in the end they performed, having thereunto persuaded some of the people which thrust him into the backe, béeing on his knées in the same chappell praying—which history as yet is found painted and set in manie places and churches of India for a memorie,' &c.   So the 'Saving-Face' story narrated at Mylapore does not deny the martyrdom, and the paintings referred to support it.

The Portuguese on arriving in India, unaware of the historical data adduced above regarding the remains of the Apostle, were wrong in supposing that the tomb at Mylapore yet held them.[1]   This, however, would not

---

[1] It will not appear surprising if the learned Assemani looked upon the statement put forward by some Portuguese and other writers, wrongly informed, that the Relics of the Apostle Thomas were discovered and found in the Indian tomb, Mylapore, on the arrival of the former.   To those who have followed the historical and traditional course of the story of the Relics thus far narrated, the meaning to be attached to Assemani's rejection of the story referred to below, will be quite clear and self-evident, viz., the Bones (not to use the misleading term *corpus*, body), could not have been found by the new European arrivals at Mylapore, when it was known, on undoubted evidence, that these Relics were in the fourth century deposited at Edessa.   If no other inference is drawn from the statement there would be no further question.   Mr. W. R. Philipps, dealing with the 'Connection of St. Thomas the Apostle with India,' reprint from *Indian Antiquary*, vol. xxxii., 1903, p. 151, expresses himself as follows: 'The opinion of Assemani, mentioned by Bickell . . . is of great weight in such a matter as this.   Assemani, who wrote at Rome early in the eighteenth century, was perfectly well informed; and no one could be more competent to pass judgment on the facts. He deemed these Indian relics of St. Thomas a Nestorian fabrication.' Now this short statement, which does not inform the reader what was Assemani's opinion as to St. Thomas and his connection with India, is misleading.   It has been construed to mean that Assemani denied the Apostle's connection with India ; and the change of type in the text adopted by the printer to enforce the conclusion has added an external weight to the passage.   If the inference is drawn that, in Assemani's opinion, the Relics of St. Thomas were never in India, it would not only be misleading, but would directly oppose the learned Orientalist's emphatic statement.   In the fourth volume of his learned work, *Bibliotheca Orientalis*, Rome, 1728, the author covers ten folio pages with his proofs in defence of the Indian apos-

imply that a minute search, by screening the earth,
would not yet yield minor fragments of bone or other
relics. The hasty and furtive manner in which the
Bones must have been removed by the merchant Khabin
would yet leave lesser relics in the tomb ; and, in fact,
the Relic held at the Cathedral of San Thomé consists
of the fragment of a rib and of the extreme point of a
lance, as were shown and declared to the writer by the
former Bishop of San Thomé, the Right Rev. Henrique
José Reed Da Silva, since retired.

IV.—TRADITIONS REGARDING THE APOSTLE

The West Coast or Malabar Traditions.—The tradition universally accepted by the Saint Thomas Christians
of this coast attest the following points :[1] (1) that

tolate of Thomas, which he establishes on the authority of the Fathers
in reply to Besnage's cavillings. He further adduces evidence from
the Liturgical Books of the Syrian churches, including the Nestorian
section, and of Syrian writers, both in proof of his apostolate as well
as of his martyrdom in India. The *corpus*—or Bones—he points out,
were transferred from India to Edessa ; and he lays emphasis on
the fact that Syrian, Greek, and Latin writers ' write of the body of
Thomas, from the fourth century, as having been removed to Edessa
of Mesopotamia.' What then does Assemani deny ? He denies that
the body was found by the Portuguese in India ; and quite rightly.
In mentioning the Nestorians in this connection Assemani was misled
by statements published in Europe. The Nestorians in India knew
perfectly well that the Relics had been long before removed elsewhere,
for they had annually celebrated in India the festival of the *Removal*
of these Relics on the 3rd of July. Read note p. 134 ; pp. 60–62 ; also
Theodore's statement, text and note, pp. 74–80.

[1] We give a summary of the traditions found prevailing in India
at the arrival of the Portuguese from their early writers in support
of what we say :—

Maffei, *Hist. Ind.* (1st ed. 1588 ; p. 85 of reprint, Coloniae, 1590) :
In Socotram insulam . . . fertur adisse primum [Apostolus Thomas],
deinde multis ibi factis christianis trajecisse Cranganorem. . . .
Colanum petiit . . . trans juga montium ad oram orientalem contendit . . . christiana re bene gesta perrexit in Sinas. . . . In Coro-
mandelem ad revisendos . . . neophytos rediit. Coromandelis caput

the Apostle Saint Thomas landed on the Malabar
coast at Kodangulur (Cranganore) ; (2) that seven
churches, or, more correctly, centres of Christianity

et regia tunc erat urbs Meliapor. . . . Inusitatae magnitudinis truncum in litus jecerat mare quod eo tempore leucas fere decem ab urbe
distabat . . . apostolus regi conditionem tulisse fertur si truncum
illum sibi ad templum vero Deo aedificandum daret . . . sese pro-
tinus ad urbem attracturum. . . . Cum rex annuisset. . . . Thomas
zona quo erat praecinctus . . . immanem stipitem facili ductu sequen-
tem . . . in ipso poemerio statuit, &c. ; he is killed by the Brahmins,
first stoned, then pierced by a lance.

Du Jarric, *Thesaurus rerum Indicar.*, Coloniae, 1615, tom. i. pp.
579-583, repeats similar details.

Gouvea, *Jornada*, Lisbon, 1606, has a similar account, with some
reference to Nestorian archives of Angamale in regard to bishops
sent to Socotra and China.

A Portuguese *Report on the Serra, written in* 1604, Brit. Mus.
Add. MS., 9853, leaf 86 in pencil and 525 in ink, supports the
tradition of the Apostle's preaching at Socotra, Malabar, and Bisnaga.
[Bisnagar, now in ruins and called 'Hampe,' in the present Bellary
district, is the name of the capital of the kings who, at the arrival of
the Portuguese in India, ruled over the Coromandel coast and held
Meliapor, 1490-1508 ; hence that portion of the eastern coast was by
them called Bisnaga.]

The Malabar Christian tradition of the arrival of St. Thomas in
their country is upheld by Colonel Yule, *Cathay and the Way Thither*,
vol. i. p. 75, note. After quoting the different names Cranganore
had borne at different periods—in the Apostolic age it was known
as *Musiris*—he says: 'Cranganore is the seat of one of the old
Malabar principalities, and famous in the early traditions of both
Jews and Christians on that coast. It was there that, according to
the former, the black Jews of the tribe of Menasseh first settled and
abode for more than one thousand years; it was there that St.
Thomas is said to have first preached on the shores of India, and
there also the Mahommedans were first allowed to settle and build a
mosque.'

M°Crindle, in his *Ptolemy*, London, 1885, p. 51, repeats: '*Mouziris*
may unhesitatingly be taken to represent the *Muyri* of " Muyri-Kodu,"
which, says Yule, appears in one of the most ancient of Malabar
inscriptions as the residence of the King of Kodangalur or Kranganur, and is admitted to be practically identical with that now
extinct city. It is to Kranganur, he adds, that all the Malabar
traditions point as their oldest seaport of renown ; to the Christian
it was the landing-place of St. Thomas the Apostle,' &c.

assigned to that early period of evangelisation, were established; of these Palur, Kodangulur, and Parur, were in the north, while the others lay to the south; some of these centres exist no longer, such as Cranganore, destroyed by the Dutch; (3) that the Apostle passed from Malabar to the Coromandel coast, where he suffered martyrdom; (4) that at some subsequent period a violent persecution raged against the Christians on the Coromandel coast, compelling many of them to take refuge among their brethren on the western coast, where they settled down; the Christianity on the Coromandel coast would thus appear to have been destroyed.

The writer feels bound to lay strong emphasis on this tradition in support of the claim of Mylapore to hold the tomb of the Apostle. He is thoroughly convinced—even quite apart from all the evidence adduced in the preceding pages—that if the claim of Mylapore to be the place of the martyrdom and of the burial of the Apostle was not based on undeniable fact, the Christians of Malabar would never have acknowledged their neighbours' claim to hold the tomb of the Apostle, neither would they ever be induced to frequent it by way of pilgrimage. Had this been a case of a fictitious claim put forth to secure public notoriety and importance, they would as probably have, anyway, set up one for themselves, and would have certainly ignored the claim of the former.[1]

---

[1] To the European scholar it may appear paradoxical that the Saint Thomas Christians on the west coast, Malabar, kept the feast of the *Translation* of the Relics of the Apostle Thomas from India to Edessa on the 3rd day of July in accordance with the Syriac Calendar; yet it is so to this day. That the festival had also been kept in India in ancient times we have the authority of the Hieronymian Martyrology, quoted in a preceding chapter. The Christians of the Syrian rite to this day call it the *dohârana, i.e.* the 'translation.' They keep no feast of the Saint on the 21st of

The tradition that the Apostle landed on the Malabar coast, coming by sea, is indirectly confirmed by what St. Francis Xavier found to be the belief existing among the Christians of the island of Socotra at the time of his visit, viz. that they were the descendants of the converts made by the Apostle Thomas (see below).

December ; this latter feast is kept in India by the native Christians on both coasts, the converts of our Latin missionaries subsequent to the establishment of the Portuguese on the two coasts. To the European mind this seems inexplicable, and in consequence the doubt has been raised by some whether the statement be true ; while others have thought this offered an argument to reject the Indian apostolate of St. Thomas. Those who have taken either view have only looked at the question superficially. The question is, What regulates the Liturgy and the Calendar of a Church ? We answer unhesitatingly, the Rite to which it belongs. If the rite of the missionary be the Latin, he will, as the missionaries of the present day practise, introduce everywhere the Latin Missal, Ritual, and Calendar. If Greek, that of the Greek Church will be adopted. If Anglican, that of the Church of England as by law established. So, if Syrian, that of the respective section of the Syrian Church to which he belongs will be introduced. The first Christianity established by the Apostle on the eastern coast, according to an ancient tradition of the Christians of the west coast (reported by Portuguese writers and mentioned in the Report of 1604, Brit. Mus.), was exterminated at an early date by persecution, and many went across and joined their brethren on the west coast. So there remained no permanently established continuous Church at Mylapore. When at a later age Nestorianism forcibly captured the episcopal sees of Mesopotamia and Persia, the clergy and bishops coming from there to India and Socotra brought with them their own Rite (if it had not already pre-existed) as well as their heretical tenets. This is how the ancient Christians in India came to adopt the Syrian Calendar and Liturgy of the Nestorians ; and this is how, followed by the priests they then had, they came to keep the feast of the Apostle not on the day of his martyrdom—which they no doubt would have done had their Church continued autonomous with a regular succession of clergy ; but the case not being so, and they having become a part of the extreme eastern section of the Church of the Syrian Rite, the Calendar and Liturgy found among them by the Portuguese was naturally that of the Nestorian Church. It is a safe axiom—Liturgy and Calendar follow the Rite. See Paulinus à S. Barthol., *India Oriental. Christ.*, Romae, 1794, pp. 132-33.

The earliest mention of the existence of Christians on that island is that by Philostorgius, the Arian Church historian, in his narrative of the mission of Bishop Theophilus to the Homeritae; the reader will find the details, belonging to the year *c.* 354, given in Chapter V., Section iii.

Cosmas Indicopleustes, before the middle of the sixth century (*Topographia Christiana*, Migne, *P. Gr.-L.*, tom. lxxxviii. col. 170), says: 'Similarly on the island named of Dioscoris [the Greek name for Socotra], situated in the same Indian Ocean, whose inhabitants speak Greek, and are a colony placed there by the Ptolemies, the successors of Alexander of Macedon, there are clergy ordained in Persia and sent there, and a multitude of Christians.'

The Arab travellers of the ninth century, whose narrative was published by Reinaud, with Arabic text and a translation in French, in two small volumes, Paris, 1845, mention Christians on the island (vol. i. p. 130): 'The same sea holds the island of Socotra. . . . The greater part of the inhabitants are Christians.'

Abulfeda (Reinaud's *Géographie d'Aboulféda*, Paris, 1848, vol. ii. pt. ii. p. 128): L'ile de Socotora a quatre-vingts parasanges de longueur. Ses habitants sont des chrétiens nestoriens.

Marco Polo, A.D. 1294, also mentions these Christian inhabitants (vol. ii., *ut supr.*, pp. 398–399) : 'Further towards the south you come to an island called Socotra. The people are all baptized Christians, and they have an Archbishop.' And again : 'Their Archbishop has nothing to do with the Pope of Rome, but is subject to the great Archbishop who lives at Bandas [Bagdad]. He rules over the bishop of that island, and over many other bishops in those regions of the world, just as our Pope does in these.'

Assemani (*Bibl. Or.*, tom. ii. p. 458 ff.) gives two lists

of the sees under the Nestorian Catholicus or Patriarch. In the second, which is that by Elias, a Nestorian Bishop of Damascus, the see of Socotra is placed under the Metropolitan of Persia, and this appears to be the older of the two lists; while in the first list, that given by Amr', son of Matthew, of about A.D. 1349 (*Bibl. Or.*, tom. ii. p. 425), Socotra is placed as the eleventh Metropolitan see under the name of Katraba. No date can be assigned to the authorship of the first list. Lequien (*Oriens Christiana*, tom. ii. col. 1290) mentions the transfer of one Elias from the see of Jerusalem to the Nestorian Metropolitan see of Damascus in the year 893, but concludes : Plane Eliam, tabulae et nomocanonis auctorem, illo de quo nunc est sermo recentiorem duxero.[1]

Nicolò Conti, *c.* 1435, visited Socotra and spent two months there (R. H. Major's *India in the Fifteenth Century*, London, Hakluyt Society, 1857, p. 20 of narrative): 'This island produces Socotrine aloes, is six hundred miles in circumference, and is, for the most part, inhabited by Nestorian Christians.'

The evidence of the local tradition mentioned before is contained in St. Francis Xavier's letter written from Goa, 18th September 1542, to the Society at Rome (Coleridge's *Life and Letters of St. Francis Xavier*, London, 1872, vol. i. p. 117). As the Saint gives the last full account of the state of Christianity on the island before its entire disappearance, we make no apology for reproducing it in full :—

'After sailing from Melinda we touched at Socotra, an island about a hundred miles in circumference. It is a wild country with no produce, no corn, no rice, no millet, no wine, no fruit trees; in short, altogether

---

[1] Elias, the author of the list, is styled the bishop of Damascus by Assemani, *Bibl. Or.*, vol. ii. p. 391, and in Index *ad verb.*, but at p. 458 he calls him the archbishop of the see. For further details regarding the see of Socotra, see vol. iv. p. 602, of same work.

sterile and arid, except that it has plenty of dates, out of which they make bread, and also abounds in cattle. The island is exposed to great heat from the sun; the people are Christian in name rather than in reality, wonderfully ignorant and rude: they cannot read or write. They have consequently no records of any kind. Still they pride themselves on being Christians. They have churches, crosses, and lamps. Each village has its Caciz [Syriac term for priest; correctly *Kàshisha*], who answer to the Parish Priest. These Caciz know no more of reading or writing than the rest; they have not even any books, and only know a few prayers by heart. They go to their churches four times a day— at midnight, at day-break, in the afternoon, and in the evening. They use no bells; but wooden rattles, such as we use during holy week, to call the people together. Not even the Caciz themselves understand the prayers which they recite; which are in a foreign language (I think Chaldean). They render special honours to the Apostle St. Thomas, claiming to be descendants of the Christians begotten to Jesus Christ by that Apostle in these countries. In the prayers I have mentioned they often repeat a word which is like our Alleluia. The Caciz never baptize any one, nor do they know the least what baptism is. Whilst I was there I baptized a number of children, with the utmost good will of the parents. Most of them showed great eagerness to bring their children to me, and made such liberal offerings out of their poverty of what they had to give, that I have been afraid to refuse the dates which they pressed upon me with such great good will. They also begged me over and over again to remain with them, promising that every single person in the island would be baptized. So I begged the Governor to let me remain where I found a harvest so ripe and ready to be gathered in. But as the island has no Portuguese garrison, and it is exposed to the ravages of the Mussulmans, the Governor would not hear of leaving me, fearing that I might be carried off as a slave. So he told me that I should soon be among other Christians who were not less, perhaps more, in need than the Socotrians of instruction and spiritual assistance, and amongst whom my work would be better spent.

'One day I went to Vespers as recited by the Caciz; they lasted an hour. There was no end to their repetitions of prayers and incensations; the churches are always full of incense. Though their Caciz have wives, they are extremely strict in regard to abstinence and fasting. When they fast they abstain not only from flesh meat and milk, but from fish also, of which they have a great supply. So strict is their rule that they would rather die than taste anything of the kind. They eat nothing but vegetables and palm dates. They have two Lents, during which they fast; one of these lasts two months. If any one is profane enough to eat meat during that time, he is not allowed to enter the church.

'In the village there was a Mussulman woman, the mother of two young children. Not knowing that their father was Mussulman, I was going to give them baptism, when they ran off, all of a sudden, to their mother to complain that I was trying to baptize them. The mother came to say that she would never let me baptize her children. She was a Mahommedan, and would never have her children made Christians. Upon this the people of Socotra began to cry out that the Mussulmans were unworthy of so great a blessing; that they would not let them be baptized however much they desired it, and that they would never permit any Mussulman to become a Christian. Such is their hatred of Mussulmans.'

The customs described as prevailing among the Christians of the island are those peculiar to Nestorian Christians.

The Carmelite Friar Vincenzo Maria di Santa Cata-
rina (*Viaggio alle Indie Orientali,* Venezia, 1683, lib. v.
cap. ix. p. 472), describing the state of the island on his
voyage home about the middle of the seventeenth century, found Christianity quite extinct, with but some faint
traces of Christian names yet lingering.

The Apostle Thomas, prior to his going to Socotra,
is said to have traversed the Ethiopia of old, preaching
the faith through the country known subsequently as
Nubia. That he had preached to the *Kushites* (the
Semitic name for Ethiopians) more than one testimony
has been adduced in Chapter II. from the Liturgical
Books of the Syrian Church. Marco Polo mentions also
the tradition in the quotation given above (p. 125), and
says that mission preceded his to India—so he had
learnt from the Christians on the Coromandel coast.
An echo of this tradition is also found in *Sermo in
Sanctos xii. Apostolos* (tom. viii. p. 11, *Oper. S. Joan.
Chrysost.,* Parisiis, 1728), wrongly attributed to this
Doctor: 'On one side Peter instructs Rome; on
another, Paul announces the Gospel to the world;
Andrew chastens the learned of Greece; Simon conveys the knowledge of God to the barbarians; Thomas
cleanses the Ethiopians by baptism; Judea honours the
chair of James,' &c.[1]

There appears to be a fixed idea in the minds of
some in connection with the preachings of the Apostles,

[1] An unsupported tradition says also that the Apostle visited
the Magi who, guided by the mysterious star, came to Bethlehem to pay their adoration to the new-born Saviour, and baptized
them. The passage is found in ' Opus imperfectum incerti auctoris'
apud Chrysost., tom. vi., ut supr., p. xxviii., *Commentar. in Matth.,*
now held to be the work of an Arian of the fifth century : Denique
cum post resurrectionem Domini Thomas apostolus isset in pro-
vinciam illam ubi reges stella Bethlehem ducti degebant adjuncti
sunt ei, et baptizati ab eo facti sunt adjutores praedicationis illius.

that after their dispersion to carry out the mandate given them by their Divine Master, they remained permanently in that country and its vicinity, to which each had mutually agreed to go, and that practically they visited no other locality.   Such an opinion is based on no authority, but is the mere outcome of a self-formed conception of things untested by such evidence as we have bearing on the subject.   The mandate itself was to go forth and preach unto all nations, Matt. xxviii. 19, *Going, teach ye all nations;* Mark xvi. 15, *Go ye into the whole world and preach the Gospel;* Luke xxiv. 47, *Penance and the remission of sins should be preached in His name unto all nations, beginning at Jerusalem;* Acts i. 8, *You shall be witnesses unto me in Jerusalem and in all Judea and Samaria, and even to the uttermost part of the earth.*

This implied that after His ascension they should tarry in the neighbourhood of Jerusalem for some considerable time to fulfil the mission entrusted to them 'beginning at Jerusalem,' viz. 'to Jerusalem, all Judea and Samaria,' before their dispersion.   This will be found confirmed also by Peter, when Acts x. 42 is read with its context.   If we test history as has come down to us regarding the separate preachings of the Apostles, the fact that they were not tied down to any one country or nation will appear evident.   They were the sowers of the Gospel seed, and the Master who had prepared the ground to receive that seed sent them to sow it broadcast all over the world.   They were the heralds of the new Gospel, which it was incumbent on them to announce to every living being.   Thus, of Peter we know that besides being specially the Apostle of the Circumcision, he practically traversed all Western Asia from Palestine to the Black Sea, and from Antioch of Syria to Pontus.   His first letter, written from Rome, which he styles Babylon because of its depravity and corruption, was addressed to his first converts residing in 'Pontus, Galatia, Cappadocia, Asia, and Bithynia,' geographically comprising the whole area above mentioned. Certain passages of the letter indicate clearly that these primitive Christian converts had already commenced to experience the hardships of persecution, and that in its cruellest form, torture by fire, it should be noted that the whole of that section of country was under Roman sway, for he openly mentions (chap. iv. 1-5, 12-16) 'sufferings in the flesh' which some had already endured, and warns them that they must 'not think it strange' if they were to be 'tried by burning heat'; this implies that fire was already resorted to, to add the acuteness of anguish to the Christian's sufferings for his faith. It should also be kept in mind that a large portion of this section of Asia likewise formed the special field of the Apostle Paul's labours as described in the Acts.

After this extensive course of apostolic preachings, Peter went to Italy and fixed his seat at Rome, yet so as to make excursions into other fields as well.[1]

---

[1] The first persecution against the Church raised by the Emperor Nero, during which the Apostles Peter and Paul and a host of first converts to the faith suffered martyrdom, may here be briefly told :—

Under secret orders from Nero, and for his personal gratification to witness a great scene of horror and tragedy, it was devised to set fire to a part of the city of Rome. The scene occurred on the 19th of July, A.D. 64 ; the fearful conflagration lasted some nine days, and it consumed the greater portion of the city. Gibbon says that of the fourteen *regiones*, or quarters into which the city was divided, four only escaped the fire, three were levelled to the ground, the other seven presented a melancholy scene of ruin and desolation. The monuments of Greek and Roman art, the trophies of the Punic and Gallic wars, the most sacred temples, with their shrines, votive offerings, and paraphernalia for the services of the State religion, were all consumed. The people, burnt out of house and home, crowded in the vicinity of the Campus Martius, where, under the tyrant's orders, sheds were erected to shelter them, and bread and provisions dis-

John again, who had been somewhat tied down to
Ephesus because of the charge of the Blessed Virgin en-
trusted to him by our Lord, after the demise of the Blessed
Mother of God, is known to have travelled to Italy and

tributed. But, angered and enraged as the populace were at the loss
and destruction of their property, the rumour that the emperor had
purposely come from Antium to witness the scene and that it had
been got up for his amusement, excited them to such a pitch that
they threatened the emperor.   Hence every step was taken to
appease the popular rage ; an inquiry was set on foot to ascertain the
origin of the fire, and thus to divert attention from the suspicions that
had been raised against the emperor.

The inquiry established that the fire originated at the covered
stalls of the *Circus Maximus* frequented by Eastern traders and that
the quarter in the vicinity of Porta Capena, occupied by the Jews, had
escaped the conflagration.   These circumstances would tend to throw
suspicion on the Jews, the more so because of their irreconcilable
attitude to the national worship.   This, coupled with the destruction
of the fanes and temples by the fire, was exploited to fix the blame
more definitely on this alien element of the population.   The Jews
held important positions in the court of the emperor, and exercised
great influence in the city ; so, to divert adroitly all suspicion from
their body, they cast it on the believers of the new faith, whom they
hated most intensely. The cry was thus turned against the Christians—
people of an unknown, mysterious faith, who seemed, even more than
the Jews, to keep aloof from Roman life, its social intercourse and
amusements. The cry once raised was taken up rapidly, the most
absurd popular rumours regarding Christians, their practices and
beliefs, were spread and accepted by the exasperated multitude.
The emperor, glad of the opportunity to divert all suspicion from his
own person, and anxious to throw a victim to popular fury, did his
best to appease and conciliate the people.   He, in consequence, threw
open the imperial gardens, which occupied the present sites of the
Vatican and the adjoining Borgo, and ordered games and sports to
be got up there for the people's amusement.   It was then that the
alleged guilt of the Christians offered the opportunity of making
them subjects of popular sport.   In the morning sports they were
brought out covered with the skins of wild beasts, and pushed into the
arena to be torn to pieces by the dogs set at them.   In the evening the
park was lit up by a novel feature of horror, never heard of before or
since.   Christians were covered with skins or other absorbent wrap-
pings, steeped with oil and tar, tied to posts, and set on fire.

This is what Tacitus tells us of these inhuman scenes (*Annales*,
xv. 44): 'The confession of those who were seized (viz., the Chris-

to have gone to Rome, where both Peter and Paul had taken up the government of that Church, and there, at the 'Porta Latina,' became a confessor of the faith by undergoing the ordeal of being plunged into a

tians) disclosed a great multitude of their accomplices, and they were all jointly, not so much for the crime of setting fire to the city as for their hatred of human kind, condemned to death. They died in torments, and their torments were embittered by insult and derision. Some were nailed to crosses, others, sewn in skins of wild beasts, were exposed to the fury of dogs; others again, smeared with inflammable materials, served the purpose of torches to illuminate the darkness of night. The gardens of Nero were utilised for the melancholy spectacle,' &c. These are the circumstances under which the first general persecution broke out against the Church, and this is how the first martyrs were done to death.

Let us now hear what some witness from the body of these Christians, and a chief amongst them, has to tell us as to the cause and motives of this outbreak of ferocity. St. Clement of Rome, *Epist. I*, cap. v–vi, referring to the cause of the persecution, says it was διὰ ζῆλον καὶ φθόνον—'owing to envy and animosity;' indicating thereby the feelings and the motive which guided the Jews to cast the blame of the conflagration on the Christians. Of Peter he says: 'Because of this (envy and hatred) Peter suffered not once or twice but often, and so through martyrdom passed to his crown of glory.' On account of the same envy and hatred, 'Paul, under the prefects [sub Tegelino et Nymphidio Sabino] suffered martyrdom.' Then, passing to the great body of the faithful, he adds : 'To these holy men who showed the way to life was joined a great multitude of the elect who suffered executions and tortures, leaving unto us a noble example. Because of this animosity women [dressed up as] Danaides and Dirces, after suffering dreadful and monstrous indignities, persevered to the end ; and though feeble of body secured the great reward.' This persecution broke out at the beginning of August, A.D. 64. The martyrdoms of St. Peter and St. Paul, A.D. 64–66, were but separate incidents in the long course of its events. See Tacitus, *ut supr.;* Dom H. Leclerq, *Les Martyrs*, vol. I., *Les Temps Néronniens* : Paris, 1902.

In the days of the Apostles there stood prominent in the vicinity of the Coliseum a huge statue of Nero. The site was not exactly known, but during recent excavations and researches made in the vicinity of the present church of Santa Francesca Romana, the site of the statue appears to be ascertained. The campanile of the church is said to occupy almost exactly the spot where had stood that statue of 'Nero-Helios,' a standing bronze-gilt figure, 120 feet high, placed in the centre of the atrium of the 'Golden-House.'

caldron of boiling oil.[1]   As these had done, so other
Apostles, Thomas among them, must have acted.

It should therefore not appear surprising if ancient
tradition reports Thomas to have preached to many
nations.   Barhebraeus (*Chron. Eccl.*, iii. 4–6) records
the tradition of the East: 'He evangelised many
peoples, the Parthians, Medes, Persians, Carabeans
[read Karmanians], Bactrians, Margians, and Indians.'
Sophronius the Greek (*apud* Hieron. *De viris illustr.*,
Appendix v.) has the following: 'The Apostle Thomas,
as has been handed down to us, preached the gospel
of the Lord to the Parthians, Medes, Persians, Carmanians, Hyrcanians, Bactrians, Magians (or Margians).'

St. John Chrysostom has the following significant
passage (*Hom.* 62, *alias* 61, *Oper.*, ed. Montfaucon,
Parisiis, 1728, tom. viii. p. 370): 'They (the Apostles) all
feared the attack of the Jews, most of all Thomas ; hence
he said, *Let us go and die with him.* Some say he wished

---

[1] This occurred when the persecution of Domitian was at its
height, and he suffered at Rome in the year 95 near the site named
afterwards, when enclosed within the walls commenced by Aurelian
in 271, 'Porta Latina.' These are the words in which Tertullian
(*De Praescil Haeres.*, 36) describes the occurrence : 'O glorious
Church of Rome ! . . . where John plunged in boiling oil suffered no
harm, and was immediately sent into exile to an island' [Patmos]. St.
Jerome, *De viris illustr.*, cap. ix., adds : 'After the death of Domitian
and the cancelling of the cruel edicts of his reign in that of Nerva,
John was able to return to the city of Ephesus,' in A.D. 97. Eusebius
has the same (*Hist. Eccl.*, iii. 18) ; here he organised the churches in
Asia, and survived till the time of Trajan (Euseb., *H. E.*, iii. 23, quoting
Irenæus). St. Epiphanius, *Haeres.*, li., n. 12, says he was past ninety
years when he returned from exile. Polycrates, bishop of Ephesus,
writing to Pope Victor, *c.* A.D. 180, says that John died and was
buried at Ephesus.   The Council of Ephesus, A.D. 431, in their letter
also attest the burial at Ephesus.   Tillemont, *Mémoir. Hist. Eccl.*, i,
article x. p. 350, ed. *ut supr.*, maintains that his body yet reposes in
the church dedicated to his honour at Ephesus [perhaps now a
mosque]. Nothing, at any rate, is now known regarding it.

K

to die; but it is not so, for he rather spoke through fear. But he was not rebuked; his weakness was yet tolerated. Eventually he certainly became the most adventurous and irrepressible. It is, indeed, wonderful, that he who before the crucifixion was feeble, after the cross and faith in the resurrection, should be the most fervent of all. So great is the power of Christ! He who was afraid to go to Bethania with Christ, he, deprived of the presence of Christ, travelled almost the whole inhabited world — οὗτος τὸν χριστὸν οὐχ ὁρῶν σκεδὸν τὴν οἰκουμένην διέδραμε [*lit.* he, not seeing Christ, almost all the inhabited world traversed]; was in the midst of the most bloodthirsty races, who sought to take his life,' &c. This implies that this Doctor of the Church was fully cognisant that, according to the tradition handed down, Thomas was the most travelled of all the Apostles; this the quotations adduced specify in detail, and they should go a long way to uphold the traditional record that has come down to us.

While these sheets were passing through the press an additional piece of traditional evidence, anterior to any quoted above, comes to hand furnished by the *Gospel of the XII. Apostles*, recovered from different Coptic papyrus and other texts. This apocryphal Gospel cannot be placed among those St. Luke had in view when he wrote: ' Many have taken in hand to set forth in order a narration of the things which have been accomplished amongst us' (Luke i. 1), for it makes free use of the texts of the four canonical Gospels, leaning chiefly on that of John, and also refers to the Apocalypse, in its rendering of the history of the last three years of Jesus. It was thus of a later date; the chief narrator of events is a pseudo-Gamaliel. Though no precise date can yet be fixed for this compilation, not unknown to early Christian writers, it will probably not be later than the second century. Our quotation from the text is taken from M. Eugène Revillout's paper (*Revue Biblique*, 1904, April and July numbers, p. 324). The second fragment of the text contains a special blessing bestowed on Peter, and subsequently on each of the other Apostles. As the full text has not yet appeared, we avail ourselves of what the writer has reproduced in the article. After giving textually the words of the blessing bestowed on Peter, he says : Après il donne une bénédiction spéciale à chacun des apôtres. Notons seulement que, pour saint Thomas qui doutait toujours, il est annoncé que sa foi serait désormais un aigle de lumière qui volerait dans tous les pays jusqu'à ce qu'ils croient en leur Sauveur, &c. The text contains many extra-canonical statements ; and what is produced here is a *post-factum* statement, embodied in the words of the blessing, of what Thomas was to have done as an apostle, viz. : ' To the doubting Thomas it was said that his faith would henceforth be an eagle of light that would fly to all countries until the peoples would believe in their Saviour.' This would not have been written of Thomas unless tradition had already reported that he had visited nearly 'the whole inhabited world' in the course of his apostolic career. The passage, in other words, reflects a much earlier tradition of fact, of which Chrysostom has left the written record which has been quoted above.

We will now sum up the traditional record of the Apostle Thomas : (1) He would have preached through the whole of that tract of country lying south of the Caspian Sea—the ' Mare Hyrcanum ' of his days—east of the mountain range of Armenia and of the Tigris, down to Karmania in Southern Persia. (2) It would be during this first apostolic tour that he came in contact with the north-western corner of India at Gondophares' court. (3) After the demise of the Blessed Virgin Mary, when, according to ecclesiastical tradition, the second dispersion of the Apostles took place,[1] Thomas commenced his second apostolic tour. Probably from Palestine he travelled into Northern Africa, and thence, preaching through Ethiopia, he passed on to Socotra, where he must have stayed some time to establish the faith. Going thence, he would have landed on the west coast of India. It is not necessary to hold that he first landed at Cranganore ; he may have landed previously anywhere to the north of the present Mangalore, if it so pleased him. But, in any such case, the fluvial configuration of the land between Mangalore and Calicut would, in all probability, have rendered travelling by land along that coast impracticable at that age, and would have compelled his taking to sea again to make a landing farther down the coast. At any rate, as in those days *Kodangulur*—the Μωζιρις εμποριόν—of the Greek and

---

[1] The tradition that the Apostles, by some supernatural intervention, received intimation to assemble at the dwelling of the Blessed Virgin, Mother of Jesus, before her demise, is, like other sound ecclesiastical traditions, based on a solid foundation. The undermentioned are some of the authorities in support of it :—

I.—St. Gregory of Tours, A.D. 590, *In Gloria Martyrum*, lib. 1. c. 4, p. 489, pars ii. vol. 1, ed. Arndt et Krusch, Hannoverae, 1885 : Denique impleto beata Maria hujus vitae cursu, cum jam vocaretur a saeculo, congregati sunt omnes apostoli de singulis regionibus ad domum eius.

II.—Modestus, Archbishop of Jerusalem, A.D. 631–634, Migne, *P. Gr.·L.*, tom. lxxxvi., col. 3300, *Encomium in dormitionem Deiparae Virginis Mariae*, sec. ix. : Divini Apostoli ex omni terra, quae sub sole est, properarunt vi superna ducti et impulsi, ut eam invenirent sanctissimam matrem, per quam electi a Christo digni facti sunt, qui in Spiritu Sancto apostolatum, sanctissimam omnium quae a Deo tribuuntur, dignitatem assequerentur : quae prope erat ut consequeretur et perciperet in caelis ipsius bona, *quae nec oculus vidit nec auris audivit nec in cor hominis ascenderunt* (1 Cor. ii. 9), quae per ipsam humano generi sunt donata.

III.—Andrew, Archbishop of Crete. He is said to be the author of the new style of hymns called *Canons*, introduced in the Liturgy of the Greek Church. He appears to have lived a long life ; first known as secretary to the Patriarch of Jerusalem, promoted in 711 to the see of Crete, and died *c.* 720 (lived 668–720). He has left three

Roman geographers, was the principal port of the coast, it would be precisely there that he would land—and this is what the traditions existing in Malabar demand. (4) From Malabar the Apostle would find no difficulty in crossing over to the Coromandel coast. He might easily travel by any one of the several passes across the Ghauts known and regularly used by the natives in ancient times for intercourse between both coasts, as being the shorter and the less dangerous route for such communication. (5) It would be on the Coromandel coast that he ended his apostolic labours. This is upheld by the joint traditions of the Christians of the Coromandel and the Malabar coasts.

The foregoing brief sketch will enable the reader to see how the various traditions regarding the Apostle mutually hang together. We have only to remark,

homilies *in Dormitionem Deiparae Virginis Mariae*, Migne, *P. Gr.-L.*, tom. xcvii.; they are marked xii., xiii., and xiv., col. 1045-1110. The quotation is taken from col. 1066: Significat ergo verbis suis vir admirabilis (Dionysius Areopagita) totum fere apostolorum sacratum chorum, ad venerabile illud magnumque Dei Matris coactum spectaculum discipulosque per universam terram dispersos una tunc fuisse congregatos.

IV.—St. John of Damascus was the great light of the Eastern Church during the eighth century. The date of his birth is unknown. He came forth as the great defender of sacred images, *c.* 726; was ordained priest by the Patriarch John, who died in 735. The iconoclast pseudo-Council, held at Constantinople in 754, hurled no less than four anathemas against him, but says he was then dead. The year of his death is unknown. This doctor of the Greek Church has left three homilies *in Dormitionem B. V. Mariae*, Migne, *P. Gr.-L.*, tom. xcvi., Operum Damasceni iii. col. 699 *seq.* In the second Oration, sec. 9 (col. 735), the presence of the Apostles at the demise of the Blessed Virgin is implied. At sec. 11 (col. 738) it is said: Deinde puris linteis purum corpus involvitur, lectoque rursus regina imponitur: Angelis utique linguis suis hymnum sibi gratissimum concinentibus; apostolis autem, Deoque plenis Patribus divinas quasdam cantiones a Spiritu Sancto inspiratas modulantibus Sec. 12. Ac tum sane, tum arca Domini e monte Sion abiens, venerandisque apostolorum humeris gestata, in caeleste templum per interjectum sepulchrum effertur.

further, how unreasonable it is to suppose that traditions converging from various points, and mutually self-supporting, can be the outcome of legendary imaginings. It is for those who contest them to prove that they are inconsistent with any known facts, and consequently baseless. Until then, they hold the field.

V.—The Question of Calamina

The name of Calamina is found in some of the writings which bear reference to the Apostle Thomas, and the same writings mention it as the place of his martyrdom, with the added information that it is situated in India. The reader will scarcely need to be told that geography knows of no place—past or present—bearing the name, and that India ignores it. It becomes, therefore, a literary puzzle, the solution of which, though not necessary to establish the fact that India had received the faith from the Apostle, yet asks for a plausible, if not satisfactory, explanation. It is this obvious desire that we will attempt to meet.

It should be borne in mind that the name does not appear in any of the older writings treating of the Apostle. St. Ephraem, from whom we have quoted largely, the ancient Oriental and Western Liturgies, or the Fathers of the Church, whose witness is given in Chapter II., never mention it; neither do the Acts of Thomas, or the versions of the same. Chronologically, the earliest mention of Καλαμίνη, or *Calamina*, occurs in Greek writers and their Latin translations of a later date, and the desinence of the word discloses a Greek, not an Oriental form. It appears first in a group of mostly anonymous writings in Greek, which give a brief summary of the doings, preachings, and deaths of the Apostles. These stories, when closely examined, are found to bear a family resemblance in shape and detail to the entries given in the *Synaxarium* of the Greek

Church for the 30th of June, on which date is kept the feast of the 'Commemoration of all the Twelve Apostles.' For a specimen of these, see either the extra vol. of November, published by the Bollandists, containing *Synaxarium Ecclesiae Constantinopolitanae,* or the *Menologium Graecum,* edited by Card. Albani, Urbini, 1727 *ad diem,* compare the same with the list of Dorotheus or Oecumenius, &c. It should be noted, however, that neither of the above Greek liturgical books makes mention of Calamina.

From this class of writings we quote the following : (1) Sophronius, whose short accounts of the Apostles in Greek are appended to St. Jerome's book, *De viris illustr.;* the authenticity of the MS discovered by Erasmus, whence these additions have come into Jerome's text, has not only been questioned but openly denied ; but it has lately been re-discovered (*an.* 1896) at Zurich, and is a MS of the thirteenth century, it is the same from which Erasmus had published the Greek extracts in 1516; but the MS does not bear the name of Sophronius ; this the first editor, Erasmus, must have by conjecture suggested, as one Sophronius, a friend of the Doctor, had translated into Greek some of his writings ; the name is here retained to specify the text (see Bardenhewer, *Les Pères de l'Eglise,* i. p. 13, and ii. p. 390) : 'Thomas the Apostle, as has been handed down to us, preached the gospel of the Lord to the Parthians, Medes, Persians, Carmanians, Hyrcanians, Bactrians, and the Magi. He fell asleep in the city of Calamina of India.' Then comes (2) pseudo-Hippolytus,[1] *On the Twelve Apostles, where each of them preached and when he met his death,* p. 131 : 'And Thomas preached to the Parthians, Medes and Persians, Hyrcanians, Bactrians and Margians, and was thrust

---

[1] T. & T. Clark's *Ante-Nicene Christian Library,* Edinburgh, 1869, vol. ix., or vol. ii. of Hippolytus, appendix to part ii. ; also Migne, *P. Gr.-L.,* tom. cxvii.

through in the four members of his body with a pine spear at Calamene, the city of India, and was buried there.' (3) Dorotheus[1] writes: 'Thomas the Apostle having preached the Gospel to the Parthians, Medes, Persians, Germans [*perhaps* Carmanians], Bactrians and Magians, suffered martyrdom at Calamite, a city of India so named.' (4) An anonymous, published with the works of Oecumenius,[2] says: 'Thomas the Apostle, as the tradition of our elders discloses, preached the Gospel of Christ to the Parthians and Medes, the Persians and Germans [*read* Carmanians], the Hyr-canians and Bactrians: he fell asleep in the city of Καλαμίνη—Calamina, India.'

From these writings apparently the name has been taken up by some later Syrian writers:—(1) Barhebraeus (*Chron. Eccl.*, tom. i. col. 34), giving a summary of the preachings of the Apostles, says: 'Thomas preached to the Parthians, the Medes, and at Calamina, a town of India, was crowned with martyrdom, whence his body was removed to Edessa.' A similar passage of his is given by Assemani, *Bibl. Or.*, iv. p. 33, from another work, *Horreum Mysteriorum: Comment. in Matth.* (2) An anonymous Syrian writer[3] says: 'The Apostle Thomas preached . . . in India interior, and taught and baptized and conferred the imposition of hands for the priesthood. He also baptized the daughter of the King of the Indians. But the Brahmins killed

---

[1] See Du Fresne and Du Cange's edit. of the *Chronicon Paschale*, Parisiis, 1688, p. 435, and Migne, *P. Gr.-L.*, tom. xcii. col. 1071, *Ecclesiastical History concerning the Seventy Disciples of the Lord, by Dorotheus, bishop of Tyre;* No. vii., *Of the Apostle Thomas.*

[2] Vol. i., Parisiis, 1630, and placed before *Commentar. in Acta Apostolor.*, who wrote the *Enarratio de duodecim Apostolis et locis ubi Evangelium praedicaverunt.*

[3] In Brit. Mus. Syr. Add. Cod. 17193, folio 80, of the year 874, published by the joint editors of the above *Chron. Eccl.*, vol. iii. cols. 9-10.

him at Calamina. His body was brought to Edessa and there it rests.'

The name has also made its way into the later Martyrologies. It may be remembered that the old Western Martyrology, known as the Hieronymian, makes no mention of Calamina, but it is found in Baronius' revision or edition of the Roman Martyrology.

We may therefore infer, in a general way, that between the latter end of the seventh and the middle of the eighth century the name $Ka\lambda a\mu i\nu\eta$ came into vogue, and got inserted into the narratives concerning the Apostle Thomas. At that stage it would be restricted to Western Asia, to generalise the term ; for in the sixth century neither Jacob of Sarug, A.D. 521–522 in the East, nor in the West does Gregory of Tours in A.D. 590, nor even Florus, who, A.D. 830, enlarged Bede's Martyrologium, make any mention of the name.

How did this fictitious name originate ? and how did it get connected with the Apostle ? Had it any connection with India, that in the minds of these writers it should be the place of his martyrdom in that country ?

We venture to offer the following as a solution of the riddle. The word 'Calamina,' as it appears to us, is a composite term, consisting of the words *Kâlâh*, the name of a place, and *Elmina*, which in Syriac denotes a port. The two words joined together with a necessary elision gives the product Calamina, or Calamine, signifying originally the 'port of Kâlâh.' That there existed in the vicinity of India a port bearing the name of Kalah is historically beyond doubt. The present form of the conjunction of the two terms is not of Semitic origin, for the words would then hold reversed positions, and would have assumed the form 'Elminah-Kalah,' by the same rule that the Aramaic form of the names of towns with *Beth* have Beth preceding the noun governed, but must be of Greek or Latin origin (see Assemani, *Bibl. Or.*, iv. p. 730, for a long list of so governed names). This of itself implies that the term 'Calamina' is not of Aramaic or Semitic origin.

The origin of this compound name may be explained in some such way as the following. Suppose a Christian of Greek origin anxious to learn something of the story of the Apostle Thomas, or of his Relics, inquired of an eastern Syrian traveller, whence were the Relics of the Apostle brought to Edessa? and received in reply the answer that they had come from Kalah [the port] 'Elmina' in the Indies; it would be sufficient to start the report that they had come from *Cala-mina* in India. As a further inference it would easily follow that that was also the place of his martyrdom. The name may have at first originated in this manner, and so got spread among Greek-speaking Christians, and thence passed into written records.

The earliest distinct mention of Kâlâh, to give it its full guttural Aramaic sound, occurs in a letter of Jesuab of Adiabene (see Assemani, *Bibl. Or.*, iii.,113 ff.), Patriarch of the Nestorians, A.D. 650–660. In his letter, No. 14, to Simeon the Primate of Persia and Metropolitan of Ravardshir (*ibid.*, p. 127) he says: Quum per legitimos traductores, perque canonum semitas donum Dei fluxerit fluatque; en plenus est orbis terrarum episcopis, sacerdotibus et fidelibus, qui tanquam stellae caeli de die in diem augentur. At in vestra regione, ex quo ab ecclesiasticis canonibus deficistis, interrupta est ab Indiae populis sacerdotalis successio; nec India solum —quae a maritimis regni Persarum usque ad Colon, Khalam [*lege*], spatii ducentorum super mille parasangarum extenditur—sed et ipsa Persarum regio vestra, divina doctrinae lumine, quod per Episcopos veritatis refulget, orbata et in tenebris jacet.

To understand the full importance of this passage of

Jesuab, it should be borne in mind that the Metropolitan of Persia, then bishop of the see of Ravardshir, was in open revolt against the authority of the Catholicus, or Patriarch, of the Nestorians; that from ages past, even at the date of the Council of Nice, A.D. 325, India had been dependent upon the Metropolitan of Persia.[1] Later, in the days of Cosmas Indicopleustes, the bishop and the clergy used to come to India, as also to Socotra, from Persia and were ordained there ; the passage will be found in the next Chapter (pp. 197, 199); this cannot be gainsaid.

[1] In the signatures to the Decrees of the first Council of Nice, registered according to provinces and reproduced by Gelasius Cyzicenus (Migne, *P. Gr.-L.*, tom. lxxxv., col. 1342 *seq.*), we find the following entry: *Joannes Persa, Ecclesiis in tota Persia et magna India* —'John the Persian [presiding over the] churches in Persia and Greater India.' The signature implies the control he, as Primate, or Metropolitan, the term then in use, held over all the churches in Persia and Greater India. It is in perfect conformity with the style of signatures appended by other Metropolitans present at the Council. Some writers have gone the length of denying the presence of a Persian bishop, while others have objected that *Persa* must imply the name of a town. These latter have read the signature in the light of those appended by bishops within the empire, who affix the title of their see after their name. But here, it should be considered, we have the case of a solitary Persian in an assembly composed chiefly of Greek bishops ; he rightly puts forward his nationality as the proper designation of himself—'John the Persian.' The denial of his presence at the Council is quite unpardonable. Eusebius of Caesarea, the father of Church history, was present at this Council, and he writes as follows (*De vita Constantini*, lib. iii. cap. vii., Migne, *P. Gr.-L.*, tom. viii., col. 51): Etenim ex omnibus ecclesiis quae universam Europam, Africam atque Asiam impleverant, ii qui inter Dei ministros principem locum obtinebant simul convenere, &c. After enumerating those who had come from Syria, Cilicia, Phoenicia, Arabia, Palestine, Egypt, and Mesopotamia, he continues : Quidam etiam ex Perside episcopus synodo interfuit. What further can be demanded to prove the presence of Bishop John the Persian? Eusebius appropriately notes that there was but one bishop from that country, for if there had been others they would have affixed their signatures after that of their Metropolitan, as was done in the case of those provinces of the empire whence more than one bishop was in attendance. Somehow this important point of early Church history has never been clearly brought forward.

Owing, then, to the revolt of the Metropolitan, the supply of the clergy for India was cut off, and became diminished even in Persia, as the contents of the letter fully disclose. This is the burden of Jesuab's complaint. Incidentally he mentions *Kalah* as the extreme eastern terminus of his jurisdiction in the direction of India and beyond India proper.

Colonel Yule, who quotes part of this extract, was not conscious that the translation given by Assemani was misleading; and thereon he further built a wrong inference of his own (see his *Cathay*, &c., vol. i. p. 72, note). The scholar who detected the error was Gilde-meister (see his *Scriptorum Arabum de locis Indicis loci et opuscula*, Bonnae, 1838, p. 60).   The passage, though, was well known to Orientals, among whom this extract of the letter ranked as a classical passage, and used to be assigned to students of the language for study.   It was thus that it came to be pointed out to the writer by a Syro–Malabar priest of his late Vicariate Apostolic on that coast, when he first com-menced his researches in the history of the Church in India.

There are two places, the reader should know, on behalf of which the name *Kalah* is claimed by scholars. It may be that both at different times and for different reasons had a claim to the name. But the evidence for the verbal appellation that has come down to us is conclusive for a place on the Malay Peninsula, which was so named either because it was adjacent to the tin mines of that coast, situated a few miles to the north of Penang, and now worked by Chinamen—or because it was the port whence the mineral named *Kalai*, tin, was exported. The name occurs in the narrative of the Arab travellers of the eighth-ninth century, first published in a French translation by the Abbé Renaudot, Paris, 1718, also rendered into English and published in London.

The Arab text was edited by Reinaud with a new translation and notes, published in two small volumes, Paris, 1845. In vol. i. pp. 93–94, the text says : Le roi du Zabedj compte encore parmi les possessions l'îsle de Kalah, qui est située à mi-chemin entre les terres de la chine et le pays des Arabes. La superficie de l'îsle de Kalah est, à ce qu'on dit, de quatre-vingts parasanges. Kalah [1] est le centre du commerce de l'aloes, du camphore, du sandel, de l'ivoire, du plomb l'alcaly. Yule comments (*Cathay*, vol. i. p. cxci., note): 'M. Reinaud objects "to the lead called *al-qula'-i*" being translated tin, though all the light he throws on it is a suggestion that it is *brass*, which Cosmas says was exported from Kalliana [Bombay]. Yet *qula'-i* is the word universally used in Hindustani for the tinning of pots and pans, and I see F. Johnstone's Persian dictionary simply defines it as *tin*. This product sufficiently fixes Kalah as in or near the Malay Peninsula. Edrisi also places the mine of *qala'-i* at that place.' Another important passage bearing on the question is to be found in the narrative of travels left by Ibn Mehalhal, who in A.D. 941 travelled overland to China and returned by sea.[2] He says, leaving China, 'he arrived at Kalah. It is the first Indian city, and the last for those sailing thence ; they cannot pass it or they would be lost. On arriving there I explored the place. Kalah is a great city with high walls and many gardens and water courses. In the vicinity I saw mines of lead called *qala'-i*, which is found in no part of the world but at *Qala'-h*.' Consult also Yule and Burnell's *Hobson-Jobson, or Glossary of Anglo-*

---

[1] This passage is thus rendered by Yule (*Hobson-Jobson*): 'Kalah is the focus of the trade in aloeswood, in camphor, in sandal-wood, in ivory, in the lead which is called Kala-i,' &c.

[2] See Abu Dolef Misaris ben Mohalhal, *De Itinere Asiatico*, edidit Kurd de Scholoezer, Berolini, 1845 ; also Yule's *Cathay*, vol. i. p. cxi., No. 84, and p. cxci. ; and Gildemeister, *ut supr.*, p. 211.

Indian Colloquial Words, &c., London, 1886, at the word
'Calay.'

The other place for which, among others, M.
Reinaud claims the name of *Kalah* is Point de Galle
(*l.c.*, vol. ii. p. 48, note 171 *et alibi;* see also *Géographie
d'Aboulféda traduite en Français*, vol. i., Paris, 1848,
Introduction, pp. cclxviii–cclxix). The whole of the
south-east coast of Ceylon was known formerly as the
'Galla country': the first word, with a slight Oriental
guttural sound added, becomes 'Kalah.' The reader
will find in Tennent's *Ceylon*, 3rd ed., London, 1859,
vol. i. pp. 582–606, the main arguments in support of
the claim either of Point de Galle, or rather of some
ancient port on that coast now forgotten—whence, for
example, the Chinese pilgrim, Fa Hian, sailed direct to
China. We append the Chinese pilgrim's narrative to
enable the reader to form his own opinion. Samuel
Beal, in his edition of the *Travels of Fa Hian and Sung-
Yun, Buddhist Pilgrims from China to India* (London,
1869, p. 165), assigns the year A.D. 400 for the journey;
and the passage relating his departure from Ceylon is
thus rendered : ' Fa Hian resides in this country (Ceylon)
for two years (and having obtained certain sacred books
in Pali) he forthwith shipped himself on board a great
merchant vessel which carried about two hundred men ;
astern of the ship was a smaller one, as a provision in
case of the larger vessel being injured or wrecked
during the voyage.' This will establish the existence
of a port, an entrepôt of commerce, between western
and eastern Asia, where large Chinese ships were found
trading, at the opening of the fifth century on the Galla
coast. This or any other port of the Galla country
could also have offered a *point d'appui* for the introduction of the composite term 'Calamina.'

Before closing this inquiry we must for a moment
return to the Nestorian Patriarch's statement regarding

Kâlâh. The passage in English would read thus : 'The
flow of sacerdotal succession to the peoples of India has
been cut off since you (the Metropolitan of Persia) fell
away from the observance of the canons of the Church ;
and not only to India—which extends from the shores
of the kingdom of Persia even unto Kâlâh, a distance of
twelve hundred parasangs,' &c.   This gives the marine
distance at which Kâlâh was placed from the shores of
the Persian Gulf.   If the point of departure be taken
from the old land station of Ormuz, and following
closely the coast line, we measure from that point the
distance to the Kâlâh of the Arab geographers on the
Malay Peninsula, passing through the Gulf of Manâr by
Jafnapatam, and across the Bay of Bengal, to the south
of the Nicobars, on to the present Qualah of the Malay
Peninsula, placed somewhat to the north of Penang, we
obtain, roughly, 58 degrees.   To convert these into land
miles we take the more or less generally accepted term
of 69 English statute miles to a degree ; this gives us
4002 English statute miles.   If we now look at Jesuab's
figures of 1200 parasangs, we have three and a quarter
miles ($3\frac{1}{4}$) to a parasang, with a remainder of but 2
miles.

But what is a parasang ?   The only clear definition
generally accepted is that it implies 'the distance a
horse is accustomed to travel by road in Persia in
one hour.'   Taking into consideration the roads, if
roads they may be called, the condition of the ordinary
caravan mount, and the weight of personal belongings
carried by the animal together with his rider, it does
not seem likely that the distance travelled would be
over $3\frac{1}{4}$ miles.   Colonel Yule, in fact (*Cathay*, vol. i.
p. 53, note), converts the parasang into English miles
at roughly that figure.   There is no reliable, much less
standard, gauge to go by in converting the parasang into
an European measure.   It should be realised, to begin

with, that Jesuab's measurement is only a fair Arab
calculation of the distance, that which our maps show
to be 58 degrees, between Ormuz and Qualah. As these
two fit into each other, by the rate of conversion adopted
as a common measure, we come to the conclusion, by a
fairly average measurement, that Jesuab's Kâlâh is the
same as that mentioned by Arab geographers, and was
consequently known already and frequented by Persian
traders by the middle of the seventh century. So that,
whilst in the days of Cosmas Indicopleustes the Nestorian clergy had penetrated as far as Ceylon, A.D. 530–
545, and Cosmas says he was unaware (see p. 199) that
there were any farther east, we are able to verify on
the authority of Jesuab, that they had, with the development of trade, penetrated as far as the Malay coast.
Might not this also offer a fair basis to fix a date
for the introduction of the word Calamina into hagio-
graphical literature ?

To test this point we propose to place together all
the data we have adduced, and see what result they offer.

A.—KALAH or CALAMINA *not mentioned by*—

(1) Jacob of Sarug (Poem, *The Palace that Thomas*, &c.),
A.D. 552.
(2) Gregory of Tours (*Gl. Martyr.*), A.D. 590.
(3) Florus of Lyons (Bedae *Martyrol.*), A.D. 830.

B.—KALAH or CALAMINA *mentioned by*—

(1) Jesuab, A.D. 650–660.
(2) Syr. MS (Brit. Mus.), A.D. 874.

The above are dated records. Now as to the undated :—

(1) Calamina is found mentioned by a series of Greek
writers, who have only left lists of the Apostles'

doings, &c., all anonymous. These, Mgr. Duchesne, aptly classifies as 'Catalogi Apostolorum.'

(2) And by Syrian and Latin writers of the ninth and tenth centuries.

We think it may be safely inferred that the origin of the word 'Calamina' should not be placed earlier than Jesuab's date ; it had not yet been introduced in 830 when Florus made his additions to Bede's Martyrology. This brings us down to the second quarter of the ninth century for Latin writers. Later, it crept into the smaller Latin Martyrologies.

If we accept a date from the middle of the seventh century to the middle of the eighth, A.D. 650–750, for the introduction of the word in the writings 'Catalogi Apostolorum,' we may perhaps not be far wrong. A closer date could only be worked out from some external circumstance, such as a dated MS, but no inference can be drawn from style, as the lists consist of only short paragraphs for each Apostle. The origin may even be later, between 750 and 850 ; and if the Syriac MS date be taken as a gauge for its introduction, the latter period would suit better. Mgr. Duchesne ventured an opinion (*Martyr. Hieron.*, ut supr. p. lxxviii.) that the 'Catalogi' writers appeared 'vix ante saeculum vii,' that would be A.D. 601. This appears to be too early.

VI.—THE 'MALIARPHA' OF PTOLEMY

What has been said above will no doubt have impressed the reader with the fact that the writers who mention Calamina take it to be the name of the place in India where our Apostle died and was buried ; yet they were mistaken as to the name. It is but natural that the reader should further inquire whether there is any

L

mention in ancient geography of the town Mailapur (*Anglicè*, Mylapore) where the tomb of the Apostle, from the evidence produced in a preceding chapter, is known to exist.

The author of the *Periplus*, of the end of the first or beginning of the second century, the earliest geographer who treats somewhat fully of India (see the edition by McCrindle, London, 1879, pp. 140–144) ends his description of the maritime shores of India with the two gulfs of Manār and Palk. It is true he gives some three names which are found in the vicinity of the estuary of the Cauvery, but he has no detailed account of the eastern coast of the peninsula, and passes on to mention *Masalia*, the present Masulipatam, as a landmark. It would seem that he never travelled beyond the gulf of Manār. It is needless, therefore, to look to him for any information regarding the Mylapore of ancient days.

We may next turn to Ptolemy. Mr. McCrindle has also given an English translation of the section of his text with a commentary regarding India (*Ancient India as described by Ptolemy*, London, 1885). The information regarding Southern India, for reasons quite independent of the editor's industry, leaves much to be desired. In tracing the geography of the Alexandrian cartographer for the Northern, Eastern, and Western sections of India, McCrindle had received very considerable aid from work which had been done by M. Vivien de Saint-Martin ; this help now failed him. Three *Mémoires sur la géographie de l'Inde* by the Frenchman were published, but the fourth, which was to take up the geography of Southern India—though promised and referred to in the third —was unfortunately never published.[1]

[1] While at Paris we made personal inquiries to trace the missing MS, and having learned that the *Société de Géographie*, Paris, was the possessor of some of M. Vivien de Saint-Martin's unedited MSS,

The withdrawal of this help brought with it another disadvantage. Saint-Martin possessed a wealth of knowledge of the geography of ancient India, and displayed a rare genius in tracing up details of the Vedic and Puranic, or Sanscrit, geography. McCrindle had now to fall back on what aid Colonel Yule could supply ; and he, excellent as he was in all appertaining to the geography of the Middle Ages and of Arab travellers, was unable to supplement what help the Frenchman had given. It will therefore not appear surprising if the result of McCrindle's work covering this section is not found conclusive to recall the memory of the Mylapore of ancient days.

Ptolemy's Geography from McCrindle :—

' Book VII.—Description of the furthest parts of Greater Asia according to the existing provinces and satrapies.

' 13. Paralia, specially so called, the country of the Toringoi.
   Mouth of the river Khabêris.
   Khabêris, an emporium.
   Sabouras, an emporium.

' 14. The Arounarnoi [Arvarnoi].
   Podukê, an emporium.
   Melange, an emporium.
   Mouth of the river Tyna.
   Kottis.
   Manarpha [or Manaliarpha], a mart.

' 15. Maisolia, &c.'

---

we inquired there, but ascertained that the missing MS was not among the few the Society possessed; nor were we able to trace it elsewhere. We then made special research to obtain further information bearing on this point. After producing what McCrindle has to say, we place before the reader the result of our further investigations carried out in Rome and Paris.

The point to be ascertained is whether the reading *Manarpha*, or *Manaliarpha*, a mart, represents the sole, or even the best reading of this passage in Ptolemy.

(1) The oldest edition we consulted was indeed a tall, venerable edition[1] in fol. max. of 1513, folio 49 (1st col.) :—

A.

In ea quae proprie dicitur Paralia Soretorum
σωρητων maritima.

Chaberis χαβηρις civitas.

Chaberi χαβηρου flu. osti.

Sobura σοβουρα emporium

Aruarnorum ἀρουαρνων.

Podyca ποδυκη emporium.

Melanga μελαγγη emporium.

Tynae τυνα flu. osti.

Cottis κοττις

Maliarpha μαλιαρφα emporium.

Mesoliae μαισωλιας.

(2) The second is Erasmus' first and separate edition of the entire Greek text : Claudii Ptolemaei Alexandrini de geographia libri octo, Basileae, MDXXXIII, in 8vo (*Bibl. Nationale*, Paris), p. 409 :—

---

[1] It bears the title, '*Claudi Ptolemaei viri Alexandrini* . . . *Geographicus novissima traductione e Graecorum archetipis castigatissime pressum.* 1. *Cl. Ptolomaei Geographiam per octo libros partitam,* &c. On the verso of folio 74 the following data are given : Anno Christi Opt. Max. MDXIII, Martii XII, Pressus hic Ptolomaeus Argentinae vigilantissima castigatione industriaque Joannis Scholti urbis indigenae.' The work is dedicated to the emperor Maximilian : it is a combined Greek and Latin text (of the *Bibl. de la Société de la Géographie*, Paris).

B.

Της ιδιως παλουμαινης παραλιας
Τωριγγων
χαβηρου ποτ. εκβολαι
χαβηρις εμποριον
σαβουρας εμποριον
Αρουαρων
ποδωκη εμποριον
μελαγγη εμποριον
Τηννα ποτ. εκβολαι
χοττις
μαναρφα εμποριον
Μαισωλιας

(3) The third is a Lyons' edition of MDXXXV in fol.:
Bilibaldi Pirkeymheri translatione ad Graeca et prisca
exemplaria a Michaele Villanouano jam primum recepti
(libri octo), Lugduni (the *Bibl. Casanatensis*, Rome).   A
second edition of Lyons of 1541 gives an identical text
in the passage :—

C.

Arouarnorum
Poduca emporium
Melange emporium
Tynae flu. ostia
Cottis
Maliarpha emporium
Mesoliae

(4) The fourth is a Latin edition : Geographia univer-
salis vetus et nova complectens—Claudii Ptolemaei Alex.
enarrationes, libri viii, Basileae Henricum Petrum Mense
Martio anno MDXL in 4° :—

D.

Poduca emporium
Melange emporium
Tynae flu. ostia
Cottis
Maliarpha emporium
Mesoliae

(5) The fifth is an Italian translation from a Greek text : La Geographia di Claudio Tolomeo Alessandrino, tradotto dal Greco da M. Giero Ruscelli, Venetia, apresso Giordano Ziletti, MDLXXIIII, Lib. vii, Tavola x d'Asia, p. 312 :—

E.

Di quello che propriamente si chiama maritima de' Soringi—
* Caberi mercato   [Cachel
   Bocca del fiume Cabero
* Sobura mercato   [Zael
    De gli Aruari
   Poduca mercato
* Melange mercato   [Magapara
   Bocca del fiume Tinna
   Cottide
   Maliarfa mercato
Et il luogo onde sciolgono coloro che navigano in Crisa.

(6) The sixth is an edition of 1605 : Claudii Ptolemaei Alexandrini Geographiae libri octo Graeco-Latini per Gerardum Mercatorem a Petro Montano iterum recogniti, Francofurti, Amsterodami, fol. 1605, p. 169 (1st col.) :—

F.

In ea quae proprie dicitur Paralia sive
littoralis Toringorum

.   .   .   .   .   .

Aruarorum
Puduca emporium
Melange emp.
* Tynnae flu. ostia   [al. Tynae
  Cottis
* Manarpha emporium   [al. Maliarpha
    Maesoliae

---

* N.B.—This sign indicates that the editor has supplied in the next column what he considers the present-day name of the place.

Greek text, p. 169, 2nd col. :—

Της ιδιως καλουμενης παραλιας

. . . . . .

Αρουαρων
ποδωκη εμποριον
μελαγγη εμποριον
τυννα ποτ. εκβολαι
κοττις
μαναρφα εμποριον
Μαισωλιας

(7) The seventh is the edition of Peter Bertius, printed in 1618: Bataviae, in fol., giving in full the Greek text and Latin translation (the Library of St. Geneviève, Paris).

Page 198, 1st col., Lat. version :—

G.

In ea quae proprie dicitur paralia sive
   littoralis Toringorum [Soringorum
Chaberi flu. ostia
Chaberis emporium
Saburas [*Palat.* Sobura emporium
  Arvarorum [*Pal.* Aruarnorum
Podoce [*Pal.* Poduce emporium
Melange emporium

P. 199, 2nd col :—

Tynnae flu. ostia
Cottis
Manarpha [*Pal.* Manaliarpha emporium
  Maesoliae

Greek text, p. 198 f. 2nd col. :—

χαβηρου ποταμον εκβολαι
χαβηρις εμποριον
Σαβουρας [*Pal.* Σωβουρα εμποριον
  Αροαρων [*Pal.* Αρουαρνων
Ποδωκη [*Pal.* Πωδουκη εμποριον
Μελαγγη εμποριον
Τυννα ποταμου εκβολαι
Κοττις
Μαναρφα [*Pal.* Μαναλιαρφα εμποριον
  Μαισωλιας

The preceding are the older editions we found useful to consult; we met with others, but they were reprints. There is only one modern print of the entire Greek text, that published by Carolus Fr. A. Nobbe, a stereotyped edition, printed in three separate 18mo vols. at Leipsic, 1843–45; it is a reprint of the Greek text of Peter Bertius of Amsterdam, 1618, quoted above. McCrindle's translation is based on Nobbe's reprint.

Of critical editions of the text there are two, both incomplete. The earlier was prepared by Fred William Wilberg, printed at Essendiae, 1838–45, in 4to, and issued in six fasciculi; it gives the readings of seven MSS collated by the editor, and of the readings of two others supplied to him; the edition goes only to the end of the sixth book. The second was by Alfred Fermin Didot, Paris, 1883, in 4to, for which some twenty codices were collated; it is also equipped with ample information in notes. The edition was to have been completed; in three volumes, two for text, and a third for maps. Only the first volume was published, giving the first three of the eight books of the geography. Lately, a Paris firm (*Librairie de Paris, Rue Jacob* 56) published the maps of the three first books as part ii. of first volume. It thus becomes clear that we have no critical text for the seventh and eighth books of Ptolemy's *Geography*. India is treated in the seventh.

The text first quoted, given by McCrindle, takes us back eventually to that of Peter Bertius. It will be useful to quote what he has written in the preface to that edition, on the intrinsic merit of the text he publishes: Quum . . . Hundius nostram operam ad novam Ptolemaei editionem efflagitaret, recepi eam in me et ope codicis Graeci in quo Fredericus Sylbergus varias lectiones Palatinorum codicum sua manu curiose admodum adnotaverat, non tantum Graeca infinitis locis auxi et restitui, sed etiam Latina maxima sui parte inter-

polavi. . . . Est ubi Latinus codex plura habet quam
Graecus ; est ubi Graecus plura quam Latinus : est ubi
ita inter se dissidunt ut quid sequaris vix scias. This
gives a fair idea of the value of this text based on a
single Greek MS. supplemented by readings from two
or three Palatine codices.

We place before the reader an analysis of the readings
of texts given above in regard to the passage which
refers to our Mailapur :—

Gr.	Μαλιαρφα	A
„	Μαναρφα	BFG
„	Μαναλιαρφα	G
Lat.	Maliarpha	ACDF
„	Manarpha	FG
„	Manaliarpha	G
Ital.	Maliarfa	E

The readings *Μαναρφα* and *Manarpha* are identical,
so they will be grouped together : the readings *Μαλιαρφα*
and *Μαναλλαρφα*—*Maliarpha, Manaliarpha*, and *Maliarfa*
will be similarly grouped.

For the first set we have texts BFG and FG.

For the second we rely upon AG and ACDF and G
and E.

This gives (5) five readings for the root *Manarpha* and
(8) eight for the root *Maliarpha*. This leaves a sufficient
preponderance to show that, though the present text
offers a variant, the balance of weight is for the root
Maliarpha, taking together Greek text printed, and independent translations from the Greek.

The form *Maliarpha* contains the two essential in-
gredients of the name Malia-pur, which would be the
form known or reported to the Greek geographers. A
Greek desinence, as customary in such cases, has been
introduced, so in place of *pur* or *phur* (which may

represent a more ancient form of pronunciation) we have the Greek termination *pha ;* nor has the sound *r* of the Indian name disappeared, but it has passed to the preceding syllable of the word. If we take into consideration the inaccurate reproduction of Indian names in Ptolemy's present text, it is almost a surprise that so much of the native sound of the name is yet retained. We will not refer to the map which accompanies Ptolemy's *Geography*, wherein the name *Maliarpha emporium* is found, for it might be said that it is the result of subsequent manipulation of these charts; but it is significant to point out that these maps place 'Maliarpha' where the present Mylapore would be shown.

The identification which we have followed up so far had been pointed out by D'Anville, the French geographer of the eighteenth century (see his *Géographie Ancienne abrégée,* Paris, 1788, ch. ix. p. 330–331); as also by Paulinus à Sto. Bartholomeo, the Carmelite missionary of the West Coast (*India Orientalis Christiana*, Romae, 1794, p. 126).

CHAPTER V

THE ALLEGED APOSTLES OF INDIA

IN opposition to the claim of the Apostle Thomas to be
the first who conveyed the light of the Gospel to India
proper, the claims of others have been put forward from
time to time by ancient and modern writers.   It will in
consequence be necessary, in order to clear up all doubt
on the subject, to look carefully into all such claims, and
examine the credentials adduced on behalf of each.

I.—ST. PANTAENUS

The first in chronological order is St. Pantaenus,
who is supposed to have left for his mission A.D. 189–
190.[1]   This claim is put forward by no less an
authority than the father of Church history, Eusebius,
the Bishop of Caesarea, A.D. 265–340.   The Roman Martyrology (ed. *ut supr.*) has the following entry on the
7th of July : 'At Alexandria [the feast or commemora-
tion] of St. Pantaenus, an apostolic man and endowed
with every knowledge, whose zeal and love for the word
of God was so great that, inflamed by the fervour of his
faith and piety, he went forth to peoples secluded in
the farthest recesses of the East to preach the Gospel
of Christ ; and returning finally to Alexandria, he

---

[1] The claim for Pantaenus has been recently urged by Rev.
George Milne-Rae, *The Syrian Church in India*, London, 1892, ch. v.
p. 62 ; and by Dr. George Smith, *The Conversion of India*, London,
1893, ch. ii. p. 11.

slept in peace under Antoninus Caracalla' [A.D. 211-217].

The Martyrology does not specify the field of his missionary labours ; and for most of his authentic history we have to depend upon some short notices by his disciple, Clement of Alexandria, and a fuller account by Eusebius (*Eccl. Hist.*, bk. v. chap. x., Eng. trans. by C. F. Cruse, London, 1851, p. 178) : 'About the same time [*i.e.* in the first year of Commodus, A.D. 180, when Julian succeeded Agrippinus in the see of Alexandria, as shown in preceding chapter (*apud* Euseb.)] the school of the faithful was governed by a man distinguished for his learning, whose name was Pantaenus; as there had been a school of sacred literature established there from ancient times, which has continued down to our own times, and which we have understood was conducted by men able in eloquence and the study of divine things. For the tradition is, that this philosopher was then in great eminence, as he had been first disciplined in the philosophical principles of those called Stoics. But he is said to have displayed such ardour, and so zealous a disposition, respecting the divine word, that he was constituted a herald of the Gospel of Christ to the nations of the East, and advanced even as far as India. There were even there yet many evangelists of the word, who were ardently striving to employ their inspired zeal after the apostolic example to increase and build up the divine word. Of these, Pantaenus is said to have been one, and to have come as far as the Indies. And the report is, that he there found his own arrival anticipated by some who there were acquainted with the Gospel of Matthew, to whom Bartholomew, one of the Apostles, had preached, and had left them the same gospel in the Hebrew, which was also preserved until this time. Pantaenus, after many praiseworthy deeds, was finally at the head of the Alexandrian school commenting on the treasures of divine truth, both orally and in his writings.'[1]

Eusebius tells us that, according to tradition, Pantaenus reached India, but does not specify the India he refers to. The general impression produced on the mind of the reader by the text quoted would be that the reference is to India proper ; and were it not for the mention made of the Gospel of St. Matthew left by the Apostle Bartholomew there would be no substantial clue to test the correctness of the impression. But this will be found sufficient to identify the India to which Pantaenus went.

The solution of the doubt demands that a country be found to which Bartholomew had gone, known under the name of India, and a people who could make intelligent use of the Gospel of Matthew left there by the

[1] St. Jerome (*De viris illustr.*, cap. xxxvi. col. 651, Migne, *P. L.*, tom. xxiii.) has the following notice on Pantaenus : Pantaenus Stoicae sectae philosophus, juxtâ quamdam veterem in Alexandria consuetudinem, ubi a Marco evangelista semper Ecclesiastici fuere Doctores, tantae prudentiae et eruditionis tam in Scripturis divinis, quam in saeculari litteratura fuit, ut in Indiam quoque rogatus ab illius gentis legatis, a Demetrio Alexandriae episcopo, mitteretur. Ubi reperit, Bartholomaeum de duodecim Apostolis, adventum Domini nostri Jesu Christi juxta Matthaei evangelium praedicasse, quod Hebraicis litteris scriptum revertens Alexandriae secum detulit. It will be noticed that Jerome states Pantaenus brought back with him to Alexandria the copy of Matthew's gospel left among the people by Bartholomew, while Eusebius makes no mention of the sort. Rufinus, in his translation into Latin of Eusebius' history (text quoted from *Avtores Historiae Ecclesiasticae* per Beatum Rhenanum apud Basileam, anno MDXXIII, an early print, lib. v. c. 10, p. 113) reads : Quem [vid. Pantaenum] ferunt cum ad Indos pervenisset, reperisse quod Bartholomaeus apostolus apud eos fidei semina prima condiderit, et Matthaei evangelium Hebraicis scriptum literis dereliquerit : quod per idem tempus supradictus Pantaenus inibi repertum detulerit. This is an important detail added by the translator; anyhow there is no further mention anywhere of this codex of the original text of Matthew, lost after its work had been completed. Pantaenus is supposed to have returned to Alexandria by A.D. 205. Rufinus, in continuation of the passage quoted, says : apud Alexandriam claram et satis nobilem vitam optimo et mirabili fine conclusit.

former. A further point for investigation is offered by the text of the gospel.

The opinion now universally accepted is that this was written in the current Aramaic, then prevailing in Palestine, for the special benefit of the new converts in Judea. Flavius Josephus has a striking passage which bears on the language question of the Jews at his time. We take it from the preface written by him to his *The Wars of the Jews*, or *The History of the Destruction of Jerusalem* (published and revised in Greek, A.D. 93; Eng. trans. by William Whiston, London, 1870, vol. i. p. 551). In section 1 he says : ' I have proposed to myself, for the sake of such as live under the government of the Romans, to translate these books into the Greek tongue, which I formerly composed in the language of our country and sent to the Upper Barbarians' [he is here using the term in the Roman and Greek sense]. In section 2 he adds : ' I thought it therefore an absurd thing to see the truth falsified in affairs of such great importance, and to take no notice of it ; but to suffer those Greeks and Romans that were not in the wars to be ignorant of these things, and to read either flatteries or fictions, while the Parthians, and the Babylonians, and the remotest Arabians, and those of our nation beyond the Euphrates, with the Adiabeni, by my means know accurately both whence the war began, what miseries it brought upon us, and after what manner it ended.'

Josephus does not tell us in what language his history of the Jewish wars was written, but styles it 'the language of our country.' The Hebrew had long before his time ceased to be the colloquial language of the Jews. About 600 years B.C. the Aramaic is supposed to have begun to supersede it; this takes us to the period of Jewish captivity. Aram, the fifth son of Sem, is the supposed ancestor of the people inhabiting both borders of the Euphrates ; and the land on both borders, in Biblical language, is called

'Aram,' more so Syria proper and Arabia Petræa. The language of Aram gradually expanded itself over the whole of the western countries, and was, in the Persian period, the official language of these provinces. The Jews, having learned it during their captivity, as the bilingual texts of the books of Daniel and Ezra attest, brought it back with them to Palestine as their colloquial tongue. Hebrew therefore does not answer to what Josephus terms 'the language of our country': the more so as he says the language was understood by 'the Parthians, and the Babylonians, and the remotest Arabians, and those of our nation beyond the Euphrates, with the Adiabeni.' The language here referred to by Josephus can be no other than the Aramaic, and it is now generally admitted to have been the language of his text. Similarly, the language in which Matthew's Gospel was written was the Aramaic tongue spoken by Christ and His Apostles. Yet the term Hebrew, applied by older writers to the text of that gospel found by Pantaenus, demands a word of explanation.

The Chaldaic form of the Aramaic dialect, used to the east of the Euphrates and in which some books of the Old Testament were written, is found in the Hebrew text of the Scriptures, written in Hebrew letters, though the language is not Hebrew, but Aramaic or Syriac : hence the language itself with reference to such books came, in a general way, to be termed Hebrew, sometimes Chaldaic, and, in our old English form, Chaldee. The text found by Pantaenus is stated by Eusebius to be written 'Εβραίων γράμμασι—' in Hebrew characters '; the translation by Vallesius renders it *Hebraicis litteris;* Rufinus, in his Latin translation of Eusebius' history, uses the terms *Hebraicis scriptum literis;* Jerome (*De viris illustr.*, cap. xxxvi.), referring to the same codex, expresses himself, *quod Hebraicis litteris scriptum.* This strict exactness of expression adopted by these three learned writers may

represent the fact that the writing was in Hebrew characters, but ought not to be extended to the language of
the text.[1] The gospel then in question being in the
Aramaic, there would be no object or use for it in India
proper, whereas in the India at the extreme section of
Arabia, where dwelt large numbers of Jews with the
Sabaeans, it would be read, understood, and be of service
to keep up the faith preached by Bartholomew after his
departure. It is to this India Pantaenus must have gone.

Proof based on ecclesiastical grounds that Pantaenus'
mission from Alexandria was to the Homeritae is offered
by Assemani. We learn from Jerome that Pantaenus
was sent to 'India' by his bishop St. Demetrius, the
successor of Julian, c. 189. If the faith was taken to the
Homeritae from Alexandria, the church would be ecclesi-

---

[1] Eusebius (*Hist. Eccl.*, lib. iii. cap. 24) treating of St. Matthew
says : Evangelium suum patrio sermone conscribens . . . relinquebat.
He quotes (lib. vi. c. 25) Origen's words : Evangelium scriptum esse
a Matthaeo . . . qui illud Hebraico sermone conscriptum Iudaeis ad
fidem conversis publicavit. St. Jerome, writing of the codex of the
gospel, kept at the Library collected by Pamphilus Martyr, says (*De
viris illustr.* de Matthaeo) : Evangelium Christi Hebraicis litteris ver-
bisque composuit. This is said in opposition to the other books of the
New Testament, which were written in Greek. It becomes apparent
from these different statements that the term 'in Hebrew,' as we
would express it in English, should be taken in the wider sense as
mentioned above. Perhaps it may not be inappropriate to support
this view by further authority. Mgr. Lamy (*Introd. in Sacr. Script.*,
Pars ii., ed. quarta, Mechliniae, 1887, c. ii. No. 5, p. 215) writes :
Omnes novi Testamenti libri Graece exarati fuerunt, excepto S. Matthaei Evangelio, cujus tamen textus graecus ad instar textus primi-
genii evasit. . . . Omnia porro antiquitatis documenta testantur
S. Matthaeum hebraice, id est in lingua aramaica palaestinensi,
quae etiam syrochaldaica vocatur pro popularibus suis fidem Christi
amplexis suum primitus conscripsisse Evangelium. Then follows a
list of Fathers who have written on the subject. The learned Professor of Syriac takes for granted that the expression ' St. Matthew's
gospel was written in Hebrew,' used by some of the Fathers, does
not imply that the language of the text was the Hebrew idiom, but
on the contrary expressly asserts the same to have been the Aramaic
or Syro-Chaldaic.

astically linked, and would look up to that see as the head centre of its faith and jurisdiction. Had it come to them from another quarter they would not go to Alexandria, but to the other see whence the Christian faith and practice had come. This is a point beyond all dispute. It is on this well-known principle that the learned Assemani argues (*Bibl. Or.*, tom. iv. p. 602): Ex his dictis patet Homeritarum, &c. Liquet etiam christianos Homeritas olim Alexandrino Patriarchae subjectos fuisse, qui et ordinatos a se episcopos illuc mittebat. The case of the Homeritae is exactly on the same lines as that of the Abyssinian Church, as we shall see shortly; and, earlier, as was shown previously (*cf.* the opening of Chapter II.), the prelates of the Assyrian or Chaldean Church acknowledged a connection and a dependence from that of Antioch. So the Church of the Homeritae in the ancient land of the Sabaeans—Arabia Felix, now El Yemen, the land of 'the Queen of the South' to which our Blessed Lord referred, adapting his language to popular ideas, that 'she came from the ends of the earth' (Matt. xii. 42), which idea is found also expressed by a classical author (Tacitus, *Historiar.*, lib. v. c. 6): Terra finesque, quae ad Orientem vergunt, Arabia terminantur—because of the mission of Pantaenus from Alexandria, who revived the dying embers of the primitive faith implanted by Bartholomew, looked to that see for a long period as the centre of its ecclesiastical dependence.

Tillemont (*Mémoires Hist. Eccl.*, tom. i. p. 387), summing up the result of his researches regarding the preaching of the Apostle Bartholomew, says: 'We have most certain evidence that he preached in the country which the ancients called the Indies, and which can be no other than Arabia Felix. . . . He took to those Indies the Gospel of St. Matthew written in Hebrew, and St. Pantaenus after a hundred years found it there.'

Rufinus, the priest of Aquileia, in his own portion

M

of the history of the Church added to his translation of Eusebius' text (*Hist. Eccl.*, lib. i. c. 9, col. 478, Migne, *P. L.*, tom. xxi.), writes : 'In the division of the world made by the Apostles for the preaching of the word of God, by drawing lots, while different provinces fell to different Apostles, Parthia fell to Thomas, to Matthew Ethiopia, and the adjacent India on this side (citerior) is said to have been assigned to Bartholomew.' [The sequel of this quotation will be given in treating of the claims of Frumentius.] As to Ethiopia there ought to be no question ; it is the Ethiopia of the ancients which was known as the land of Kus,[1] not Abyssinia, to which country, in more modern times, the name Ethiopia was confusedly attached. Matthew the Apostle, then, preached the faith in ancient Ethiopia ; it was sometimes called the India 'interior,' and would so appear to those who wrote of it from Egypt or Palestine. This is precisely the case with Rufinus, who, born *c.* 345, died 410, had lived between Egypt and Palestine from 374 to 398, spending the last ten or eleven years of his life in Italy when he published his works, most of which were probably written while in the East, for during the last troubled years of his life he would neither have had the leisure nor time sufficient to compose what has come down to us under his name (see Bardenhewer, *Les Pères de l'Eglise*, ii. pp. 360–61). In the above quotation he tells us that while Matthew went to Ethiopia, ' the adjacent India on this side ' was assigned to Bartholomew. This clearly designates the lower extremity of Arabia, on the opposite shore of the Red Sea, and so in a manner

---

[1] We insert here the important witness borne by Flavius Josephus (*Opera omnia*, Graece et Latine recognovit Guill. Dindorf, Parisiis, 1845, vol. i., *De Antiquitate Judaeorum*, lib. i. c. vi. n. 2) on the bearing of the name *kus*: Ex quatuor enim Chamae [*Cham*] filiis, Chuso [*Chus*, Kus] nihil detrimenti tempus attulit : nam Aethiopes, quorum princeps fuit, nunc quoque tam a se ipsis quam ab Asianis omnibus Chusaei [Kus] nominantur.

adjacent to Ethiopia. This further implies that, according to Rufinus, the Apostle's mission was to the Sabaei, who inhabited the lower extremity of Arabia.

Should there be any doubt as to the correctness of this inference, it ought to be completely removed by what Socrates says, dealing with the same subject (*Hist. Eccl.*, lib. i. cap. 19, col. 126, Migne, *P. Gr.-L.*, tom. lxvii.): Cum apostoli praedicationis causa ad gentes profecturi, eas inter se sortito dividerent, Thomas quidem Parthiae, Matthaeus vero Aethiopiae apostolatum sortitus est,[1] Bartholomaeo India quae Aethiopiae confinis est, obtigit. 'When the Apostles about to disperse among the nations to preach (the faith), divided

---

[1] An echo of those early traditions regarding St. Matthew's preaching of the Gospel, as reported by Rufinus and Socrates, has been handed down by the missionary Friar, afterwards Archbishop of Cambalec, John of Monte Corvino. In his second letter dated from Cambalec, Quinquagesima Sunday, 1306 (13th February), which has come down to us in two separate sections, as explained in our Chapter III. p. 89, he writes in the second section recovered more recently, that during his stay in India 'a solemn deputation had come to him from a certain part of Ethiopia, begging him either to go thither to preach, or to send other good preachers ; for since the time of St. Matthew the Apostle, and his immediate disciples, they had had no preacher to instruct them in the faith of Christ, and they had an ardent desire to attain to the true Christian faith (Yule's *Cathay and the Way Thither*, vol. i. pp. 208–209).

We add the following from Wadding's *Annales Minorum*, tom. vi. p. 91, anno 1307, n. vi. *In margin* B. Oder. ad an. 1306 mittunt ei nuncios Æthopes—Ultra ea quae scripsit anno superiori frater Johannes a Monte Corvino, *inquit beatus Odericus*, hoc anno narrat in alia a se scripta Epistola, quod solemnes Nuncii venerunt ad eum de quadam parte Æthiopiae, rogantes, ut illuc pergeret ad praedicandum, vel mitteret Praedicatores bonos, quia a tempore beati Matthaei Evangelistae, et discipulorum ejus, praedicatores non habuerunt, qui eos instruerent in fide Christi, et multum desiderant ad veram Christi fidem pervenire ; et si Fratres illuc mitterentur, omnes converterentur ad Christum et fierent veri Christiani ; nam sunt plurimi in civitate qui solo nomine Christiani dicuntur et Christum credunt, sed de Scripturis et sanctis doctrinis aliud non sciunt, simpliciter viventes, cum non habeant praedicatores et doctores.

these among themselves by lot, Thomas obtained the apostolate to Parthia, Matthew to Ethiopia; to Bartholomew fell that India which is near to (bordering on) Ethiopia.'

The mission field of St. Pantaenus, then, was not to 'the India of the Brahmans' as St. Jerome, deceived by appearances, has stated.[1]

We may here appropriately add a few words regarding the copy of the Gospel of Matthew found years later with the body of St. Barnabas on the island of Cyprus. A general impression prevails that the copy was written in Hebrew. The Roman Martyrology under 21 September, the feast of St. Matthew the Evangelist, says : Hujus evangelium Hebraeo sermone conscriptum, ipso revelante, inventum est una cum corpore beati Barnabae apostoli, tempore Zenonis imperatoris. The reader will notice that the earlier expression used by historians, *Hebraicis litteris scriptum*, is here changed into ' Hebraeo

---

[1] Epistola lxx. ad Magnum Oratorem urbis Romae, Migne, *P. L.*, vol. xxii. col. 667, n. 4, *Scriptores Ecclesiastici saecularibus litteris eruditi :* Pantaenus Stoicae sectae philosophus, ob praecipuae eruditionis gloriam, a Demetrio Alexandriae episcopo missus est in Indiam, ut Christum apud Brachmanas et illius gentis philosophos praedicaret.

St. Jerome has another passage in his writings bearing on India, which may be reproduced here for the information of the reader (*oper. ut supra.*, tom. xxii, Epistola cvii. ad Laetam, n. 2, col. 870) : De India, Perside, Aethiopia monachorum quotidie turbas suscipimus. The letter is written from Palestine ; the reference to ' India '—whence also almost daily crowds of monks arriving were entertained by him, will appear quite inexplicable if it be applied to India proper. The other countries specified, whence they came in large numbers, are Persia and Ethiopia ; but no mention is made of Arabia the nearest to Palestine, whence they could easily have come in large bodies as he says. May not Southern Arabia be the India he refers to? If this be so, as appears most probable, may not the India of the first quotation also refer to Southern Arabia? This would show that while both passages referred to the same country, Jerome erroneously transferred the Brahmans from India proper to El Yemen.

sermone.' But such was not the case. It has often occurred to us to question the accuracy of this statement. The view which impelled us to the doubt arose from the fact that Barnabas' preaching, from what can be ascertained from the canonical books, was to Greek-speaking populations, and he himself was a Cypriote. Of what use then would the original Aramaic text of that gospel be to him? Satisfactory evidence is forthcoming that places the subject in a clear light.

Theodore Lector, in the first half of the sixth century (*Excerpta Hist. Eccl.*, lib. ii. ed. Valles, Moguntiae, 1679, and Migne, *P. Gr.-L.* tom. lxxxvi. 1*a*, col. 183), says: Barnabae apostoli reliquiae in Cypro suo sub arbore siliqua repertae sunt : super cujus pectore erat evangelium Matthaei ipsius Barnabae manu descriptum. Qua de causa Cyprii obtinuerunt ut metropolis ipsorum libera esset ac sui juris, nec Antiochenae sedi amplius subjaceret. Id evangelium Zeno deposuit in palatio in aede sancti Stephani. Further details are given in the Bolland. *Acta SS.* Junii, tom. ii., where is published the *Laudatio S. Barnabae Apostoli auctore Alexandro Monacho Cyprio* (c. iv. n. 41, p. 450). Invenerunt etiam evangelium supra Barnabae pectus impositum . . . and n. 44, p. 451 : evangelium illud in urbe Constantinopolim attulerunt. Erant autem libri tabellae thyinis lignis compositae. Evangelium illud imperator in manus sumpsit, et deosculatus est, auroque multo exornatum in palatio suo reposuit, ubi ad hodiernum usque diem servatur, et in magna quinta Paschae feria quotannis in palatii oratorio Evangelium ex eo libro recitatur. This writer lived during the reign of Justinian, 518–527.

A Bollandist Father, in a subsequent volume (Septr., tom. vi. col. 206), quoting this passage, draws the obvious conclusion: 'Haec lectio demonstrat Graece scriptum fuisse illud exemplar' : and this offers a fresh proof that

Matthew's Gospel from the Aramaic, called also Hebrew, had been translated into Greek in the first century. A further conclusion also follows that this gospel existed as a distinct work, and had been used by Barnabas in the first century.

II.—St. Frumentius

We proceed to examine the credentials of the next supposed Apostle of India. The Roman Martyrology places the feast of St. Frumentius on the twenty-seventh of October. 'Among the Indians [the feast] of Saint Frumentius, bishop, who first there while a captive, later ordained a bishop by St. Athanasius, preached the Gospel in that province.' Rufinus informs us that he personally received from the lips of Edesius, the Saint's relative and fellow-captive, the narrative he hands down. There seems no doubt in this case that Rufinus thought he was dealing with India proper. These are his words :—

'Between which [the "citerior India" of St. Bartholomew previously quoted] and Parthia placed midway, but a long way in the interior [which would probably imply to the south] lies India the Farther, inhabited by peoples of many and divers tongues, and which, as remote, no ploughshare of apostolic preaching had touched, but which, from some similar cause, in the days of Constantine, received the first seeds of the faith.

'A certain Metrodorus, a philosopher, impelled by a desire to travel through the world and see the different countries thereof, is said to have penetrated into Farther India. Meropius of Tyre, also a philosopher, anxious to emulate his example, desired for similar reasons to visit India. He took with him two young relatives whom he was training to liberal culture ; the younger of these was named Edesius, while the elder bore that of Frumentius. Having completed his travels and seen all he wished, and picked up what information he wanted, while on his return, the ship put into port to take in water and provisions. It is the custom of the barbarians of those parts that when intelligence reaches them from their neighbours that peace with the Romans is broken, they attack all Romans whom they find in their country and kill them. The philosopher's ship is invested, and all the ship's company are put to death together with him. The boys are discovered under a tree learning their lessons; touched by their youth, the barbarians bring them to the prince.

'Edesius is made a cupbearer at court, while Frumentius, who appeared possessed of greater intelligence and ability, is raised to the office of treasurer and secretary by the ruler : they were both held in esteem and regard by the prince. The king before his death gave the young strangers their liberty and freedom to act as they liked, leaving behind a widow and a young son. But the queen begged them, as being the most trustworthy in the kingdom, to remain and help her in the government of the country until her son came of age. She was specially desirous of retaining the services of Frumentius, who displayed conspicuous and sufficient ability to govern the kingdom, while the younger, though of a simpler mind, displayed fidelity and goodness of heart. Frumentius while holding the government of the country, God moving his mind and heart, sought out from among the Roman traders such as were Christians, authorised and encouraged them to erect places of worship in different parts where Romans could, according to their usage, assemble for prayer. This he himself did to a much greater extent, and encouraged others as well to follow his example, helping them in every way by grants of sites for the erection of these churches, and all else that was necessary ; and he displayed the greatest interest to sow there the germs of Christian faith.

'When the young prince had attained manhood, the two strangers decided on leaving in spite of entreaties to remain. Having faithfully handed over everything, they took leave of the queen and her son and returned to our world. Edesius hastened to Tyre to see his parents and relations, but Frumentius, deeming it unbecoming to conceal the work of the Lord, went to Alexandria. There he explained the state of things and disclosed what had been done to promote the cause of religion. He urged the bishop to select a worthy person and commission him to the charge of the many Christians now gathered together, and of the churches which had been erected.

'Athanasius, who had recently been ordained to the office he held, having duly weighed and considered in the assembly of the clergy what was said and had been done, "Whom else," he exclaimed, "shall we find endowed as thou with the spirit of God, and competent to do what is required?" Having ordained [1] him, he bid him with God's blessing return whence he had

---

[1] Tillemont (*ut supr.*, tom. vii., chapter on Frumentius, p. 287) fixes the date of his consecration and return to Abyssinia at *c.* 330. But since he wrote, the ' Paschal' or *Festal Letters* of St. Athanasius have been recovered in a Syriac translation ; a summary was translated in English and edited by Cureton, London 1848; a full Latin translation was published by Cardinal Mai in *Nova PP. Bibliotheca*, Romae, 1853, tom. vi. 1st pt., and is also to be found in Migne, *P. Gr.-L.*, vol. xxvi. col. 1351-1444. These letters make it certain that Athanasius succeeded St. Alexander in the see of Alexandria in May 328 (see Cureton, *op. cit. praef.* xxxvii.). He died after a very stormy episcopate, full of exile and persecution, but at the close of his career, as the Lesson of the Breviary aptly remarks, ' ex tot tantisque periculis divinitus ereptus, Alexandriae mortuus est in suo lectulo,' 2nd of May 373, having governed his see for just forty-five years. If we adhere closely to what Rufinus says, 'Athanasius who had been recently ordained to the office [episcopate],' we can take for the consecration of Frumentius the year 329, *i.e.* a year earlier than that assigned by Tillemont, in whose time the exact year of Athanasius' election was disputed. The death of Constantine the Great occurred in 337. With these settled dates before us, it becomes clear that there was no

come. On his return to India as bishop, so great were the favours of grace God bestowed upon him, that the wonders of the apostolic age were seen anew, and an immense number of these people were converted to the faith. It is since then that India has had a Christian people, churches, and priesthood. These things,' adds Rufinus, 'we have not picked up from popular rumour, but heard them from the lips of Edesius, afterwards an ordained priest of Tyre, who had formerly been the companion of Frumentius.' (Rufinus, *Histor. Eccl.*, lib. i., cap. 9, col. 478–480, Migne, *P. L.*, tom. xxi.)

Had we no other source of information which could throw light on the scene of Frumentius' apostolic labours, we would be forced to admit, however it might seem on other grounds, that the events described may have taken place in some part of India remote from that of the labours of the Apostle Thomas, and of which, owing to some unexplainable cause, no local trace or memory had survived. But fortunately we possess the means of identifying the India of Frumentius by the testimony of St. Athanasius himself and of the Emperor Constantius. The imperial letter, addressed to two[1] princes of the Auxumitae (Abyssinians), is unanimously assigned to the year 356. The emperor demands of them that Frumentius, who had been consecrated and sent by Athanasius, be sent back to Egypt to render an account of his faith and doings to George (the Arian intruder in the see of Alexandria) and to the bishops of Egypt, who would test his fitness and the validity of the consecration he had received. St.

reason to question, as some have done, Rufinus' statement that in the days of Constantine the first seeds of the faith were sown by Frumentius, whether as a captive or a bishop.

[1] Rufinus, in his narrative, speaks of one prince, whereas the emperor addresses two princes of Auxum ; we do not pretend to explain the discrepancy, but we must take it to be the fact that two princes were then holding power in the country.

Athanasius incorporates the letter which had come to his knowledge in his defence (*Apologia*) addressed to the emperor. Both the comment and the letter are given below.[1]

[1] Sancti Athanasii Apologia ad Constantium (Migne, *P. Gr.-L.*, vol. xxv. 631–635):—

29. Itaque hi cum rumores essent, ac sus deque omnia abirent, ne sic quidem meam minui alacritatem, sed pergebam ad tuam pietatem; eoque diligentius quo confiderem ea praeter pietatis tuae sententiam perpetrari; atque ubi res gestae humanitati tuae compertae forent, te, ne in posterum ea fierent, curaturum, ratus nequidquam id religiosi esse imperatoris, ut episcopos exsulare, virgines nudari, aut ullo modo ecclesias turbari patiatur. Sed haec nobis animo versantibus, ecce testis quidem increbuit rumor litteras Auxumeos tyrannis esse datas ut curarent Frumentium Auxumeos episcopum illinc abduci; me quoque perquirerent usque ad barbarorum terras, et ad praefectorum commentaria, ut vocant, transmitterent: populos ac clericos omnes adigerent ad communicandum cum Ariana haeresi; si qui non morem gererent, illos interficiendos satagerent.

31. Constantius Maximus Augustus Æzanae et Sazanae.

Maximae nobis curae et studio est, ut Deus cognoscatur; hoc in negotio enim arbitror, parem pro communi hominum genere sollicitudinem gerendam esse, ut ad Dei notitiam deducti, vitam cum spe transigant, in nulloque discrepent circa justi ac veri disquisitionem. Cum tali igitur nos providentia dignos habeamus, unam eamdemque doctrinam apud utrosque in Ecclesiis vigere praecipimus. Quare Frumentium episcopum quamprimum mittite in Aegyptum apud honoratissimum Georgium episcopum et alios Aegypti episcopos, quibus in primis ordinandi ac ejusmodi res dijudicandi auctoritas inest. Nostis enim et meministis, nisi quae apud omnes in confesso sunt, soli ignorare simulatis, Frumentium in hunc vitae gradum promotum esse ab Athanasio sexcentis criminibus obnoxio; qui cum nullam e sibi illatis accusationibus probe diluere potuisset, statim quidem cathedra excidit: ac cum nullibi vivendi locum reperiat, errabundus ab alia in aliam regionem vagatur, quasi eo pacto se malum esse effugere possit.

Si igitur sponte Frumentius obtemperet universi rerum status rationes redditurus, compertum omnibus erit eum ab Ecclesiae legibus et a fide, quae jam obtinet, nullatenus discrepare; cumque judicatus fuerit, totiusque vitae suae experimentum dederit, ejusque rationem apud eos reddiderit ad quos pertinet hujusmodi negotia judicare, ab eis constituatur; si tamen verus episcopus juxtaque leges ordinatus haberi velit. Quod si procrastinaverit ac judicium subterfugerit, palam certe erit ipsum scelestissimi Athanasii sermonibus seductum

Lequien (*Oriens Christiana*, vol. ii. col. 643-44) makes the remark that Constantius' letter to the princes, written for the purpose of effecting the expulsion of Frumentius from Abyssinia and of his being sent to George, the intruder, was sent at the suggestion of the same George, known as of Cappodocia, then the second Arian intruder into the see of Alexandria, appointed to supersede Athanasius by a Synod of some thirty bishops held at Antioch. He captured the see by the aid of the Roman military garrison, but subsequently met his death at the hands of the populace, owing to his tyrannical conduct, in an insurrection that took place in the following reign of Julian the Apostate.

The efforts made to oust Frumentius from his see and to capture it for the benefit of Arianism, failed of effect in spite of the full weight of imperial support,[1] as will be shown more fully in treating of the next case.

impie de Deo sentire, ita nempe affectum ut ille affectus declaratus est scelestus cum sit. Verendumque est ne Auxumim praefectus vestrates nefariis et impiis sermonibus corrumpat ; nec solum ecclesias confundat et turbet, in Deumque blasphemet, sed etiam singulis nationibus hinc vastationis et excidii auctor sit. Caeterum habeo ipsum Frumentium non pauca edoctum, magnamque in publicum bonum utilitatem consecutum venerabilissimi scilicet Georgii consortio, nec non reliquorum, qui in iis docendis apprime versati sunt ad suas sedes reversurum in omnibus ecclesiasticis rebus apprime eruditum.

Deus vos custodiat, fratres honoratissimi.

In the admonitum prefixed to this *Apologia*, col. 593-594, it is stated of the Apologia : . . . ad annum 356 eam haud dubianter referimus. *Cf.* Cod. Theodos., tom. ii. *De Legatis*, where a decree of Constantius is found regarding the expedition of imperial messengers to the Auxumitae and Homeritae, rightly supposed to have been enacted on the occasion of the despatch of this imperial letter. The law bears the date of 15th January 356. Theophilus' mission should then be placed earlier, in *c.* 354, as the imperial letter to the Auxumite princes followed upon the failure of that mission.

[1] At the close of his letter the emperor styles these princes—fratres honoratissimi—'most honoured brethren,' an appellation he would not have bestowed upon them had they not become Christians. This discloses the success of Frumentius' apostolate among the Auxu-

III.—THEOPHILUS THE INDIAN

We now leave "India citerior," the Arabia Felix of the ancients, and the India of Frumentius, Abyssinia, to deal with a third mission which is also said to be connected with India. This is the mission which the Emperor Constantius equipped and sent, before A.D. 356, c. 354, at the head of which he placed a certain Theophilus, called the Indian. The emperor, who in 350 had subdued one rival, and later crushed the usurper Magnentius, thus becoming the sole ruler of the Roman empire, set his heart on establishing Arianism even in the churches outside the boundaries, as he had supported it in those within the empire. This was the impelling motive that suggested the despatch of the mission assigned to

mitae. Rufinus also says that 'an immense number of these people were converted to the faith.' The early Arab narratives tell a similar tale. D'Herbelot, *Biblioth. Orientale,* ad verb. 'Habasch,' says: 'The bishop whom St. Athanasius sent them, Salamah, who was the first to baptize them,' &c. The Abyssinian Church keeps the feast of St. Frumentius on the 26th July and 18th December. In both entries, as Ludolf (*Calendar. Aethiopicum,* in his *Histor. Aethiop.*) observes, 'mutato nomine' he is styled 'Salama'; he also mentions Codex Paris Bibl. Regiae, No. 796 (*ibid.,* p. 74), which contains a life of Frumentius, and produces from the same an extract in support of the change of name. St. Athanasius' feast is also kept by the Abyssinian Church, 7th of January, and he is styled 'St. Athanasius the Apostle.'

Another passage of the imperial letter demands a word of comment: 'For you *know indeed and remember,* unless you alone pretend to be ignorant of what is known to all, that Frumentius was raised to this grade of life by Athanasius, guilty of more than six hundred crimes.' Constantius shows full knowledge of how things stood at Auxum. In spite of the emperor's emphatic language Frumentius retained the support of the princes. But how came the emperor to be so accurately informed of the state of matters ecclesitical there but by Theophilus—of whom we shall presently treat—on his return after the failure of his mission to Auxum? The expression 'and remember' points to some intimation made to the princes and known to the emperor. The letter would thus offer internal evidence that it was written after the return of Theophilus' mission.

Theophilus. Philostorgius[1] is the sole historian of this event.

'Constantius,' he records, 'sent an embassy to the people formerly known as the Sabaeans, but now the Homeritae,' to whom the Apostle Bartholomew had previously preached the faith, revived as we have seen by Pantaenus. 'These [Sabaei] are Abraham's issue by Chittura [Ketura]. The country was known to the Greeks as "Arabia Magna" and "Arabia Felix," extending to the farthest ocean. Saba was their capital, whence once went forth the Queen of Sheba to see Solomon.' The race, he adds, practises circumcision on the eighth day, and is mixed up with a large number of Jews residing among them. It was to these that Constantius sent the mission. The historian notes carefully the object, 'that they might be brought over to the true faith,' which shows clearly that the chief object held in view was to ensnare these Christians into the fold of Arianism. An ostensible object set forth was that of obtaining permission from the ruler of the country to erect churches for the benefit of Roman subjects frequenting those lands for purposes of trade, as also for natives who might be converted. The mission was amply supplied with funds for the erection and equipment of the churches that were to be built.

Theophilus, who was at the head of the mission, is called 'the Indian.' Of him the historian says, qui

[1] This author wrote his history in twelve books, A.D. 423, the first letter heading the commencement of each book formed his name —Philostorgius. The original has not come down to us, but we have a compendium (Photius, *Bibliotheca*), and a few extracts, chiefly contained in Suidas' *Lexicon*. Photius (*ibid.*) thus briefly expresses his opinion on the work : 'It is an eulogium of heretics and an accusation of the orthodox ; a vituperation rather than a history' ; the writer was an Arian. The Compendium and Extracts are to be found in the Corpus of Greek Ecclesiastical Historians with notes and Latin translation by Valesius, reproduced by Migne, *P. G.-L.*, tom. lxv.

Constantino imperium administrante, admodum juvenis obses a Divaeis missus fuerat ad Romanos—'Theophilus, while very young, was sent an hostage to the Romans during the reign of Constantine [the Great].' The island home of Theophilus is by the historian named Διβους and the inhabitants Διβηνῶν; the Latin form in which these names are reproduced is *Divu* or *Divus*, that of the inhabitants *Divaei*. Ammianus Marcellinus, a contemporary historian, A.D. 362, makes mention of islands with a similar name (*History*, bk. xxii. ch. 3): Legationes undique solito ocius concurrebant ; hinc Transtigritanis pacem obsecrantibus et Armeniis, inde nationibus Indicis certatim cum donis optimates mittentibus ante tempus ab usque Divis et Serendivis. —'Legations were coming in from everywhere earlier than usual' [the occasion is the accession of Julian the Apostate, the reference is to the sending of legations by border nations on friendly terms on the accession of a new emperor, and the historian, Ammianus, it should be remembered, is a pagan] ; 'on the one hand the nations across the Tigris and the Armenians asking for peace, on the other hand' [what follows is Yonge's transl., Bohn ed.] 'the Indian tribes vied with each other, sending nobles loaded with gifts even from the Maldive Islands and Ceylon.'

That the Maldives were specially designated by the name reproduced from the Greek text of Philostorgius, besides the support received from a contemporary writer just quoted, is amply upheld by a long series of quotations given by Colonel Yule and Burnell (*Hobson-Jobson ;* A Glossary of Anglo-Indian Colloquial Words, new edition by William Crooke, London, 1903) :—

'*Maldives :* The proper form of this name appears to be *Male-diva*. . . . The people of the islands formerly designated themselves and their country by a form of the word for " island," which we have in the Sanscrit *dvipa* and the Pali *dipo*. We find this reflected in the Divi of Ammianus [the Greek of Philostorgius has already given Διβους] and in the *Diva* and *Diba-jat* (Pers. plural) of old Arab geographers, whilst it survives in letters of the eighteenth century addressed to the Ceylon Government (Dutch) by the Sultan of the Isles who calls his own kingdom *Divehi Rajje*, and his people *Divehi* mihun.

'Year 851, Yule refers to the Arab geographers, *Relations*, &c., traduit par Reinaud, Paris, 1841, vol. i. p. 45 ; these give the islands the name *Dibajat* (see also *Discours préliminaire* same vol. p. xxxiii.)

'Year 1030, By Al. Beruni (in Reinaud's *Fragmans*, p. 124) those of one class are called *Diva-Kurah* (or the Cowrie Divahs) because of the cowries which are gathered from coco-branches planted in the sea ; the others are called *Diva-Kaubar*, from the word Kaubar, which is the name of the twine made from the coco-fibres with which vessels are stitched.

'Year 1343, Ibn Batuta, tom. iv. p. 110 ff, speaks of his arriving from Calicut at the island called *Dhibat-al-Mahal.*'

All these passages refer to the Maldives.

As to the modern name of the islands, the *Maldives*, Yule has the following :—

'Something like the modern form first appears in· Ibn Batuta ; he calls them *Mahal-dives*, and says they were so called from the chief group *Mahal*, a palace. . . . But Pyrard de Laval, the author of the most complete account existing [of these islands] also says that the name of the island was taken from *Malé.* This name is given by Cosmas Indicopleustes to the coast of Malabar, and it is most probably this same name that enters into the composite *Maldives.*'

With reference to the true bearing of Ammianus' passage — ab usque Divis et Serendivis — a further remark may be offered that it has reference to the Maldive group generally, that the object of the passage is to show that delegations also hastened from the Indian peoples, even from the Divi and the Serendivi, pointing to them as the outer extremes of India in the natural order in which they would occur.

There is a remark made by the historian regard-

ing Theophilus which has an important bearing in fixing
his island home. He has told us that Theophilus, while
very young, was sent to the Romans as 'a hostage';
most probably he was not the only hostage demanded
from the islanders. Now it may be asked, for what
purpose would the Roman power demand hostages
for good behaviour from these islanders? Most probably this precaution was taken as a check on the
piratical habits of the dwellers who would pillage
and rob vessels crossing to India, from the east coast
of Arabia or *via* Socotra, which happened to have
stranded on those coral reefs. This would also be the
route of the entire Indian commerce bound westward,
which in those days passed chiefly through Alexandria
and was thence diffused through the empire, while the
route through Persia continued to be 'closed during the
long wars between that country and the empire. The
same predatory habits have prevailed down to our times;
for though the Maldives are now better controlled by the
Collector at Calicut, who is the representative of British
authority to the petty Sultan of the island and his suzerain
the Rajah, or the Bebee, of Cannanore, the same cannot
even now be said of the inhabitants of the adjoining
group, the Laccadives, who more than once of late
years have forced the British authorities to send punitive
expeditions to exact reparation and inflict punishment
for pillage committed on stranded ships. The last occurrence of the sort happened within the last couple of
years. The mention that Theophilus was an ' Indian,' in
the sense of the historian, and that he was surrendered
as a hostage to the Romans, are two points which of themselves would point to the group of the Maldives as his
home. The Laccadives would hardly have been inhabited
at so early an age; besides the two form but one continuous group of coral reef formations in those seas.

To return to Philostorgius' account. The youth

received his education while among the Romans, having
lived long with them; he became conspicuous for his
piety and embraced the monastic profession. From the
approval bestowed on his faith and the mention that
he had received deacon's orders from Eusebius [of
Nicomedia], the court prelate, there can be no doubt
that Theophilus had embraced the Arian heresy.
Photius, the abbreviator of the narrative, here inserts
an observation of his own: 'This refers to the past,
but when he was appointed to this mission he received
episcopal consecration at the hands of those of his
communion.' Philostorgius continues: 'Theophilus
was successful in his mission to the Homeritae.'
Among other presents which he took with him for the
rulers and chiefs, he embarked also 'two hundred
superb Cappadocian horses.' The king was converted
by the legate's preaching, and built of his own accord
three churches. Philostorgius here takes notice of the
large proportion of Jews in the country and of their strong
opposition to Christians ; on this occasion though,
owing to the great success of Theophilus' mission, 'the
usual Jewish fraud and malice,' he adds, 'was compelled
to conceal itself in deepest silence.' One of the churches
erected was at the metropolis Tapharon,[1] another at

---

[1] This city is named in *Periplus* Saphar, a variation of Taphar,
Tapharon ; it is there, § 23, styled 'the Metropolis of Karibael, the
rightful sovereign of two contiguous tribes, the Homeritai and the
Sabaitai.' McCrindle (in his ed. of the *Periplus Maris Erythraei*,
London, Bombay, and Calcutta, 1879, p. 80), adds the following comment : ' Saphar, the metropolis of the Homeritai—*i.e.* the Himeryi—the
Arabs of Yemen, whose power was widely extended not only in Yemen,
but in distant countries to the east and west.' Saphar is called Sapphar
by Ptolemy ; it is now Dhafar, Dsoffar, and Zaphar. In Idrisi it appears as Dhofar, and he thus writes of it ; ' It is the capital of the
district of Jahssel. It was formerly one of the greatest and most
famous cities. The Kings of Yemen made it their residence, and
there was to be seen the palace of Zeddan. These structures are now
in ruins, and the population has been much decreased, nevertheless
the inhabitants have preserved some remnants of their ancient riches.'

the Roman emporium projecting on the outer sea named Adane,[1] the third in that part of the country—ubi Persicum est emporium[2] celebre, in ostio maris Persici quod inibi est, situm—'where the celebrated Persian emporium at the entrance of the Persian Gulf is situated.'

The ruins of the city and palace still exist in the neighbourhood of Jerim. The place is mentioned in the Ming Annales of China as *Tsafarh*, and as being a Mahommedan country. *Marco Polo* (Yule's 2nd ed., vol. ii. p. 441) gives the following description of the place: 'Dufar is a great and noble and fine city, and lies 500 miles to the north-west of Esher. The people are Saracens and have a Count (Sheik) for their chief, who is subject to the Soldan of Aden; for this city belongs to the Province of Aden. It stands upon the sea and has a very good haven, so that there is a great traffic of shipping between this and India (viz., the Kingdom of Ma'bar, p. 324), and merchants take hence great numbers of Arab horses to that market, making great profit thereby. This city has under it many other towns and villages.' It was pre-eminently 'the frank-incense land' of the ancients.

[1] Adane in the *Periplus*, § 26, is called, 'Eudaimon Arabia, a maritime village subject to that kingdom of which Kharibael is sovereign. It is called Eudaimon, "rich and prosperous," because in bygone days, when the merchants from India did not proceed to Egypt, and those from Egypt did not venture to cross over to the marts farther east, but both came only as far as this city, it formed the common centre of their commerce, as Alexandria receives the wares which pass to and fro between Egypt and the ports of the Mediterranean. Now, however, it lies in ruins, the emperor [Augustus] having destroyed it not long before our own times.' It will hardly be necessary to tell the reader that Adane is the well-known port of Aden. During the Middle Ages it regained its former commercial importance and prosperity. It was found by Marco Polo in this flourishing state, and he says that all the Indian trade was landed there, and thence merchants trading with Egypt would convey it in small vessels for a journey of seven days, when it would be landed, loaded on camels, and conveyed to the Nile, a distance of thirty days' journey, and thence by river to Alexandria. The Portuguese under Albuquerque captured the place and destroyed it later on. But owing to the natural advantages of its situation, though placed on a barren rock, it has in our days under British sway more than regained its former importance.

[2] The emporium localised *in ostio maris Persici* but not named, is Oman, our present Sohar; the gulf in front still retains the older name and is marked in charts 'the Gulf of Oman.' The following is

Under such happy circumstances Theophilus arranged matters among the Homeritae to the best advantage. He consecrated the three new churches and supplied them with ornaments; then he sailed for his native island, one of the group of the Maldives, as indicated above. The narrative continues: · Thence he sailed to other parts of India and reformed many things which were not rightly done among them; for they heard the reading of the Gospel in a sitting posture, and did other things which were repugnant to the divine law; and having reformed everything according to holy usage, as was most acceptable to God, he also confirmed the dogma of the Church.' This denotes an attempt to introduce his heretical tenets. The Arian historian's last remark has justly excited the indignation of Photius : ' Nor with regard to divine worship,' as this impious historian remarks, ' was any emendation necessary, as from the earliest antiquity

from Colonel Miles (*J. R. A. Soc.,* new series, vol. x., 1878, p. 164, : 'The city of Oman is Sohar, the ancient capital of Oman, which name, as is well known, it then bore ; and Pliny seems to be quite right in correcting former writers who had placed it in Carmania.' The *Periplus,* § 36, says : 'If you coast along the mouth of the gulf, you are conducted by a six days' voyage to another seat of trade belonging to the Persis called Omana.' Philostorgius has called it ' Persicum emporium.' It is difficult to say for what reasons it came to be known as the ' Persian' emporium. It would perhaps not be amiss to suppose that the appellation may be due to a prior supremacy of Persia over that portion of Arabia ; anyhow this was not the case in Philostorgius' time, for the port then formed part of the territories of the prince ruling at Tapharon who erected there the third Christian church. Pliny (vi. 32) writes of it : Homana quae nunc maxime celebrari a Persico mari negotiatores dicunt; here the reason assigned is that it lies in the Persian Gulf. Idrisi calls it ' one of the oldest cities of Oman and one of the richest. It was in ancient times frequented by merchants from all parts of the world, and voyages to China used to be made from it.' Marco Polo mentions it under the name of Soar, as one of the ports that exported horses to southern India. In modern times it has been superseded by Muscat situated farther south.

they had continuously believed the Son to be of a different substance from the Father.'

To ascertain which were the above 'other parts of India' Theophilus visited, it will be as well to follow the sequel of the narrative given by Photius. Philostorgius then makes him leave Arabia and proceed to Abyssinia: 'From this Arabia Magna Theophilus proceeds to the Ethiopians, who are named Auxumitae. They dwell on the first shore of the Red Sea, which the ocean there forms, indenting the continent.' So the journey does not take Theophilus to Socotra; but on his return to 'Arabia Magna,' after the visit to 'other parts of India' from his island home, he is sailing straight through the Straits of Bab-el Mandeb and entering the Red Sea. This disposes of the myth of a modern writer, who makes Theophilus a native of Socotra, quite forgetful of the fact, as will presently appear, that he never visited the island, according to Philostorgius (Milne-Rae's *Syrian Church in India*, p. 98).

The question will now arise, To what 'other parts of India' did Theophilus sail when he left his island home? We may, on the same basis, shape the question differently: To what 'other parts of India' could he have gone from his home in the Maldives? Geographically there are but two places—Ceylon and the Malabar coast, both at a short sail from the Maldives.

Of Ceylon, apart from the consideration that Ceylon was well known to Romans and Greeks under the name of Serendivus and Taprobana, and would have been mentioned by its distinctive name if the reference was to that island, we have no authority based on history, that Christians existed on the island at the middle of the fourth century, the date of the mission we are dealing with. When we hear of Ceylon, almost a hundred and eighty years later, from Cosmas Indicopleustes, who visited it after the first quarter of the sixth century (he was writing his book in 535) he mentions the presence of Christians and of clerics. The passage (Migne, *P. Gr.-L.*, tom. lxxxviii. col. 446) reads : 'There exists on the island, which is named Sielediva by the Indians and called Taprobona by the Greeks, a Christian Church of strangers from Persia, also a priest ordained in Persia and sent there, also a deacon with other ecclesiastical ministry [clerics]. The natives, however, and the kings are of a different religion.'[1]

This distinctly shows that such Christians as Cosmas found in Ceylon were a colony of Persian traders with Persian clergy to attend to their spiritual wants. This system has been kept up in the large Indian seaport trading centres even to our times, Armenians taking the place of the Persian clergy. As to native converts, Cosmas pointedly says there were none. We are thus justified in inferring that 'the other parts of India' visited by the emperor's legate does not apply to Ceylon. This forces upon us the one remaining conclusion that 'the other parts of India' visited by Theophilus can be no other than the Malabar coast on which he found the organisation of a native Christian church which the subsequent narrative discloses. Nor will this take the reader by surprise : he knows already some details of the Apostolate of Saint Thomas in India ; he has learnt of his martyrdom, of the existence of his primitive tomb at Mylapore on the east coast ; and he is acquainted with the traditions of the Saint-Thomas Christians on the west coast, who, as also the former Christians of Socotra, lay claim to be the descendants of the converts of the Apostle. If then, he learns of Theophilus' visit to that coast about the

---

[1] Exstat autem ea in insula (quae ab Indis Sielediva, a Graecis Taprobona vocatur) Ecclesia Christi advenarum ex Perside, ac presbyter in Perside ordinatus eoque missus, diaconus item cum reliquo ecclesiastico ministerio : indigenae vero et una reges alieni cultus sunt.

year 354, and of his finding there a Christian church in working order, it will be nothing more than what he is prepared to expect. The English translation of the passage in which the historian mentions the visit paid to these Christians by the imperial legate has been given above ; we reproduce here the Latin version by Valesius : Ad alias Indiae regiones perrexit, multaque quae apud illos non rite fiebant, emendavit. Nam et lectiones Evangelii audiebant sedentes, et alia quaedam peragebant quibus divina lex repugnabat. Verum cum Theophilus singula juxta sanctiorem ritum, Deoque magis acceptum correxisset, Ecclesiae quoque dogma confirmavit (Migne, *P. G.-L.*, tom. lxv. col. 482–490). The statement implies (1) a resident congregation of the faithful, (2) church services regularly held at which the gospels were read, and (3) consequently a ministering clergy. This discloses a Christian community constituted in parochial form ; and if there be any doubt as to whether the congregation be indigenous or foreign, such doubt (4) ought to be set aside by the peculiar custom found among them, mentioned by the historian, and referred to below, which Theophilus is said to have reformed.

At this period the Christians on this coast must have held the faith unadulterated. But the case was quite different at the period of Cosmas' visit before 535. Nestorianism, in the person of its author, was condemned, close upon a century after Theophilus' visit, in the Council of Ephesus, 431 ; Theodosius, in 435, passed a law against Nestorianism ; and in the year 496, Acacius, the Catholicus of Seleucia, died peacefully. With him ended the series of the Catholic occupants of that see. Babaeus, a fervent Nestorian, succeeded him. He, in 499, held a synod authorising marriage among the clergy and monks, and condemning celibacy (Assemani, *Bibl. Oriental.*, tom. iv. pp. 80, 83). So with the close of the fifth century Nestorianism had captured all the

Catholic churches within the kingdom of Persia. Thus this heresy early in the sixth century would have installed itself in all the churches of the Farthest East, dependent as they were from the see of Seleucia; all intercourse, besides, with those within the Roman empire was severed by the active part the kings of Persia took in hindering such communication.[1]

Philostorgius, in referring to the visit paid to the Christians in 'the other parts of India' by Theophilus, mentions as a custom prevailing among them that they

[1] Besides the passages given in the text, Cosmas makes mention in another (*Topographia*, ut supr., col., 170) of the churches in Ceylon and India : In Taprobana insula ad interiorem Indiam, ubi Indicum pelagus exstat, ecclesia christianorum habetur, ubi clerici et fideles reperiuntur, an ulterius etiam ignoro—that these were foreign Christians consisting probably of traders we have already learnt from him, and he adds, ' whether also farther [East], I know not.' He then continues : Similiter in Male, ut vocant, ubi gignitur piper. In Caliana vero (sic nuncupant) episcopus est in Perside ordinari solitus : similiterque in insula quae Dioscoridis vocatur in eodem mari Indico. This is followed up by an extensive enumeration of churches in Asia, Africa, and some parts of Europe. Commenting on this passage the learned Assemani (*Bibl. Or.*, tom. iv. p. 91) writes : Cosmas Indicopleustes in sua Topographia christianae religionis in Perside, Indiaque faciem saeculo sexto ejusmodi exhibet. Omnes, inquit, quotquot in Perside, India et Arabia Felice christiani degebant Catholico Persidis subditi erant, a quo etiam ordinabantur earum regionum episcopi. Ipsius Cosmae aevo, hoc est anno circiter 530 Patritius Thomae Edesseni magister ad Archiepiscopales totius Persidis thronos evectus est. Catholicus Persidis in Calianam episcopum ab se ordinatum mittere solebat. In Male, sive Malabar, aderat christianorum ecclesia ; similiterque in Sieldiva insula (Silan) ecclesia christianorum, cum presbytero et diacono in Perside ordinatis ac reliquo ecclesiastico ministerio. Item apud Bactros, Hunnos, reliquos Indos, &c. Persidis autem Archiepiscopus, ut notat cl. Montfaucon, Nestorianus erat, ut alii omnes episcopi et presbyteri ejusdem subditi ; then follow quotations from Cosmas' work. This shows clearly that the churches comprised in Cosmas' enumeration were addicted to the Nestorian heresy. Consequently by the year 530 the Christians in Male, Malabar, had been captured in the Nestorian net. The credit of detecting that Cosmas himself was a Nestorian is due to La Croze ; see his *Histoire de Christianisme des Indes*, La Haye, 1724, pp. 27–37. Assemani also (*ut supr.*, pp. 405–406) gives him full credit for it.

remained seated while the gospel was being read at the liturgy.[1] The habit of the west coast people of sitting down on the floor as often as permissible is quite characteristic, and it may be that it also extended to their remaining in that posture at the reading of the gospel. The propensity to 'squat' which the incident indicates would only be applicable to an indigenous, and would not apply to a foreign, congregation. As to what other, if any, abuses were suppressed it is needless to speculate, for were they of any importance the historian would not have omitted to mention them, as his propensity to enlarge upon and magnify the success of

---

[1] The usage of standing while the gospel is read during mass has probably come down from Apostolic times, like most principal rites connected with the Liturgy. Mention of this custom is made in the *Apostolical Constitutions*, which, though apocryphal, drawn up by one or more authors, is admitted by all scholars to record the early practices of the Church and its discipline (lib. ii. cap. 57) : 'When the gospel is being read let all the presbyters, the deacons, and all the people stand in perfect stillness.' St. Anastasius I., Pope (398–402), is reported in the Breviary Lessons to have 'ordained that whenever the holy gospels are read presbyters be not seated but stand with heads bent (*curvi*).' St. Isidore of Pelusium (died *c.* 440), *Epist. Hermino Comiti.*, writes : 'When the True Shepherd becomes present through the opening of the adorable gospels, the bishop both rises and lays aside the *omophorion* which he wears symbolical of him.' The omophorion is one of the sacred vestments used by Greek and Eastern bishops. It consists of a band of woollen material ornamented with crosses and gold braiding; it can be raised over the head or dropped on the shoulders, the ends falling forward. It symbolises the idea of carrying a sheep on one's shoulders, and the reference is to this. Amalcarius, a priest of Metz and Chorepiscopus, writing about 836 (*de Eccl. Offic.*, lib. iii. cap. 18), of the gospel, says : 'Up to this time we sit ; now we must stand at the words of the gospel.'

The practice of keeping a sitting posture, observed by Theophilus among the peoples of 'the other parts of India,' is not the only known instance of deviation from the ecclesiastical usage. Sozomen (*Hist. Eccl.*, lib. vii. cap. 19) tells us that 'among the Alexandrians this new and unbecoming custom, that while the gospels were read the bishop did not rise' prevailed ; and he adds, 'which I have neither seen nor heard done elsewhere.'

Theophilus' mission is too apparent. Photius is quite right in stigmatising as a piece of impudence the further statement that these Christians had all along held the Arian belief, denying the equality of substance in the Son and the Father.

After mentioning the departure, as above, of the mission for Abyssinia, the writer proceeds to give the configuration of the Red Sea. It 'extends for a great length and divides itself into two gulfs; one lies towards Egypt, and is named Clysma from the place where it ends, and across this gulf the Israelites passed dry-shod on their departure from Egypt. The other gulf extends to Palestine by the city known from remote antiquity as Aila [Elath]. At the outer bay of this sea [viz., to the south] to the left dwell the Auxumitae, so named from Auxum their capital. Before, how-ever, reaching the Auxumitae, to the east, in the outer sea, dwell Syrians also so called by the inhabitants.' This refers to the island of Socotra, and we shall find that it was not visited by Theophilus. These Syrians, he says, were placed there by Alexander, having been removed from Syria; even in his day they made use of the Syriac language and were quite dark in complexion; 'but Theophilus did not go so far,' he adds. This passage is quoted by geographers as relating to Socotra. Indicopleustes has a similar passage (*Topographia*, lib. iii., Migne, *ut supr.*, col. 170): Similiter [*i.e.* there are Christians] in insula quae Dioscoridis vocatur, in eodem mari Indico sita, cujus incolae Graece loquuntur, suntque coloni a Ptolomaeis Alexandri Mace-donis successoribus istuc deportati, clerici reperiuntur ex Perside, ubi ordinantur, eodem transmissi : ibi etiam christianorum multitudo versatur. Cui insulae adnavi-gavi, neque tamen eo discensum feci. Verum cum quibusdam ejus incolis Graece loquentibus colloquia miscui qui in Aethiopiam [Auxum ?] proficiscebantur.

As to the visit paid to Abyssinia by the imperial mission, we are simply told in a couple of lines that Theophilus went there, arranged affairs suitably and returned to the Roman dominions. This excessive curtness discloses the utter failure of the embassy to the petty princes of the Auxumitae, where St. Frumentius at the time was firmly established.

Of Theophilus we learn from Photius' epitome this further detail, that on his return he was honourably received by the emperor, but obtained no appointment to any episcopal see. Suidas, however, in his *Lexicon* (ed. Bernhardy, Graece et Latine, Halis et Brunsvigae, 1853, ad verb. Θεοφιλος, col. 1150), has saved the last portion of the narrative: 'Theophilus on his return from India fixed his residence at Antioch; he was in charge of no particular church, but acted as a bishop at the service of all, so that all freely went to him as if he were their bishop [which could only be true in regard to the scattered Arians living in the vicinity of Antioch] since the emperor held him in great respect: wherever he went he was cordially received and held in esteem for his virtues.'

CHAPTER VI

DID THOMAS, A DISCIPLE OF MANES, GO TO INDIA?

CERTAIN writers have suggested, while others have alleged that Thomas, a disciple of Manes who sent him, it is said, to India, has been mistaken for St. Thomas the Apostle. The purpose of this chapter is to show that there are no grounds for the supposition that the said Thomas ever went to India, and consequently less for the allegation.

St. Epiphanius, the bishop of Constantia, in Cyprus, A.D. 315–402, has fortunately left us a very full and complete account of the tenets of Manes, an arch-propagator of falsehood. These tenets wrought for a long time much mischief and loss to the Church, and were the cause of large numbers of her members falling away at different periods, seduced by the attraction of a double principle of good and evil, coeval and eternal—a doctrine which seems to have always had a special fascination for weak humanity, since it is found to be a principle permeating nearly all primitive religions.

The authority of St. Epiphanius does not rank high with some; they consider he was not sufficiently cautious in accepting and testing the sources of his information. In the case of Manes and his disciples, however, Epiphanius specifies his authorities, which are almost all obtained first hand, and he largely utilises the contents of the contemporary historical document which fortunately has come down to us entire in a Latin translation, while that in Greek, one time much diffused, exists only in fragmentary quotations.

In his book 'Against Heresies,'[1] dealing with false teachings, both prior and subsequent to the birth of Christ down to his own times, the bishop of Constantia deals very fully with the errors of Manes and the doings of his followers. The name of this teacher of a new religion, rather than the originator of a new heresy, was Cubricus ; he was the bondsman of a loose woman who had inherited great riches and who had made him a freedman. At her death he inherited all she possessed. Cubricus, by origin a Persian, then assumed the name of Manes, and commenced to build up a system for his peculiar philosophical and religious ideas; he at the same time enrolled a small band of followers. While so engaged, he heard of the serious illness of the son of the King of Persia. Blinded with pride and ambition, he believed he could discover some remedy, or a charm that would enable him to cure the young prince, from the books of one Scythianus and a certain Terbinthus, who had studied the art of Indian magic, and were the former lovers of his late mistress. Manes had come into possession of these, together with the riches left by the deceased men. This, at one stroke, would raise him to prominence and place the project he contemplated under high patronage. So he went to the Court and offered his services to restore the prince to health. The offer was accepted, but he failed in his efforts, and the young prince succumbed under his treatment. The king, attributing the death to Manes, and enraged at the loss and imposture which had been practised upon him, cast Manes into prison.

---

[1] Epiphanius, *Adversus Haereses* seu *Panarium*, Haeres. 66, Migne, *P. Gr.-L.*, tom. xlii. col. 30 *seq.*

Manes had previously heard of Christianity and of its diffusion over the world, and he bethought himself that it would be as well for him to obtain a more accurate knowledge of this religion. With this object he sent some of his disciples to Judea to obtain for him the books of the Old and New Testament. When the disciples returned with the sacred Scriptures they found their master deprived of liberty ; they, however, obtained access to him in prison and delivered the books.

By the aid of large bribes, we are informed, Manes was able to make his escape, and took up his abode on the borderland between the Persian and Roman territories. While thus at a place named Arabion he heard of Marcellus, a Christian of high repute, wealth, and authority, living within the Roman boundaries of Mesopotamia. He bethought himself that if he succeeded in inducing a person of such distinction to adopt his principles, it would assure him a firm footing and the prestige necessary to propagate them. In doubt how to make his first advances, he hesitated whether he should meet Marcellus personally, or first open the way by letter ; judging the latter course the safer, he wrote to him. This letter of Manes, setting forth his double principle ruling the world, coupled with some tincture of Christianity, is given by Epiphanius.

It so happened that when Turbo, the messenger and adherent of Manes, brought the letter to Marcellus, Archelaus, the bishop of Cascara (*Kaskar*) in Mesopotamia, lying in the outskirts of Seleucia, was paying him a visit. On reading it Marcellus, a religious man, was so taken by surprise at the nature of the contents that he communicated them to the bishop. They decided eventually that a reply should be sent. It is here reproduced as a sample of an Eastern non-committal message.

'Marcellus, the nobleman, to Manes, known to him by letter, greetings.

'I read the letter you wrote and have entertained Turbo with my customary hospitality. But the meaning of the letter I cannot understand, unless, perhaps, you come personally and explain by word of mouth everything, as by your letter you promise. Farewell.'

The reply was sent expeditiously by one of Marcellus' servants, Turbo being unwilling to undertake the return journey. While awaiting Manes' appearance, the bishop and Marcellus closely examined Turbo, who willingly unfolded to them all that he knew of his master's teaching, and in the meanwhile removed to the bishop's residence. Archelaus was thus able to draw up a statement of the tenets of the new false religion, which enabled him to nip in the very bud Manes' attempt to introduce it among the faithful. The bishop's statement of Manes' false principle; his refutation of it at a public discussion held with him at the residence of Marcellus; his letter to the priest of a village of his diocese where Manes after the previous disputation attempted to propagate his errors (this letter was written in reply to one from the priest himself asking the bishop to solve some difficulties proposed by Manes, or to come personally and refute them); an account of a second disputation between Manes and the bishop at the village in question; an address by the bishop to the people on the subject of Manes; and finally, particulars of his death—all these have been fortunately preserved for us in the Latin translation mentioned above.[1] We have thus first-hand knowledge of the errors of this man and of some of his disciples.

After this double defeat at the bishop's hands, the

---

[1] *Acta disputationis Archelai episcopi Mesopotamiae et Manetis heresiarchae*, published by Laurentius Alexander Zacagnus in his

King of Persia, hearing of Manes' whereabouts, had him captured in the village where the second dispute took place. He was ordered to be executed, and his skin stuffed with straw was hung up outside the city gates, as Socrates, the Church historian, who wrote about 450, mentions.[1] The tragic death of the author did not, however, kill his errors.

St. Epiphanius concluding the narrative (*Oper. c.*,

Collectanea Monumentorum veterum graece et latine quae hactenus in Vaticana Bibliotheca delituerunt, Romae, 1698, pp. 1–102. This old Latin translation is now the only form in which the complete work exists, with the exception of Greek fragments preserved in Epiphanius' text, *Haeres.* 66; and in St. Cyril of Jerusalem, *Catechesi Sexta.* The Acta were also published by Gallandus, *Bibl. Patrum*, tom. iii. pp. 569–610; by Mansi, *Concilia*, tom. i. p. 1129 *seq.*; by Routh, *Reliquae Sacrae*, 2nd ed., Oxford, tom. v. Zacagnus states in his preface that the work must have been originally written in Syriac, and gives internal reasons; he also adduces the authority of Jerome, who says (*De viris illustr.*, cap. lxxii.): Archelaus episcopus Mesopotamiae librum disputationis suae, quam habuit adversus Manichaeum exeuntem de Perside, Syro sermone composuit, qui translatus in Graecum habetur a multis. Claruit sub imperatore Probro qui Aureliano et Tacito successerat (A.D. 276–282).

An important doctrinal treatise against Manes' error has survived in a Greek translation written by Titus, bishop of Bostra, *c.* 360, published in the *Thesaurus monumentor. eccl. et historicor.* sive Henrici Canisii lectiones antiquae, edit Jacobus Basnage, Amsterdam, 1725, vol. i. pp. 56–62. St. Jerome (*De viris*, cap. ciii.) has the following : Titus Bostrensis episcopus sub Juliano et Joviano principibus fortes adversus Manichaeum scripsit libros et nonnulla volumina alia. Moritur autem sub Valente; (between 364–378). Bostra, the metropolitan see of Arabia, to the Jews Bosra, was a former city of the Moabites (Lequien, *Oriens Christiana*, tom. ii. col. 853).

[1] Socrates, *Hist. Eccl.*, lib. i. cap. xxii., ed. Henrici Valesii : Rex Persarum comperto quod Manichaeus in illis partibus moraretur, inde abrepto cutem detrahi jussit eamque paleis oppletam ante civitatis portas appendit. Atque haec nos nequaquam commentati sumus, sed ex disputatione quadam Archelai Cascharorum urbis in Mesopotamia episcopi, a nobis lecta excerpsimus. Hic enim Archelaus ait se cum Manichaeo ipso coram disputasse, et ea quae superius a nobis relata sunt de illius vita commemorat.

col. 47) says : ' This man so died and left the disciples
I have mentioned, Adda, Thomas, and Hermeas,
whom before his death he had sent to different
places. Hermeas, with whom many are acquainted,
went to Egypt ; nor indeed is this heresy so old as
to prevent those who had spoken to Hermeas, the
disciple of Manes, from narrating to us what concerned him. Adda went to the further region [which
here implies the countries east of the Euphrates],
Thomas to Judea, and from these the sect has acquired
vigour and growth down to our days.' In the Latin
version of the *Acta disputationis Archelai episcopi*, at the
close of the eleventh chapter (division by the editor
Zacagnus) we have the following : Haec est omnis
doctrina quam tradidit tribus discipulis suis et jussit
eos in tres mundi plagas proficisci. Adda partes sortitus est Oriētis ; Thomas vero Syrorum terras suscepit ;
Hermas vero ad Aegyptum projectus est, et usque in
hodiernum ibi degūt, dogmatis hujus gratia praedicandi.
'This forms the entire body of his teaching which he
(Manes) handed down to his three disciples, ordering
them to proceed to three different countries of the world.
Of whom Adda was destined to the East, Thomas went to
the land of Syria, and Hermas to Egypt, and up to this
day they dwell there to propagate these doctrines.' In
the *Acta*, at a later stage, Archelaus again mentions these
three disciples of Manes (chapter liii.) : Tunc visum est ei
mittere discipulos suos cum his quae conscripserat in
libellis ad superioris illius Provinciae loca, et per diver-
sas civitates et vicos ut haberet aliquos se sequentes et
Thomas quidem partis Aegypti voluit occupare, Addas
vero Scythiae, solus autem Hermas residere cum eo
elegit. In this second passage missions are assigned to
two only, Thomas, who is sent to Egypt, and Addas, to
Scythia. Epiphanius had the document before him
from which he quoted, and of which St. Jerome (*De*

viris illustr., cap. lxxii.) says : 'Written originally in the
Syriac they are in the hands of many in a Greek translation.' But Epiphanius had also almost contemporary
witness, as we have seen, of the preaching of these disciples, and has told us that Thomas's mission was to Judea
and not to Egypt, while of the mission to Egypt he had
good oral evidence that Hermeas was sent there; this
latter statement, as well as the general agreement between
the first statement in the *Acta* and that given by Epiphanius show that there is some vagueness in Archelaus'
later passage. It remains, however, clear that there is
no mention of India, and that Thomas was never sent to
that country.

The learned Petavius adds that 'he (Archelaus) was
the first to oppose this monstrous heresy, and is therefore worthy of special praise, and he wrote an account
of the disputation he had with the impostor and disclosed all the secrets of this nefarious superstition.
From this narrative of Archelaus all others who have
given the history or handed down the tenets held by this
heretic have drawn their materials.'[1]

We said above that certain writers—who have not
looked into the evidence of the case—have alleged that
one of the disciples of Manes went to India, and that
this gave rise to the supposition that the Apostle Thomas
had not preached the faith there. On what foundation
does this allegation rest ? There is a passage in Theodoret[2] (died 457–458) : Habuit autem hic Manes ab
initio discipulos tres Aldam, Thomam, et Hermam. Et
Aldam quidem ad praedicandum misit in Syriam, ad
Indos vero Thomam. As the ·*Acta disputationis* and
Epiphanius, both older authorities than Theodoret, agree

---

[1] Epiphan. *Haeres.* 66, *ut supr.*, § xxv., col. 71–72, in a note to
his Latin translation of the above work.

[2] Theodoretus episcopus Cyrensis, *Compendium Haereticar.
Fabular.*, Migne, *P. Gr.-L.*, tom. lxxxiii., Theodor., oper. iv. col. 379.

O

perfectly on the missions assigned to the three disciples of Manes, Theodoret's statement must give way to the former.[1] There remains one remark to offer. Theodoret is at fault in the name of the disciple Adda, whom he calls $\Lambda\Lambda\Delta\Lambda$ in place of $\Lambda\Delta\Delta\Lambda$. Bearing in mind that the MSS existing in the fifth century were mostly written in uncial letters, the change is easily explained—the bottom stroke of the Δ was overlooked. Theodoret or his amanuensis must have had a faulty manuscript before them, or mis-read the same. This would also explain how Thomas comes to be sent to India. Epiphanius, in the quotation given above, has in the Greek text Θωμας επι την Ιουδαιον, it is easy to see how the last word might be hastily read or transcribed Ινδιαν. This appears to be a reasonable explanation of the inaccuracy of Theodoret's statement (see Assemani, *Bibl. Or.*, tom. iv. p. 28).[2]

---

[1] Even such a scholar as Tillemont, misled by Theodoret's passage, writes in his *Mémoires Hist. Eccl.* (Venice, 1732, tom. i., note 4, p. 613): 'There is reason to fear that an apostle of Manes (Thomas) was mistaken for Thomas the Apostle of Jesus Christ.' He failed apparently to consult St. Epiphanius, and was unaware of the existence, or of the publication by Zacagnus, of the *Acta disputationis.* Backed by the opinion of Tillemont, Theodoret's misreading was made much of by certain Protestant writers of the seventeenth and eighteenth centuries in their attacks on the Jesuits. Having Theodoret's authority for saying that Thomas the disciple of Manes went to India, they affirmed this had given rise to the notion that the Apostle of the same name had preached the faith there. The suggestion occurs *passim* in a certain class of writings, and thence it has crept into works of a more serious stamp.

[2] Bardenhewer, in his *Les Pères de l'Église* (French translation, Paris, 1899, vol. ii. pp. 59–60), on a statement of Photius (*Bibliotheca*, cod. 85, cols. 287–288, Migne, *P. Gr.-L.*, tom. ciii.) would make the *Acta disputationis Archelai* an ingenious piece of forgery of a later date. Let us see what Photius says. While giving a summary of the writings of Heraclian, bishop of Chalcedon (between 491–518) against Manichaeans, he says : Recensit item eos qui ante se in Manichaeorum impietatem calamum strinxerunt. Hegemonium, nimirum, qui disputationem Archelai adversus ipsum (Manetem) perscripsit (αναγραφαντα—recorded). From the evidence of earlier writers produced, the passage cannot be reasonably taken in the sense assigned by the learned professor. The

Latin copy and the Greek extracts attest the *Acta* to be of Aramaic origin, apart from the authority of St. Jerome—no mean authority on a question of Eastern literature. Nor should the fact be overlooked that Epiphanius, a native of Judea though he wrote in Greek, knew besides, according to Jerome (*Adv. Ruf.*, ii. n. 22; Migne, *P. L.*, xxiii. col. 446), Hebrew, Syriac, Coptic, and had also some knowledge of Latin, quoted long passages from these Acts; he wrote his *Adversus Haeres.* between 374–377. Surely all these authorities cannot be set aside. The only plausible meaning that can be assigned to the passage of Photius is that Hegemonius may have been the author of the Greek translation. Finally, Harnack, writing on these *Acta* and Tatian's *Diatessaron*, considers himself justified in concluding that the *Acta*, of which he made a special study, reproduced quotations of the Gospels from the *Diatessaron*. This offers additional internal evidence that the writing originated in Mesopotamia and was the work of a Syrian, not a Greek, author, and was written in the Aramaic tongue.

Since writing the above we have consulted Dom Remy Ceillier, who discusses (*L'Histoire générale des auteurs sacrés et ecclésiastiques*, new ed., Paris, 1868, vol. ii. p. 453) the passage quoted from Photius. The opinion he arrives at is the following : On peut concilier ces deux versions en supposant que cet Hégémone traduisit en grec les *Acta* de la dispute d'Archelaus, ou qu'il les publia de nouveau en y ajoutant plusieurs circonstances dont Archelaus n'avait pas fait mention ; car il est certain que ces Actes sont de deux auteurs—more probably were slightly supplemented, if at all ; this may also account for the discrepancies of the later citation with the earlier discussed above.

APPENDIX

A CRITICAL ANALYSIS OF THE ACTS OF THOMAS THE APOSTLE

SECTION I

PREAMBLE

WHEN dealing with the question raised by these Acts, of the historical existence of the King of the Indians named Gondophares, we were able to show (see Chapter I.) that the statement is amply supported by historical evidence. This ought to offer encouragement to proceed a step further and to inquire whether the Acts contain other points of reliable history.

1. CRITERIA

Before doing so, we deem it advisable to ask the reader to follow us through a few preliminary remarks, which a closer study of the Acts has shown should be kept in mind while endeavouring to discriminate between what may be termed the kernel, or main facts of the narrative, contained in the present form of the Acts, and the ample enlargements the text has undergone. For this purpose we should first of all place ourselves in the circumstances of the age when they were most likely written; examine the channels then available for the transmission of news between distant countries; take into consideration whether the story was written on the spot where the events took place, or if the narrative came to be committed to writing in a far distant country from that in which the scenes occurred.

Should the latter be the case, and that the facts had to be obtained at second-hand, passing from mouth to mouth and travelling over long distances before reaching the place where they took concrete form in writing, it is clear that a great many precautions are necessary to ensure a reliable rendering of the events. Few are the instances in the early ages when travellers have given us their experiences at first hand. Most of the narratives which have survived and have reached us show that they are based on unwritten reports. Having then, often, nothing better than hearsay reports to go upon, the writer, after carefully examining the facts put before him, would have to choose what he can accept, and exclude what he feels bound to reject. Similarly he will have to depend on his own judgment in setting and co-ordinating them as to time and place.

He has yet a further difficulty to surmount; he has to clothe them in his own language. Any one who has made the experiment of putting hearsay narratives on record, is conscious of the danger he lies under of unwittingly stating what is inaccurate, or of giving a wrong meaning or colour to what he reports. The difficulty increases very considerably when he happens to be unacquainted with the country he deals with and its customs and usages. In such a case, however painstaking, he is morally certain to be led into inaccurate statements. Unknown perhaps to himself, he will alter the sequence of events when not interdependent, or he will misplace them geographically or chronologically—showing them as having occurred in one part of the country when they may have taken place in quite another, or at a different period.

Dealing with oral reports coming from afar and not received at first hand, one has to bear in mind that all this dislocation and distortion of the story may already have happened before the narrative reaches him, owing to its having passed through different oral channels.

2. ARE THE ACTS A ROMANCE?

It may be asked, What object is served by placing these different criteria before the reader?

If the Acts of Thomas are to be taken as pure romance, like a large portion of the present-day literature, then, indeed, these preliminary remarks would be out of place ; for we would not be dealing with facts having any historical basis, but with a work of fiction. But if they are taken to contain a record of historical, or partly historical, events of an early age, then the reader will find, from what will come before him, that the above criteria are absolutely necessary to guide him in forming a sound opinion on the merits or demerits of the story as a whole, or of its component parts, where analysis enables us to separate its different elements.

3. Two Different Ancient Views of the Same

What is the history of these Acts?

They are, by Catholic writers of great authority, such as SS. Augustine and Epiphanius and some others, said to have been used by the Manichaeans and by several branches of the early Gnostic sects, to have been read in their assemblies, and to have practically replaced the Holy Scriptures among them. This discloses the fact that they were made use of by these sects for a doctrinal purpose, in order to set up some theory or tenet of their own which they sought to inculcate on their followers and propagate among others. A novel written expressly for the purpose would answer as well; it would then hold, as incrusted fossils, the doctrinal features embedded in the narrative, but it would be the pure outcome of imagination. Of the present Acts of Thomas it can be said that, in a certain sense, they have been dramatised and utilised for a similar purpose, and how far this is true we shall have an opportunity to judge in the sequel.

We have also to consider that there are other Catholic writers, as St. Ephraem, and later St. Gregory of Tours, not to mention others of lesser weight, who recognise as historical, incidents mentioned in the Acts; and the latter also informs us of the existence of a narrative which he describes as *historia passionis eius* [*Thomae*]—according to which the Apostle Thomas suffered martyrdom in India. This can be no other than the *Passio B. Thomae*, which is an abbreviated form of the story, of which a fuller account exists also in Latin, under the name *De Miraculis B. Thomae*.

We are thus face to face with two facts: one, that certain Πράξεις or Περίοδοι or Μάρτύριον—*Acta* and *Passio* of the Apostle were monopolised by certain heretics for the purpose of propagating their tenets; the other that a certain history of his martyrdom in India does exist, and is referred to as containing a historical narrative concerning the Apostle.

4. Gnostics and the Acts

To clear up the point whether the Gnostic sects set up a composition of their own—in other words, a romance to disseminate their errors under the shadow of the Apostle's great name—it will be as well to ascertain first if there be any other pre-existing story or acts of a martyr used by them at an early age for any similar purpose. If this be found to be the case, it will almost be safe to conclude, even on this ground alone, that the same had occurred in the case of the Acts of Thomas. This is precisely what we find has happened. The acts of a virgin martyr of the apostolic age have been tampered with and adapted for doctrinal purposes by these heretics. They are the Acts of St. Thecla, a convert of the Apostle Paul and of about the middle of the first century. Treatment of this side issue follows in Nos. 13-15.

5. Reasons in Support

A pre-existing book held in esteem and veneration would suit the purpose of these sects much better than any new production; hence the reason for utilising the Acts of a martyr, and more so those of an Apostle, is obvious. There is the prestige of the name which would at once attract readers while concealing the design. In the primitive ages of the Church the books which were read by Christians were the Scriptures and the Acts of Martyrs, for in those days of persecution the fervour of their faith urged them to prepare themselves to undergo, when called upon, every sort of torture to secure the martyr's crown, and for this purpose the reading of the *Passiones Martyrum* was the most effective help. Such acts, then, would be the most convenient channel heretics could employ for the purpose of spreading their tenets. A third reason which may be suggested is that it would not be a book that could be cast back at them as their own composition; and if the false principle was cautiously allowed to drip through the web of the narrative, as is the case with the Acts of Thomas, it would easily pass undetected, and hence be more easily absorbed and assimilated.

6. Criteria Applicable to the Acts

Under the circumstances described above, in which the early Acts were compiled, as will appear in the sequel, the reader will perceive the utility of keeping in mind what we have so far discussed, and of applying these criteria to the present Acts of Thomas. The criteria are fully applicable to a composition like this, which, as will be seen, originated in Mesopotamia; it recorded events that must have taken place in India, which was connected to the former by commerce, was difficult of access, while the channel of communication would have been oral—through travellers.

SECTION II

PRELIMINARY QUESTIONS

7. Abdias, his Compilation

The first edition of a compilation which contained the 'Passiones' and 'Miracula' of the Apostles was published by Frederick Nausea, under the title 'Anonymi Philalethi Eusebiani in vitas miracula passionesque apostolorum Rap-*sodiae, Coloniae, 1531.' Wolfangus Lazius published almost the same collection, but it is not known from what text, with the title 'Abdiae Babyloniae episcopi et apostolorum discipuli de historia certaminis apostolici libri x, Julio Africano, cujus subinde meminit Hieronymus, interprete, Basiliae 1552'; the preface bears the date of 1551. That by Nausea now represents a codex that no longer exists, probably it was used up in printing that edition. The one by Lazius, though inaccurately entered in the new Catalogue of the Bibliothèque now being printed, may be detected under the name 'Abdias' by the date of the year 1552: it was printed repeatedly, both at Cologne and at Paris, until the edition 'Codex Apocryphus Novi Testamenti, Hamburgi, 1703,' by J. A. Fabricius, in two volumes, superseded it. Fabricius, in 1719, issued a second enlarged edition in three volumes, also at Hamburg.

Max Bonnet, who made a special study of this class of writings bearing chiefly on the Apostles, and issued, as we shall have occasion to note, critical editions of some, holds that Nausea's edition gives a faithful rendering of the original text, while Lazius has given himself some freedom in his editing of the same. See his remarks in preface to St. Gregory of Tours 'Liber de Miraculis Beati Andreae Apostoli' (*Opera Gregorii Tvronensis*, tom. i. pt. ii. p. 824, forming vol. i., of Scriptores Rerum Merovingicarum, Hannoveriae, 1885, in 4to).

We reproduce the heading of the first book of Lazius, the rest repeat the same at each life: 'Historiae apostolorum auctore Abdia Babiloniae episcopo et ipsorum apostolorum discipulo, quam ex Hebraica lingua in Latinam Africanus vertit.' It will scarcely be necessary to warn the reader that the name of Africanus has been gratuitously introduced; but we have also the name of Abdias and mention of the Hebrew language. A modern editor of some of these apocryphal (anonymous) writings, published in an important series, scoffs at the mention of Hebrew on the title-page: he was unaware that it offered him an early hint that some of the texts it gives are of Semitic origin. During the Middle Ages and later the 'Chaldee' as of old and the Chaldean as now, representing the Assyrian form of the Aramæan or Syriac language, was commonly termed Hebrew, and the writing was often reproduced in Hebrew characters, as may to this day be observed in the case of the books of the Old Testament composed in Chaldaic.

It has been asked, What proof is there that some of the texts came from a Semitic source, or that there ever was such a person as Abdias? To the former of these two questions incidental references as well as direct proof will be forthcoming, but to the second an answer may here be given. The Eusebian text of what is termed by some 'The Abgar Legend' offers us a name almost the same in the Greek form. This Rufinus, in his ancient Latin version of that history, corroborates. The Eusebian text (*Hist. Eccl.*, lib. i. c. xiii. col. 127, Migne, *P. Gr.-L.*, tom. xx., Eusebii, tom. ii.) recites that, after the cure of Abgar by the messenger sent by Judas Thomas the Apostle, namely, Thaddeus the Apostle, it continues: 'Nec vero ipsum solummodo (curavit) sed et Abdum quemdam Abdi filium,' &c. The Greek text (col. 128) gives the name Ἀβδος. Dr. Schwartz's critical ed. of Euseb. *H. E.*, Leipsic, 1903, Part I., p. 94, gives—ἀλλὰ καὶ Ἀβδον τον τον Ἀβδου. Rufinus (in a valuable edition of his Latin translation, published *per Beatum Rhenanum—*

apud inclytam Basileam An. MDXXIII. — under the title
Avtores Historiae Ecclesiasticae, p. 22) translates: 'Non solum
autem illum sed et Abdon quemdam Abdiae [*al.* Abdei], filium,'
&c. Theodore Mommsen's crit. text of Rufinus' translation,
published with Schwartz's text, *ut supr.,* p. 95, reproduces a verbal
reflection of the Greek text—'sed et Abdum quendam Abdae
filium.' Cureton (*Ancient Syriac Documents,* London, 1864), in
his English rendering of an ancient Syriac version of a fragment
of Eusebius' history, translates the same passage: 'not himself
only, but also Abdu, son of Abdu,' &c. The Syriac of the *Doctrine
of Addai the Apostle,* edited with text, translation, and notes, by
George Phillips, London, 1876, gives the corresponding passage
of the same narrative, p. 8 : 'And also with respect to Abdu,' &c.
We may then infer that the Semitic form of the name is Abdu ;
this Eusebius rendered in Greek Aββos; and Rufinus, at the end
of the fourth or beginning of the fifth century, gives the Latin
form of the same name as Abdos, Abdias, and Abdeus.

In Eusebius' text 'Thaddeus the Apostle' is described 'one
of the seventy.' The Eusebian narrative is taken, as he expressly
states, from the Syriac ; it must be from the same Edessan document from which the *Doctrine of Addai* takes its narrative, and
this in Phillips' translation of the Syriac text, p. 5, reads,
'Judas Thomas sent to Abgar Addai the Apostle, who was one
of the seventy-two Apostles.' If we turn to St. Jerome, we
find him stating most positively (*P. L.,* tom. xxvi., Hieron., tom.
vii., *Commentar. in Matth.,* col. 61) : 'Thaddaeum apostolum
ecclesiastica tradit historia missum Edessam ad Abgarum regem
Osroenae,' &c. The Syriac text of *Addai* offers evidence to
show that the text contained at first the words 'Addai the
Apostle'; but it, to later Eastern ideas, would appear strange
and undignified that one Apostle should depute another to per-
form a certain work for him, so the title 'Apostle' is retained
and an insertion is intercalated to meet the difficulty—'who
is one of the seventy-two Apostles ;' a form of expression quite
unusual, hence savouring of being an addition by a later hand.
Eusebius curtails it to 'one of the seventy.' The true reading
is confirmed also by the above-quoted assertion of Jerome, that
'ecclesiastical history hands down that the Apostle Thaddeus
was sent to King Abgar of Edessa,' where, after curing him, he
cured also Abdias, the son of Abdias: 'Addai' is the Aramaic
form of the name Thaddeus.

So we have not only the name, but we can see the probability that this Abdias, cured by a miracle, may have attached himself to the person of the Apostle Thaddeus. This latter inference we shall presently find supported by one of the texts of the short histories of the Apostles in the collection above mentioned. We take our quotation from Nausea's edition (*Passio sanctorum Apostolorum Simonis et Judae*, c. vi. fol. lxxii.): ' ordinaverunt autem in civitate illa [Babylon] episcopum nomine Abdiam'; it then adds, 'qui cum ipsis venerat a Judaea,' &c, which latter insertion would be by way of an inference. Lazius, in his edition of the text, does not leave it to be inferred, as in that given by Nausea, that the name of the city was Babylon, but expressly inserts the name. It should further be borne in mind that the Apostles James, son of Alpheus (Matt. x. 3), and Thaddeus, named Jude by Luke (vi. 16), and Simon the Canaanean, were brothers; for the two former we have the authority of Matthew and Luke, and for Simon the constant tradition of the Western and Eastern Churches. Jude-Thaddeus suffered martyrdom in Persia with his brother Simon; the joint feast is kept on 28th October. Jude-Thaddeus could therefore have appointed Abdias bishop of Babylon.

That no direct evidence has come down to us from other sources that Abdias was the first bishop of that city proves nothing. Even in the case of large and important places within the Roman empire we possess no list of the early bishops, much less need we expect to find those of cities outside the empire recorded and handed down in some prominent record. Yet we have here a mention, the rejection of which cannot be warranted on the sole ground that it is found in an anonymous writing. On the other hand, it will appear obvious that during the Apostolic age, when a sufficient number of conversions to the faith demanded the nomination of a bishop, the selection would fall on some well-tried disciple who had accompanied an Apostle and had been trained in such a school, and not on a neophyte, however zealous and fervent. The 'non-neophytum' principle (1 Tim. iii. 6) would naturally be enforced.

No texts in the Syriac have yet appeared which would cover anything like the ground of the Latin compilation published under the name of Abdias. Many manuscripts still remain to be printed; as to whether such writings in Syriac cover a large field we have yet to learn, since no collection of the existing Syriac texts has yet appeared. There is, however, hope that in

the near future this want will be supplied. The editors of the
new series, *Corpus Scriptorum Christianorum Orientalium*, J. B.
Chabot, J. Guidi, H. Hyvernat, and B. Carra de Vaux, propose
to publish Eastern works written by Christians in the following
languages : Syriac, Ethiopic, Coptic, Arabic, and, perhaps later,
Armenian may also be included. The series will embrace four
sub-heads for each language. Under the sub-head *Apocrypha
Sacra* for Syriac, four volumes are reserved for writings bearing
on the New Testament, treating of the Blessed Virgin, the
Apostles, and the Cross. These may give us the supplementary
texts. It will hence be wise to keep an open mind on the subject, the more so as recent researches have singularly re-habili-
tated many a piece of early ecclesiastical literature which had
been placed under ban by a long succession of savants.

8. Acts of Thomas, Original Language

Selecting the Acts of Thomas for special treatment—which
are also incorporated in the Abdias Latin collection—it will be
necessary to ascertain in what language they were originally
written. The Semitic text of the Acts of Thomas has been
fortunately submitted to scrutiny and compared with its Greek
representative to ascertain the primitive language of the composition. The work has been done by Professor F. C. Burkitt,
who has found the Syriac to be beyond doubt the original text.
We therefore recommend to the reader in search of such techni-
cal proof the Professor's *Early Christianity outside the Roman
Empire*, Cambridge, 1899, pp. 63–79 ; *Journal of Theological
Studies*, for 1900, pp. 280–290 ; *ibid.*, for 1902, p. 95.

The different copies of the Acts now extant give us no fair
idea of what the original short form of the narrative must have
been. The large amount of unnecessary incidents, and yet more
the redundant discourses put into the mouths of persons brought
on the scene, of which the Syriac offers the most exaggerated form,
can by no means have formed part of the original composition.

9. The Syriac Text of the Acts

A complete copy of the Syriac text of these Acts of Thomas
exists in the British Museum in Add. MS 14,645, dated 936,
edited by Dr. Wright, *Apocryphal Acts of the Apostles*, London,

1871, in two volumes, one of text and the other giving the English translation by the editor. Of those published in the former, the Acts of John the Evangelist, and on his Decease; on Matthew and Andrew, as also that of Thomas, are in Syriac. There are besides three other copies of our text which have come from the East: one was procured by Sachau and is in Berlin—a modern transcript; a second copy, probably taken from the same original also, is at Cambridge; the third, also a modern transcript as we believe, was procured for the Borgian Museum, Rome, by the late Syrian Archbishop of Damascus, David, together with a large number of other Syriac MSS, some of which were copies. All these latter have now passed to the Vatican Library with the other MSS which had been collected either by the founder, Cardinal Borgia, or by the late Cardinal Barnabò. Besides Wright's edition of the text, the Rev. Paul Bedjan has also given a separate edition in vol. iii. of his *Acta Martyrum et Sanctorum*, Leipsic-Paris, 1892, incorporating readings from the Borgian MS. This edition contains several additions to Wright's text taken from the Berlin MS (Duval, *Litt. Syriac*, 2nd edition, 1900, p. 98, note).

Fragments of these Acts, from a palimpsest Sinaitic codex, have been read and published, with an English translation by Mr. Burkitt, in Appendix vii. to *Studia Sinaitica*, No. ix., text and translation, London, 1900, Clay & Sons, edited by Agnes Smith Lewis; also *Horae Semiticae*, Nos. iii. and iv., text and translation, Cambridge University Press, edited by the same lady. The text yielded by the palimpsest, of which only eight pages were found decipherable, would cover the space of about five pages of Wright's edition. Burkitt holds these fragments to be 400 years older than any known text; this would give us A.D. 936-400 = A.D. 536, or the second quarter of the sixth century. The reader should, however, be warned that the learned Professor worked on photos taken by Mrs. Lewis, and had not the opportunity of handling the original sheets.

A small poem in Syriac of the Acts of Judas Thomas by a Nestorian of the eighteenth century, Giwargis of Alkosh, will be found in P. Cardahi's *Liber Thesauri de arte poetica Syrorum*, p. 130.

10. THE GREEK VERSION

The best edition of the Greek and Latin versions has been given by Professor Max Bonnet, of Montpellier, *Acta Thomae:*

*Graece partim cum novis codicibus contulit, partim primus edidit—
Latine recensuit*, Lipsiae, 1883.[1] The Greek text is found entire
in only one codex, Paris-Graec. 1510 (olim. 2452); this Bonnet
discovered and has reproduced. He considers the MS to be of
the eleventh century; the catalogue marks it of the twelfth.

11. THE LATIN VERSIONS

Of the Latin versions Bonnet says (*praef.* xiii.): 'Acta Thomae
latina habemus bina, pleniora altera altera breuiora, neutra ex
alteris hausta.' The third statement that they are independent
of each other is of considerable importance, as this implies that
they descend from independent sources. The former of these
versions, 'on the authority of the codices,' is called *De Miraculis
Thomae*, the other *Passio Thomae*. The difference of names is
important. St. Gregory of Tours, A.D. 590, knew only the
latter—Thomas Apostolus secundum historiam Passionis ejus.[2]
The point is of importance for more than one reason, and
will turn up again for consideration. Bonnet terms the version
'Passio' (p. xiii.) 'minoris pretii librum.' This is true in
two ways, it is not as good a compilation as the other *De
Miraculis*, and is written in an inferior style; but he remarks
'sed a multis deinceps lectum.' The ruggedness of its style
may also be a reason for holding it as the more ancient version
of the two, even apart from the witness of Gregory of Tours.
Bonnet admits further that there may have been from the beginning two Latin versions of the Acts, as there were two of
Hermas's book, *Pastor ;* and, we may add, as there were of
the letters of St. Ignatius of Antioch, as well as of other early
writings.

Anyhow, note should be taken of the fact that St. Gregory,
who had made a special study of early literature of this class,
and to which he himself was a large contributor, does not
mention the present compilation *De Miraculis*.

Of the Acts of Thomas, the shorter version, *Passio*, was the

---

[1] These texts are now incorporated in Part II. of vol. ii. of the Leipsic
edition of the *Acta Apostolorum Apocrypha*, 1903.

[2] *Liber in Gloria Martyrum*, cap. 31, p. 507, *Opera Gregorii Tvronen.*
tom. i., *Scriptores rerum Merovingicarum*, of the series *Monumenta Germaniae Historica*, in quarto, Hanover edition; this gives a critical edition of
the text for all the works of the Bishop of Tours.

first that was printed. Boninus Mombritius included it in his *Sanctuarium*, tom. ii. folio 333, Mediolani, *c.* Anno 1480.

The book *De Miraculis* was first edited by Frederick Nausea, Coloniae, 1531, and next by Wolfangus Lazius, Basileae, 1552; it was reprinted by J. A. Fabricius in his *Codex Apocryphus N.T.*, Hamburgi, 1703 and 1719.

12. OTHER VERSIONS

Besides the above work, one somewhat similar is found also in Ethiopic. Mr. Malan gave an English translation of it under the title *Conflicts of the Apostles*. Mr. E. A. Budge published the same work with the title—*The Contendings of the Apostles— Gadla Hawarsjat*, London, 1901, in 2 vols., text and English translation. Budge found Malan's edition unsatisfactory, as it reproduced a modern faulty MS; the text which he published comes from two MSS, formerly belonging to King Theodore of Abyssinia, brought from Magdala in 1868. The MSS are probably of the fifteenth and seventeenth century; the oldest known MS is at Paris, and is dated A.D. 1379. Dr. M. R. James has also published some writing called *Acts of Thomas*, but this is said to be a different work. We have had no opportunity of consulting the Ethiopic versions; but it may be taken as a general rule that similar versions offer very little help in reconstructing the text of an ancient work—*The Didascalia of the Apostles*, published by Thomas Platt, Ethiopic text and translation, may be cited as a case in point—since they are never first-hand translations, based frequently on a prior Arabic version, and are comparatively of modern date. We take from Mr. W. R. Philipp's paper, *The Connexion of St. Thomas the Apostle with India*, printed in the *Indian Antiquary* of 1903, what will give some idea of the contents of the Ethiopic Acts of Thomas given in Mr. Budge's work. There seem to be two narratives. The first of these takes the reader down to Act vi. of the Syriac text (see No. 24). The other comprises two sections; the first is styled 'The Preaching of Saint Thomas in India.' It appears to be a garbled account, of which some details are taken from the known Acts, and others, to a certain extent, invented. The second section contains 'The Martyrdom of Saint Thomas in India.' This portion appears to be based on a new narrative, the new names retaining some semblance to the older ones of the known Acts; the story can give no help in elucidating the Syriac text.

An Arabic edition, text and translation of the *Conflicts* or *Contendings*, has been lately issued by Mrs. Agnes Smith Lewis, under a new title, *The Mythological Acts of the Apostles* (*Horae Semiticae*, Nos. iii. and iv. *ut supr.*). The Arabic is supposed to represent a Coptic text, of which up to the present only fragments are known to exist. As this Arabic text gives a version of the doings of the Apostle Thomas, the Coptic most probably contained it. The Ethiopic version mentioned above now turns out to be, as we surmised, a translation from this Arabic text.

The manuscript of an Armenian version is at Berlin; the text is unpublished and consequently not available for comparison with the present text of the Syriac. Armenian versions, however, are often more helpful, and bear a closer relation to older originals. Even in literature of this class the Armenian has been found serviceable; it has been employed with advantage along with the Syriac version in the study of some Acts, as the reader will have occasion to see.

13. ACTS OF THECLA

The *Acta* of St. Thecla, the Virgin, Protomartyr of her sex, have remained under a cloud for a long period, although several Fathers of the Church refer to them approvingly, and quote the story of her triumph on the chief lines of that early narrative. Among these, Basilius, bishop of Seleucia in Isauria (died A.D. 458), has written two books, *De vita et miraculis S. Theclae*, libri. ii., Migne, *P. Gr.-L.*, tom. lxxxv.; also Nicetas David, bishop in Paphlagonia (died A.D. 890), a homily on the Saint, *ibid.*, tom. cv. cols. 822–846. The *Acta*, or the saintly virgin, are mentioned by St. Methodius of Tyre,[1] bishop and martyr, A.D. 312, *ibid.*, tom. xviii.; St. Gregory of Nazianzus, *ibid.*, tom. xxxv. col. 1105, xxxvii. cols. 593, 639, 745; St. Gregory of Nyssa, *ibid.*, tom. xliv. col. 1067, *Homil xiv.* in *Cantica Canticorum;* St. Epiphanius, *Haeres.*, lxxviii. n. 16, and *Haeres.*, lxxix. n. 5; St. John Chrysostom, *Homil xxv.* in *Actus Apostolor.*, tom. ix., ed. Montfaucon; St. Ambrose, *De virginibus*, Migne, *P. L.*, tom. xvi. col. 385 ff; *De virginitate*, col. 290; and *Epist. ad Vercell. eccles.*, tom. xvi. col. 1250.

The *Acta* were first published by Grabbe (*Spicilegium SS.*

---

[1] Carl Schmidt, *Acta Pauli* (infr.), styles him, p. 148, bishop of Olympus in Lycia.

P

Theclae, also a third apocryphal letter of Paul to the Corinthians
and their reply, as also the Apostle's Martyrdom. Of these, the
text of the letters had come down in a Syriac version and was
published among the works of St. Ephraem, while the two others
existed as separate writings. What is new is the knowledge that
the *Acta Theclae* formed part of this early apocryphal writing.
The words of Tertullian, written at the opening of the third
century, condemning Gnostics, who put forward a claim on behalf
of women to baptize and preach, now bear a much fuller meaning than had hitherto been assigned to them (*de Baptismo*, c.
xvii.): Quodsi qui Pauli perperam inscripta legunt, exemplum
Theclae ad licentiam mulierum docendi tinguendique defendunt,
sciant in Asia presbyterum, qui eam scripturam construxit, quasi
titulo Pauli de suo cumulans, convictum atque confessum, id se
amore Pauli fecisse loco decessisse. The brunt of the charge on
which the presbyter was deposed is here assigned to his having
issued his work as that of Paul. This meaning was not fully appre-
ciated before, but the present Coptic text, reproducing the title
of the Greek text, lets us know that it was κ' [κατά] τον ἀπόστολον,
usurping thus the canonical heading reserved to the books of the
New Testament. Tertullian probably had before him a Latin
text which incorporated the *Acta Theclae*.

St. Jerome (*De viris illustr.*, c. vii.) has the following passage
on the subject: Igitur Περιόδους Pauli et Theclae et totam baptizati leonis fabulam inter apocryphas scripturas computamus,
quale enim est ut individuus comes apostoli (*i.e.* Lucas) inter
ceteras res hoc solum ignoraverit? sed et Tertullianus vicinus
eorum temporum refert, presbyterum quendam in Asia σπουδαστὴν
apostoli Pauli, convictum apud Joannem, quod auctor esset libri,
et confessum se hoc Pauli amore fecisse, loco excidisse. To
Jerome also the Περιόδους Pauli contained the *Acta Theclae*.

After carefully comparing the German translation of the Coptic
text given by Schmidt with the English version of the Syriac text
by Dr. Wright, we find that, with the exception of several large
and small lacunæ which exist, the two versions run on parallel
lines as independent renderings of the same text, even to the
rendering of delicate expressions of thought. While the Syriac
is made more readable by connecting passages between the
sentences, the Coptic is severely abrupt and generally cramped
in expression. Occasionally the Syriac will add a development
to the thought expressed, while the Coptic is curt. After each

lacuna of the MS, when the Coptic resumed the narrative, it will be found to agree textually with the complete Syriac version: so that it can be asserted in all fairness that from the opening sentences recovered from the Coptic MS down to the two last lines of the same, also fortunately recovered, both versions, excepting lacunæ, reflect the same original, of which they are independent renderings. We are thus enabled to infer that were the text of the MS complete we should find both substantially the same.

Some of the lacunæ, however, have deprived us of important historical passages. The first of the larger lacunæ occurring at p. 7 of the text (the second of the Acts of Thecla), would have contained the narrative of the meeting of Onesiphorus with Paul ; the text retains—'on the royal road which '—and here the lacuna commences, omitting the important mention of Lystra. The second large lacuna, of some sixteen lines, pp. 8 and 9, has dropped the teaching of Paul at the house of Onesiphorus, when in the form of a series of new Beatitudes, attributed to the Apostle, in imitation of those found in the Gospel, the first germs of Gnostic error are gradually introduced, culminating in an open assertion that wedded life is an improper state. The third lacuna, pp. 17 and 18, cuts off the entire narrative of the ordeals to which Thecla was subjected at Iconium at her first trial and condemnation ; a few lines only have survived which tell us that she ascended the pile and the crowd set fire to it. The fourth consists of an entire sheet, leaving a blank of two pages. This lacuna would have contained Thecla's second trial at Antioch on the charge proffered by Alexander, the High Priest of Syria. Because of these, the account given by the Coptic papyrus misses some of the principal details of the narrative.

The German professor contends, against the view upheld by Professor W. M. Ramsay and Corssen, that the Acts of Thecla had no separate written form apart from the work he publishes ; and that Basileus of Seleucia, who, as we said, wrote two books on the life and miracles of the saint, based his information on this text. It becomes of importance, if not necessary, that we should thoroughly test the point so raised before proceeding further. The lacunæ indicated above will considerably militate against the case for a separate and prior existence of Thecla's Acts being argued fully ; we shall be compelled, therefore, where the Coptic is deficient, to recur to the Syriac on the grounds stated above, and indicate what it would have contained were it unmutilated.

Schmidt attests that the *Acta Pauli* disclose no doctrinal feature opposed to the early teaching of the Church (except, he says, a passage on p. 9 of the MS; this includes the section of the Beatitudes). Supposing the editor is right in his general appreciation of what that text assigns to Paul in other parts of the *Acta*, will the assumption also hold good as to that which gives us Thecla's Acts? We are of opinion it will not. Among the Beatitudes attributed to Paul, as explained above, the Syriac has the following, which is lost in the Coptic by the second extensive lacuna: 'Blessed are they who have wives as though they had them not, for they shall inherit the earth.' This comes as the fifth Beatitude in the Syriac, while the first surviving in the defective Coptic corresponds to the seventh of the former. The doctrine contained in the above is opposed both to the Gospel and the Pauline teaching; read 1 Corinthians, vii. 2–5. The doctrine is suggested in what survives of the text.

At p. 12 of the German translation of the papyrus text the same principle is again brought forward, but placed this time in the mouth of others. Thamyris is made to say: 'Who is this tempter who is within, with you (referring to Paul) deceiving the souls of young men and of virgins that they be not married, but remain as they are?' Demas and Hermogenes are made to reply: 'This man, whence he comes, we cannot find out, but he separates the young men from their wives and the virgins from their husbands, saying there will be no resurrection for them (p. 13) unless they remain holy (and) soil not their flesh, but (keep) it pure.' This is no other than the Gnostic error taught in the second and third centuries; particulars may be found under Nos. 28 and 29.

The question now arises, Did the presbyter of Asia, author of the *Acta Pauli*, denounced by Tertullian, embody this feature of doctrine in his work, or did it pre-exist in the *Acta Theclae*? If he has shown no Gnostic leanings in the rest of the compilation, will it not be legitimate to infer that the insertions are not his, but had been previously incorporated into the writing? The case being so, we are forced to admit that the *Acta* of Thecla had preceded the presbyter's work.

We may now briefly invite attention to other arguments derived from Thecla's text set forth by Ramsay, of which we shall indicate here only two; see No. 14. (1) The Acts recite that Onesiphorus went from Iconium on the royal road which led to Lystra, and was there waiting for Paul's arrival, who was coming from Antioch (of Pisidia). For the argument deduced from the state of the routes of communication existing about A.D. 50 between Iconium, Lystra, and Antioch correctly given in the text, but altered shortly after that date, a circumstance which a later writer would not have known, we refer the reader to Ramsay's book quoted at No. 14. (2) Another, and in our opinion the most cogent argument in support of the early existence of the Acts of the virgin-martyr, *i.e.* shortly after the middle of the first century, will be found in the very correct presentation of the position held by Queen Tryphaena at Thecla's trial at Antioch, given in the same, but which was completely altered after A.D. 54; see No. 14.

Before closing this digression we will invite attention to another point given in the Coptic MS. The Greek text (Grabe, tom. i. p. 108) assigns the cause of Thecla's condemnation at the second trial to Ιεροσιλια. The Latin version recites: 'erat autem eulogium [causa] eius scriptum SACRILEGIUM.' The Coptic (transl. of Schmidt) renders it thus: 'And the cause which was written behind her was this—she had stolen from the temple.' The rendering is simply absurd; the text mentions neither temple nor theft, but the action of Thecla who snatched the crown worn by Alexander, the High Priest, and cast it on the road. The only way of accounting for this blunder is to suppose that the Coptic language offering no equivalent for the word 'sacrilege,' the translator was bound to substitute its meaning; but he offers one which is not applicable to the subject. The crime of sacrilege may be committed either by theft from a temple, or by profanation; the latter, which was applicable to the text, the Coptic translator overlooks, because, perhaps, in his days sacrilege chiefly implied theft from a temple; but this discloses a low intellectual standard.

Modern students, encouraged by what they found in the writings of the Fathers referring to the story of Thecla, have begun to examine the *Acta* more closely; not only such parts of the narrative as would constitute its essential portion, but also some striking details contained therein, and have ascertained that many of these do belong to her age and are of undoubted historical accuracy (see No. 14).

14. Reconstruction of the 'Acta'

To M. Edmond Le Blant (*Les Persécuteurs et les Martyrs*, Paris, 1893) is due the credit of first advancing proofs of substantial value. The chief points he brings out may be thus briefly summarised. (1) Thecla's appeal when indecently approached by Alexander, 'Respect the stranger,' &c. (2) The sentence affixed to the post to which she was fastened, 'Sacrilegium.' (3) When so exposed, she was given a cloth or shift to cover her person and a girdle, the *cingulum*, to fasten it, for Roman law severely punished any nude exposure of the person of a female under sentence. (4) Thecla's request to the governor on her condemnation that her virginity should be respected—a request supported by usage, and promptly granted.

But for a thorough critical examination of the *Acta* the reader must consult Professor W. M. Ramsay, *The Church and the Roman Empire before A.D. 170* (7th edit., London, 1903, chap. xvi. pp. 375 ff.). We offer a condensed summary of this able treatment of the subject, which may also help the reader to form a more accurate opinion of the treatment which the Acts of Thomas require. He starts with the point that the present form the narrative assumes in the *Acta* is not the work of one author. He proceeds to investigate whether the component parts can be separated, and to what date they can be assigned; further, if the earlier or original parts came down as a traditional legend, or belonged to a literary composition; and follows up this investigation with an inquiry as to what historical value this early writing possesses. The cardinal feature of the inquiry turns on the historical reality of the Queen, Tryphaena, who bears a prominent part in the tale. She is there shown to have become a second mother to the Christian virgin, and to have protected her honour and eventually to have saved her life.

The historical evidence of her reality is offered by her coins.

Von Gutschmidt, says Ramsay, was the first to point out that Queen Tryphaena was probably a historical character. He appealed to certain rare coins of the kingdom of Pontus, which show on the obverse the bust of a king with the title —ΒΑΣΙΛΕΩΣ ΠΟΛΕΜΩΝΟΣ, on the reverse the bust of a queen with the title ΒΑΣΙΛΙΣΣΗΣ ΤΡΥΦΑΙΝΗΣ, and he urged that the queen whose bust appears on Pontic coins

was the Queen Tryphaena of the *Acta*. Obvious difficulties
arose against the identification. The Tryphaena of the *Acts*
was apparently a Roman subject residing at Antioch [of Pisidia],
who complained of her isolation and friendlessness. The
Polemon of the coins was a powerful king known to have reigned
in Pontus from A.D. 37 to 63, and was a Greek. His wife could
not, on any reasonable hypothesis, be an elderly woman in A.D. 50,
as Tryphaena is represented in the tale. Further research,
carried on chiefly by Von Sallet, Waddington, and Mommsen,
disclosed that Tryphaena was 'cousin once removed of the
Emperor Claudius, her mother Pythodoris being his full cousin;'
the mother of Pythodoris and of Claudius were sisters and daugh-
ters of the Triumvir Marcus Antonius. Queen Tryphaena in her
own right was queen of Pontus, and was married to Cotis, king of
Thrace, where, being only queen-consort, her name does not
appear on those coins. The coin bearing the inscription given
above represents Polemon as a young man, and the lady on the
reverse is a mature woman; they could not be husband and
wife, but were mother and son, she reigning in her own right as
Queen of Pontus, which her son Polemon was to inherit. The
coin is of the year A.D. 37, when her son, aged about nineteen,
was made king, and she herself was about forty-six years of age.
In A.D. 50 she was, therefore, nearly sixty. This would suit the
Acta perfectly. (For particulars of Queen Tryphaena's family, see
Theodor Mommsen, *Ephimeris Epigraphica*, 1872, vol. i. pp.
270 ff; and vol. ii. pp. 259 ff.),

Mr. Ramsay (p. 388) says: 'It should be kept in mind that
the Emperor Claudius died in 54 A.D. and Nero succeeded him;
the new emperor rather made a point of throwing contempt and
ridicule on his predecessor. After a few years he even stripped
Polemon of his kingdom of Pontus, leaving him, however, a
principality among the mountain districts of western Cilicia.
The picture given in the *Acta* of Tryphaena's situation, while
true to the time in which the scene is laid, ceases to be so after
a very few years had passed; after 54 she was no longer a
relative of the emperor, and in all probability she lost most of
her personal influence with the Roman officials.'

Mr. Ramsay points out 'as a striking instance of the historical value of early Christian documents, that, apart from the coins
the only deep mark the dynasty has left in literature is in a
Christian work,' the *Acta* of Thecla. The reader should not

fail to take note of the very striking historical coincidence and similarity there exists between the case of Queen Tryphaena of Pontus, mentioned in the *Acta*, and that of Gondophares, king of the Indians, in the Acts of Thomas. In both cases the written record of their existence was retained exclusively in ecclesiastical literature, and both again only in recent years obtained confirmation of historical value from coins discovered bearing their effigy and their legend.

It was, as has been already said, owing to the protection offered to Thecla by this queen, to whom the Roman authorities showed every deference, that the virgin's life was saved. This can now cause no surprise, since her close relationship to the emperor Claudius and her own rank are known. This position is very faithfully reflected in the story told in the *Acta*, which would not be the case had they been the product of a later age, as all memory of her position would by then have been lost owing to the want of any literary record of the queen and the position she held.

The *Acta* contain two trials of Thecla, one at her native city of Iconium, which is said to have been presided over by a Roman governor, and where the charge laid against her was that she would not marry Thamyris to whom she had been betrothed, and was in consequence condemned to be burnt alive. The trial, in the form it bears in the present text, is rejected by Ramsay on two grounds : that Iconium at that date had not yet obtained the privilege of a governor; the other that the case was not one that could be taken into court, much less could she for such refusal be condemned to capital punishment, a sentence which no inferior magistrate could inflict but which was reserved exclusively to the governor. He ascribes all these additions to a later hand which manipulated the older text. The only way, he maintains, that Thecla's refusal to marry Thamyris could be treated, would be restricted to the family circle. Some trace that such was once the form of this part of the tale is found in a homily of about the year 300, wrongly attributed to Chrysostom (see *Homil.* in *S. Theclam*, opera, 2nd edit. of Montfaucon, Paris, vol. ii. pp. 896–99). The author therein gives quite a different account of this portion of the story. He narrates how every effort was made to bring family influence to shake the virgin's resolution ; how, also, according to the custom of the age, the servants were introduced weeping to implore their young mistress not to reject her marriage pledge. It is possible she may have been produced before a local magistrate to intimidate her even by threats, but she must eventually have been allowed to go free. She then wandered about seeking for Paul, guided by rumours of his movements. Her lover pursued and overtook her; when on the point of becoming a victim to his violence, she prayed to heaven for help. Here the fragment ends most inappropriately. This older form of the tale must have had no presiding Roman governor, no condemnation, and consequently no sentence of punishment as is given in the first trial. This places the story on its true historical basis, and it implies as well that the Gnostic doctrinal additions, and the introduction on the scene of persons mentioned in the *Acts of the Apostles* and in the *Epistles of St. Paul*, as Onesiphorus, Titus, Demas, and Hermogenes, are the outcome of later enlargements by an unwise admirer of the Apostle in the latter, and by heretics in the former case.

The trial, on the other hand, of Thecla at Antioch—not of Asia, as some have erroneously supposed, but of Pisidia—is upheld; the details of which, as given in the better texts, are shown to fit in admirably with the known circumstances of time and place, and reflect the prevailing social customs of that part of Asia. Alexander, whom the text represents as an important personage and a resident in the city, was going to hold games with the production of wild beasts in the arena, called by the Romans *Venatio*.[1] Such games were only given in large provincial capitals, and though Antioch had no resident governor, the position of Alexander justifies the surmise that the governor had accepted an invitation to grace the festivities with his presence, and the coming of the governor, the celebration of the games, and possibly an invitation, would naturally explain the presence of Queen Tryphaena at Antioch from her estates situated in the vicinity of Iconium.

The charge laid by Alexander against the Christian virgin would be construed as one of sacrilege, since, according to Ramsay, Alexander was 'the high priest of Syria,' whose official dignity was considered to have been outraged when Thecla tore

---

[1] The reader may usefully refer to Dom Leclercq's article, 'Ad Bestias,' *Diction. d'Archéologie Chrétienne et de Liturgie*, Paris, 1903, cols. 449-462, for an elaborate account of such Roman sports, including the *condemnatio ad bestias*, and the incident of St. Thecla.

off the crown from his head and flung it on the ground and rent his garment.[1] As to Alexander's conduct: when the assault was committed, he was then going to the games escorted by his followers; he met Thecla entering the city, and, attracted by the charm of her beauty, he embraced and kissed her. From a Roman social point of view, it is explained, he took her for a dancing girl, whose status would not be outraged by such attention as he had paid her. That this represents the true view of the case will be found supported by what is narrated in the *Acta*. Thecla, at the outrage offered to her, cried out bitterly (Wright's translation, p. 131), 'Do not force the stranger! Do not force the handmaid of god [the servant of God]! I am a noble's daughter of the city of Iconium.'

On the occasion when Thecla was going to be removed from Queen Tryphaena's protection to be exposed to the wild beasts in the arena, the latter exclaims in grief (p. 134): 'Thy help O God (I implore); for lo, twice is there mourning in my house, and I have no one to help me; for my daughter lives not, she is dead, and there is none of my kinsmen to stand at my side, and I am a widow.' The points here put forth admirably suit her position; she had mourned her husband and her daughter; into the latter's place, as the tale says, she had taken Thecla, and she was, besides, away from her sons, who were Kings of Thrace, Pontus, and Armenia, and on Roman territory. The latter fact is also capable of a reasonable explanation. Her lonely presence there would probably be the result of friction between herself and her son, the King of Pontus. She had reigned before him in her own right, and it is most probable that her son after a time preferred to be unfettered by her presence; on that account she may have left the kingdom, or she may have been exiled.

We will quote a passage describing what happened when Thecla was fastened to the post bearing her sentence of condemnation, 'Sacrilegium,' and a lion or lioness was let loose upon her (p. 139): 'Queen Tryphaena, who was standing by

---

[1] Under Roman rule there existed *sacerdotes provinciae* and *flamines*; the former presided over public sports, the latter were priests of the emperor in the sense of the divine honours rendered to them in municipal functions. Alexander is thus the 'Sacerdos provinciae' presiding at the games, and is invested with (pagan) sacerdotal office; see *Diction. d'Archéol. Chrét. et de Liturg.*, ut supr., article 'Adoratio,' col. 542 f.

the door of the theatre, fainted away and fell down on the ground, because she thought that Thecla was dead. And when her slaves saw that she had fainted and fallen down, they broke out into wailing, and rent their garments and say, "The Queen is dead!" And when the hêgemôn (governor) heard them say "The Queen is dead!" (he stopped the games) and the whole city trembled. And Alexander was afraid, and he ran (and) came and said to the hêgemôn: "Have pity on me, sir, and also on this city, and release this (woman who was) doomed to be devoured by beasts, that she may go away from us, so that the city too may not perish, lest perchance, when Cæsar [Claudius] hears of these things which we have done, he may destroy the city, for Queen Tryphaena is of the family of Cæsar, and lo, she was standing beside the door of the theatre, and she is dead."' The *Acta* state further that the governor caused criers to proclaim (p. 140) to the people: 'Thecla who is God's [of the god], and Thecla who is righteous, I have released and given unto you.' The Greek text says: 'I release to you Thekla the servant of the god.' By this it is implied, in the sense understood by pagans—as Thecla had twice asserted herself to be the handmaid of God—that she was a woman who had given herself in celibacy to a god, and her innocence under the circumstances is proclaimed. All this admirably reflects the social state and public opinion prevailing in that corner of Asia which was the scene of the events described.

It should also be noted that at this trial Thecla's religion was not openly brought into question, therefore it must have taken place before the edicts of Nero, who ruled A.D. 54–68, against the new faith, were published; these ordered the extreme penalty of the law for the profession of the Christian faith unless the person recanted.

Mr. Ramsay puts a new construction on the passage of Tertullian given above (we have partly reflected his opinion in our translation). He maintains that Tertullian was aware of the existence of a narrative older than that which he attributes to the presbyter of Asia; his words show that the book was not composed but constructed by him—'eam scripturam construxit, quasi titulo Pauli'—and, if any ambiguity or doubt of the right meaning yet prevails, this is entirely removed by the short formula added to the preceding words—'de suo cumulans'— adding of his own. Ramsay, after Zahn, ascribes the known remark of St. Ignatius the martyr (A.D. 107) regarding the exposure of Christians to wild beasts, 'as they have done to some, refusing to touch them through fear' (*Ep. ad Roman.*, c. v.), to what is said of Thecla's escape when exposed to the wild beasts, whether a lion or lioness and a bear.

The details now contained in the opening section of the *Acta*, Ramsay assigns to a later period. They reflect, in fact, a period in the second century when persecution against the professors of the faith was thoroughly established by the new legislation introduced by Nero and extended by his successors throughout the empire. The historical allusions of this section he ascribes to two successive dates. About the year 130 the tale was enlarged by one who accepted it as true, but who wished to connect it with persons and incidents known and mentioned by St. Paul, whose names occur in the canonical books. A further reconstruction, he suggests, took place between 140–160 : and this caused the introduction of the trial scene at Iconium, which had then become a chief town governed by an official of consular rank. Mr. Ramsay has purposely abstained from dealing with the doctrinal features of the story; we therefore think it right to suggest that they could not have been inserted much later than the second period mentioned above, when the second interpolator, the Gnostic scribe, deftly interjected the germs of Gnostic antipathy to wedded life; for the text of the newly recovered *Acta Pauli* contains them.

We should not close this section without placing before the reader the latest discovered testimony to the authenticity of the *Acta Theclae* borne by the lady pilgrim (Gamurrini, *S. Silviae Peregrinatio*, Romae, 1887). She writes in her journal (p. 73) : Sed quoniam de Tharso tertia mansione, id est in Hisauria est martyrium sanctae Theclae, gratum fuit satis, ut etiam illuc accederem praesertim cum tam in proximo esset. And at p. 74 : ibi ergo cum venissem in nomine Dei, facta oratione martyrium, nec non etiam lectus omnis actus sanctae Theclae, gratias domino nostro egi infinitas, qui mihi dignatus est indignae et non merenti in omnibus desideria complere—'The Martyrion of St. Thecla is situated in Isauria at a distance of three stages from Tharsus, and it was most gratifying to me to visit it; the more so since I was in the vicinity. When by God's blessing I arrived there, I prayed at the Martyrion, read also the entire Acts of St. Thecla, and gave infinite thanks to our Lord who granted me, so unworthy, the happiness of fulfilling all my wishes.' The visit was paid by the lady pilgrim about the year 388; she is held to be Egeria or Etheria, a Spanish lady (see Dom. M. Ferotin's *Le véritable auteur de la Peregrinatio Silviae*, Paris, 1903).

15. INTERPOLATED BY GNOSTICS

We now pass on to consider how these early writings were manipulated by Gnostics. The quotations will be taken, as before, from Wright's translation. From the outset, advantage is cleverly taken of Paul's arrival at a house at Iconium—the supposed house of Onesiphorus [1]—to introduce Gnostic tenets attacking the propriety and sanctity of the married state. These are introduced in the discourse given, which is stated to have been on concupiscence of the flesh and on future resurrection. The fact that Thecla was betrothed to Thamyris was too good an opportunity to be overlooked, so Thecla's home is conveniently placed adjoining that of Onesiphorus, and she becomes an assiduous listener to the Apostle's supposed Gnostic teachings.

Her mother becomes impatient at the daughter's conduct. She remarks to her future son-in-law, ' I say to thee, Tamyris, he (Paul) has perverted the whole city of the Iconians, thy betrothed too, and many other women; and young men go to him and he teaches them to live purely.' Thamyris, driven well-nigh to despair by the attitude of his bride in spite of all his remonstrances, finding two men, who had come out of the house where Paul lodged, disputing in the street, rushes out to meet them and inquires, ' Who is this man within, with you, who leads astray the souls of young women and of virgins and commands that there should be no marriage feasts, but that they should live as they are?' Demas and Hermogenes, who turned false to the Apostle (2 Tim. iv. 9; i. 15), are here represented to be the two companions who had come out of the house. They reply, ' We do not know him; but he separates young men from the virgins and the virgins from the young men.' When Paul is dragged before the hêgemôn, the cry put in the mouth of the populace is,

---

[1] It should be known he had been a frequent host of the Apostle elsewhere and had visited St. Paul while in captivity, and Paul showed himself very grateful for such kindness and attention, 2 Tim. i. 16; iv. 19.

'Drag him along, he is a magician, for he has corrupted all our wives.' Paul is scourged and cast out of the city.

We learn from St. Epiphanius, *Haeres*. xlvii., that the sect of Gnostics was spread largely over that portion of Asia to which these *Acta* belong: Horum ingens est hodie numerus in Pisidia eaque Phrysiae parte, &c.—praeterea in Asiae provinciis et in Isauria, Pamphilia, Cilicia, Galatia, &c. Thecla was greatly venerated in those parts, as the homilies of the bishops of these countries attest. It was therefore a master-stroke on the part of the heretics to secure the *Acta* and make them an early purveyor of their doctrine.

The skeleton of this writing, skilfully reconstructed by Ramsay (end of chap. xvi), shows that the original narrative would mention her having heard Paul preaching, perhaps in the streets, and that she embraced the Christian faith and eventually decided to devote herself to God and to preserve her virginity. On this account she had to face domestic trials, which induced her to leave her home and follow Paul. On her entering Antioch of Pisidia, the incident occurred which caused her to be charged with the crime of 'sacrilege' against the person of the high priest of Syria, on which account she had to appear for judgment before the governor. Having upheld her conduct, she was sentenced to be exposed to wild beasts, and this occurred at the games then being held there. The account contained the intervention of Queen Tryphaena with the incidents connected with her. Her subsequent traditional history makes her lead a life of active usefulness in spreading the faith; she spent her later years in a sort of retired life with other holy virgins, on the spot where the lady pilgrim went to pray at her Martyrion, and where she found a convent of holy women, under the direction of a person whose acquaintance she had made in the Holy Land.

16. Acts of Andrew also Adopted by Them

It is singular that no mention is made by St. Epiphanius that the *Acta* of Thecla were utilised by the Gnostics, though he mentions her (*Haeres*., lxxix., n. v., and compares her to the Blessed Virgin, and again, *Haeres*., lxxviii., n. xvi.); the reason perhaps might be that the *Acta* were not read at their assemblies, as will be seen were such Acts of the Apostles as they had revised for their purposes. The Acts of an Apostle could be made to pass as Scriptural writings, but not the former. Epiphanius makes express mention that they used the Acts of Andrew as well as those of Thomas; the quotation will be found in the sequel. It would appear that the modified form of the Acts of Andrew used by them has not come down to us, for those which we possess do not disclose the peculiar tenets of the sect, while those of Thomas attest how thoroughly they had been adapted for doctrinal purposes.

Acts of Andrew consist of two sections. One reports his doings when, on a mission assigned to him by our Lord, he went to the relief of the Apostle Matthew, who was imprisoned and deprived of his sight.[1] The country mentioned cannot be identified from the text, but it would appear to be in Africa, as the inhabitants are described to be cannibals. The other section treats of his doings in Greece and the Asiatic borderland, until under Ægeas he suffered martyrdom in Achaia.

Of the Acts of Andrew we have a Syriac text covering the ground of the first section in Wright's *Apocryphal Acts of the Apostles*. These await at the hands of a competent scholar treatment similar to that which the Acts of Thomas received from Burkitt. We are not aware of any Syriac text or translation of the Acts of Andrew covering the narrative of the second section. Greek texts or versions of these Acts were published by Tischendorf, *Acta Apocrypha*, 1851, pp. 105 ff.; but a much fuller second edition has been published by Hermann Mendelssohn, in Leipsic. The second volume of this series (badly numbered; the series comprises three volumes), marked Part ii. vol. i., 1898, edited by Max Bonnet, contains the following Greek texts—(1) *Ex Actis Andreae*, pp. 38–45; (2) two sets of *Martyrium Andreae*, pp. 46–64; (3) *Acta Andreae et Mathiae*, pp. 117–127—in Bonnet's *Supplementum Codicis Apocryphi*, ii., Paris, 1895; (4) *Acta Andreae cum laudatione*, pp. 3–44; (5) *Martyrium Andreae*, pp. 44–64. There are two *Passiones* in

---

[1] The Greek narrative of Andrew's voyage to the relief of his fellow-Apostle gives the name 'Mathias,' while the Syriac text all through shows that the visit was made to relieve the Evangelist Matthew. The country is in Africa, and we know from traditions reported in Chapter V. that it must have been to Matthew, who was preaching the Gospel in Ethiopia of old. The Syriac form of Matthew is Matthaī, and in familiar form, Matthū. Perhaps Matthai has been erroneously turned into Mathias.

Latin: (1) *Passio Andreae*, 'quam oculis nostris vidimus omnes presbyteri et diaconi ecclesiarum Achaiae' (in former vol.) pp. 1–37; (2) *Passio Andreae*, 'Conversante et docente,' &c. (in *Suppl.*, ii.) pp. 66–70. We have also in Latin (3) *Liber de Miraculis B. Andreae Apostoli;* this has been edited by Bonnet with the critical text of the works of St. Gregory of Tours, issued by Arndt and Krusch (*ut supr.*, pt. ii. 826–846).

17. St. Gregory of Tours, Author of 'De Miraculis Beati Andreae'

There can be no doubt that St. Gregory of Tours is the writer of the above book. Ruinart, the Benedictine editor of Gregory's writings (*Opera omnia*, Lutetiae Parisiorum, 1699, in preface n. 77) says: Librum de Miraculis sancti Andreae sub Gregorii Turonensis nomine invenimus in codice bibliothecae nostrae sancti Germani a Pratis ab annis circiter sexcentis scripto, qui liber in aliis quoque codicibus habetur sed absque Gregorii praefatione. Hanc autem praefationem sicut et brevem operis epilogum Gregorii fetum esse styli et scribendi ratio vix dubitare sinunt. The above-mentioned codex is marked by Bonnet (*ut supr.*, pt. ii. p. 823) 4*b* in his references; it is the 'Parisiacus Lat. 12603 (S. Germani a Pratis) saecl. xiii.' To the possible objection that Gregory does not include it in the list of his own works, Ruinart replies: Neque id mirandum videri debet siquidem nec librum ibi recensuit Missarum Apollinaris Sidonii cui alias [*Hist. Franc.*, lib. ii., c. xxii.] se praefationem adjunxisse memorat; nec passionem Septem Dormientium Ephesinorum quam e Graeco in Latinum a se translatam fuisse ipsemet alibi testatur.

Bonnet supplements the above by adducing cogent evidence from the text of the book itself. The author, in chap. xxxvii. (*oper. cit.*, p. 846) of the book, says: Nam ferunt, hoc oleum usque ad medium basilicae sanctae decurrere, sicut in primo miraculorum scripsimus libro; this is no other than his well-known work 'in Gloria Martyrum,' which, according to Gregory, comprises eight books, of which it is the first, while the eighth or last is 'in Gloria Confessorum.' See detailed list in *Prologo Gl. Confessor.*, op. cit., p. 748. Gregory continues: Passionis quoque ejus ita ordinem prosecuti non sumus, quia valde utiliter et eleganter a quodam repperimus fuisse conscriptum. The 'a quodam' excludes the *Passio*, with the letter of 'the priests and deacons of

Q

Achaia,' and so refers to the other *Passio Andreae* 'Conversante et docente.' From this we learn that Gregory did not re-edit the *Passio* he knew, as it was 'utiliter et eleganter conscripta.' We shall have occasion to refer to these different features of Gregory's work.

This book, *De Miraculis B. Andreae*, is bodily incorporated in the Latin compilation that goes by the name of Abdias. Ruinart was then mistaken in supposing that Gregory had taken his text from that collection. Migne reproduces the same mistake in his reprint of Gregory's works. We find it necessary to reproduce here the *pro-* and the *epi-logue* of this book, as both are wanted for comparison with a text that will follow.

The Prologue (p. 827).

Inclita sanctorum apostolorum trophea nulli credo latere fidelium, quia quaedam exinde evangelica dogmata docent, quaedam apostolici actus narrant, de quibusdam vero extant libri, in quibus propriae actiones eorum denotantur. De plerisque enim nihil aliud nisi passionum scripta suscipimus. Nam repperi librum de virtutibus sancti Andreae Apostoli qui propter nimiam verbositatem a nonnullis apocryphus dicebatur; de quo placuit, ut, retractis enucleatisque tantum virtutibus, praetermissis his quae fastidium generabant, uno tantum parvo volumine admiranda miracula clauderentur quod et legentibus praestaret gratiam et detrahentium auferret invidiam quia inviolatam fidem non exigit multitudo verbositatis, sed integritas rationis et puritas mentis.[1]

The preface tells us of the existence of a book, *De Virtutibus sancti Andreae apostoli*. Bonnet (p. 821, i. 13) remarks : Quanta autem fuerit illa 'multitudo verbositatis' quam Gregorius a se amputatam ait, sciet qui contenderit cum c i. Acta Graeca a Tischendorfio edita (*Acta Apostolor. Apocryph*, p. 132 *seq.*) It gives us also an interesting sketch of the 'trophea' of the Apostles, viz., of the writings which narrated their doings. For some, there were special books giving their history, but for many there only existed the acts of their martyrdom. To enable the reader to expand his ideas still further, it will be useful to know that there existed special extensive compilations

---

[1] The prologue in Cod. 4*b* bears the heading 'Praefatio Gregorii episcopi Turonensis in libro miraculorum beati Andreae apostoli,' at the close, 'Incipit textus ipsorum miraculorum.'

known by the name 'Passionale,' containing the above stories.
The Cod. Paris. Lat., 12603, Bonnet's 4*b*, is but a fragment surviving from the wreck of a large 'Passionale,' for the present first
folio bears an old number ccc (folio 300 = 600 pages), and after
Gregory's *De Miraculis B. Andreae* in the MS—sequunter tria alia
scripta de sanctis—(Bonnet, *ibid.*, p. 823 l. 2) These collections
were made use of by the faithful as most acceptable narratives of
the Doings and Martyrdoms of the Apostles and other Saints of
God; they were read at their festivals, and by pious pilgrims when
visiting their shrines.

The Epilogue (p. 846).

Haec sunt quae de virtutibus beati Andreae apostoli prae-
sumpsi indignus ore, sermone rusticus, pravus conscientia,
propalare, deprecans eius misericordiam, ut sicut in illius natale
processi ex matris utero, ita ipsius obtentu eruar ab inferno, et
sicut in die passionis eius sumpsi vitae hujus exordium, ita me
sibi proprium adscire dignetur alumnum. Et quia de maioribus
meritis revocat nos pars magna facinoris, hoc tantum temerarius
praesumo petere, ut cum ille post iudicium dominico corpori
conformatus refulget in gloria, saltem pro immensis criminibus
mihi vel veniam non negandam.[1]

In the prologue as well as in the epilogue, Gregory styles
the book, on which he based this narrative of his, containing
a selection from the miracles attributed to the Apostle, 'De
virtutibus beati Andreae'; to his new work he gives the title
'De Miraculis beati Andreae Apostoli'; so the title 'De Miraculis' is selected by him to differentiate between the new and
the older work. There is a remark of Bonnet's worth mentioning
why the author's name does not appear in all the codices of this
work, but only in one. In his praefatum (*op. cit.*, p. 821 l. 25 ff.)
he says :—

Ego ne codicem 4*b* adhibuerim (to prove the authorship),
nam a docto et acuto alique librario Gregorii nomen e c. xxxvii.
erutum, quam a reliquis omnibus omissum esse, credibilius est.
Sed hoc ipsum quod sine nomine liber traditus est, maximo mihi
argumento esse videtur recte eum Gregorio tribui.

---

[1] Several codices here mark the end of the book; 4*b* closes, 'Finit
Gregorii Turonensis episcopi liber de virtutibus et miraculis beati Andreae
apostoli.'

The further argument is drawn from similarity, and the faulty style of Gregory's Latin. He concludes (p. 822 l. 30) :—

Sensibus quibusdam non satis aptis, &c., non offendentur, qui reputabunt talia inveniri etiam in ceteris libris qui secundis et tertiis curis a Gregorio pertractati sunt: hunc properante calamo conscriptum, sine nomine scriptoris emissum, minus studii poposcisse.

Briefly, the faulty nature of the composition is to Bonnet, the editor, a reason why Gregory allowed the book to go forth purposely without his name, though in the writing he incidentally admits himself to be the author, rather than that all the codices overlooked the title borne on the front of the writing, save one, the codex 4*b*. The aptitude of the remark will be found useful in dealing with the next question.

18. St. Gregory, probable Author of 'De Miraculis Beati Thomae'

Among the Acts of Thomas there is a book also bearing a title similar to the preceding, *De Miraculis Beati Thomae*, as we have already seen. Can this compilation as well be the work of Gregory of Tours?

Bonnet, who has given a critical edition of the text, informs us (*praef.*, p. xviii.) that for the publication of the edition he consulted four codices, besides Nausea's edition of the text, and four 'correctores,' ranging in dates from the ninth to the thirteenth century. Of these codices two also contain Gregory's *De Miraculis B. Andreae*. He argues from similarity of style, of verbal expressions, and of thought between the preface of *De Mir. B. Andr.* given above, and that found at the opening of *De Mir. B. Thomae*, for identity of authorship. The latter we here reproduce to enable a comparison to be made with the two former given above :—

Beatum Thomam cum reliquis discipulis ad officium apostolatus electum, ipsumque a domino Didimum, quod interpretatur geminus, uocitatum fides euangelica narrat, qui post dominicae gloriam ascensionis Thaddaeum, unum ex septuaginta discipulis, ad Abgarum regem Edissenae ciuitatis transmisit, ut eum ab infirmitate curaret iuxta uerbum quod a domino scriptum est. Quod Thaddaeus ambienter impleuit, ita ut uniens imposito regi crucis signaculo ab omni eum languore sanaret.

Thomas autem apostolus Christi morabatur in Hierusalem, tunc diuina commonitione iussus est Indiam ingredi, ut scilicet populo qui iacebat in tenebris lumen ostenderet ueritatis.

Nam legisse me memini quendam librum in quo iter eius uel miracula quae in India gessit explanabantur. De quo libello, quia a quibusdam non recipitur, uerbositate praetermissa pauca de miraculis libuit memorare, quod et legentibus gratum fieret et ecclesiam roboraret.

We will comment separately on the sections of the prologue. Bonnet, comparing it with the previous extracts of *De Mir. Andr.*, says (*Acta Thom.*, praef., p. xiii.) :—

Prorsus autem ad eundem modulum liber de miraculis Thomae conformatus est, eadem est sermonis cum sermone Gregoriano, eadem sententiarum similitudo; nihil deest nisi disertum testimonium quale in Andrea superest ab ipso Gregorio scriptum.

He mentions also that the similarity of style was suggested to him by R. A. Lipsius. After a close examination and analysis of terms, phrases, and ideas in the book, he says, he came to think the idea was almost his own, so thoroughly did he feel convinced of the identity of authorship. It will now be an easy task, with the help of the copious *lexica* appended to Arndt and Krusch's critical edition of the works of Gregory, and Bonnet's special work dealing with *Le Latin de Grégoire de Tours*, Paris 1900, to further complete the study, should any scholar feel inclined to undertake it.

In support of the above conclusions of the learned Frenchman, we invite the special attention of the reader to the title and to some additional remarks we propose to submit. In a previous work we have found Gregory sorting out the miraculous, and giving his compilation a specialised title, 'De Miraculis,' though his text bore the title 'De virtutibus.' So here, whatever text he utilised, unfortunately in this case the name is not given, he felt bound to give his book a title that would differentiate it from others, so he returns to his former specialised title used in the case of the Apostle Andrew, and styles it 'De Miraculis B. Thomae.' In this case the name is less appropriate, for while the former contained a continuous narrative of successive wonders worked by Andrew, in this case the miraculous is less prominent; but events are given, and, above all, it redounds in discourses, though largely curtailed, as he says, 'verbositate praetermissa,' compared with the Greek version of the Acts.

In this second work the omission of Gregory's name would be called for still more imperiously by reasons of self-regard and prudence, since the style of the writing is much inferior, a great deal more rugged, and apparently left unpolished; neither would he for the same reasons disclose himself in the text.

An additional point in support of this view is supplied by the fact that, as in the case of Andrew, whose *Passio* though known to him was left untouched, so in the case of Thomas, the *Passio*, which was similarly known to him (Oper. *Gregor. Tvron.*, ut supr., *in Gl. Martyr.*, c. 31, p. 507): 'Thomas apostolus secundum historiam passionis eius in Indiam passus declaratur,' is left unutilised, and a new work is compiled from other writings, perhaps also in Latin, but now lost because, perhaps, superseded by this new work.

We have yet to return to the first portion of the introduction to the *De Mir. B. Thomae*. There we have evidence connecting the Apostle Thomas with his colleague Thaddeus, whom he sent to fulfil the promise given, or said to be given, by our Lord in writing to King Abgar, that after His ascension he would be cured of his disease. This does not imply that the writing was by our Lord; a verbal message to the messenger put down in writing by him would easily be styled a letter in the East, or a written message might have been given by one of the Apostles on behalf of their Master. The reader will here recall to mind what was previously said bearing on this subject under No. 7. But it may be asked, Whence did Gregory derive the information he incorporates in his introduction? It is not contained in the Syriac text of the Acts of Thomas, nor in the Greek version, nor in the Latin *Passio*. From whence could the bishop of Tours have obtained it? The Syriac text, *The Doctrine of Addai*, quoted above, has it; this was never before turned into Latin, but Gregory was precisely the person who could have had access to it. It is known that this indefatigable seeker and early compiler of the acts of Martyrs and histories of Saints had left us a Latin translation of the Story of the Seven Sleepers of Ephesus. Ruinart had informed us that it was a translation from the Greek. But Bonnet, who gives also a critical text of this 'Passio SS. Martyrum Septem Dormientium apud Ephesum' (Greg. Tvron., *oper.*, pp. 848–853), informs us that the codex ends with the following clause :—

Explicit Passio Sanctorum Martyrium Septem Dormientium

apud Ephesum, translata in Latinum per Gregorium Episcopum interpretante Johanne Syro, quae observatur 6 kal. Augusti.[1]

This may then be the source whence the MS text of the *Doctrine of Addai* also came to be known to Gregory. However, it is just possible that Gregory may have read the story in Rufinus' Latin translation of the Eusebian history of the Church.

It may, by way of illustrating the above, be interesting to know the continuous historical connection between early Christianity in Gaul and the churches of the East. Large colonies of Eastern Christians existed in Gaul from early ages down to the times of Gregory of Tours. The earliest mention will be found in the letter of the churches of Vienne and Lyons addressed to their brethren in Asia and Phrygia, &c. (quoted by Eusebius in his *Hist. Eccl.*, lib. v. c. i., *seq ;* see Ruinart, *Acta Sincera Martyr.*, notes to this letter ; also Leclercq, *Les Martyrs*, tom. i. pp. 90 ff.). The forty-eight martyrs of Lyons suffered death *c.* 177, probably a little earlier. Gregory himself supplies two passages which will disclose more intimately the nature of this intercourse between Syrian Christians and those of Gaul. The first quotation is from his *Histor. Francor.* (ed. *ut supr.*, pt. i. lib. viii. c. i. p. 326) :—

Sed cum ad urbem Auriliansem venisset (rex Guntchramnus) &c., processitque in obviam eius immensa populi turba cum signis atque vexillis, canentes laudes. Et hinc lingua Syrorum hinc Latinorum, hinc etiam ipsorum Judaeorum in diversis laudibus varie concrepabat, dicens : Vivat rex regnumque eius in populis annis innumeris dilatetur.

The second passage is also from the same history (lib. x. c. xxvi., p. 488) :—

Ragnimodus quoque Parisiacae urbis episcopus obiit. Cumque germanus eius Faramodus presbyter pro episcopatu concurreret, Eusebius quidem negotiator genere Syrus, datis multis muneribus in locum eius subrogatus est ; hisque, accepto episcopato, omnem scolam decessoris sui abiciens, Syros de genere suo ecclesiasticae domui ministros statuit.

This last quotation also shows that true Syrians bore Greek names ; or, may be, living away from their own country, adopted Greek equivalents of their names, for the knowledge of Greek was very general, then and before, throughout the East.

---

[1] A reference to *in Glor. Martyr.*, of the same edition, c. xciv., shows that the new text reads : Quod passio eorum quam Syro interpretante in latinum transtulimus, plenius pandit.

SECTION III

THE ACTS OF THOMAS DISCUSSED

19. INTRODUCTION

The discussion of preliminary questions being closed, we take up the contents of our Acts for examination. The English translation of the Syriac text by Dr. Wright will be utilised, and whenever text is referred to in the sequel without qualification the reference is to this translation.

Neither the text nor the Greek version has a preface, and the Latin *Passio* follows them ; the reason why the Latin *De Mir.* has one has been explained. The introduction in the text and Greek version referring to the departure and the arrival of the Apostle appear identical. The *De Mir.* varies the narrative by making Thomas start from Palestine—Jerusalem is mentioned; the Latin *Passio* makes Caesarea the scene of preliminary negotiations. The introduction recites that our Lord admonished Thomas that he should go to India; he is disinclined to accept the mission. Our Lord is then said to have sold him to Hâbbân, a messenger or agent of the Indian king, Gûdnaphar in the text, Γουνδαφόρος and Gondophares in the versions, who had come to seek and engage the services of a qualified builder ; they take ship and sail, and arrive after a rapid passage.

The text, which throughout names Thomas the Apostle Judas Thomas, makes the start from the 'south country'; this implies a Babylonian writer, or one from the Euphrates valley. The Syriac MS of the text here drops a name unfortunately, which so far has not been supplied by the more recent Syrian copies imported from the East; but it can perhaps be supplied from Jacob of Sarug's poem (A.D. 500–521) on the 'Palace the Apostle built in India.' In the poem[1] *Mahuza* is mentioned in connection with merchants, but Schröter is unable to decide whether the start was from Mahuza, or whether only the merchants came from there. Assemani, as will be seen presently, decides that point. This may possibly be the name that has dropped out of the British Museum Codex of the Acts. As to

---

[1] See R. Schröter's two papers in *Zeitschrift der Deutschen Morgenländischen Gesellschaft*, vols. xxv. and xxviii. ; vol. xxv., p. 349, verse 20.

Mahuza, Assemani (*Bibl. Or.*, i., pp. 332 f.) has the following comment on this passage of the poem :—

Alter sermo sub nomine Jacobi inscribitur de 'Palatio quod Thomas Apostolus in excelsis aedificavit.' Indiarum rex quum magnificas sibi aedes excitari cuperet, peritumque ad id opus artificem undequaque conquireret, Thomam Apostolum ab Haban quodam mercatore ex Mahuza Mesopotamiae regione, tanquam servum illuc adductum mercede conduxit.

If Assemani is right in his reading of the poem, of which there will probably be little doubt, 'Mahuza' would be the missing word and would fit our text, which reads at present, 'a certain merchant, an Indian, happened to come into the south country from ——, whose name was Hâbbân.'

Schröter first edited a text of the poem from a British Museum Codex ; later, he consulted two Vatican codices (see pp. 584–626, vol. xxviiii. of above publication). The Vatican Syriac Codex 117 agrees generally with the British Museum text ; but Vatican Codex 118 contains a much longer poem—Schröter considers this to be the original form of the poem—while the text has been shortened in Codex 117, and in the British Museum MS. Vatican Codex 118 gives a fuller introduction than either of the other MSS. It opens thus : ' The tale of the Apostle Thomas is a sea unspeakably vast. Permit me, O Lord, to dive into this sea and to bring up from its depths the pearl Thomas has stolen from thy side. He who steals from the thief is sure of success. He stole being worthy, permit me to steal though unworthy,' &c. The poem deals with the I. and II. Acts of the text, viz., the incidents of the bridal feast, and of the building of the palace. But it nowhere mentions the name of Gondophares, though his brother's name, Gad, is mentioned ; the former is always styled simply the king.

20. THOMAS'S FIRST MISSION

A word or two more has to be said on the contents of the introduction. The text, after giving the names of the eleven Apostles (the Greek version repeats the same, but both Latin versions omit them) and saying that the world was divided among them, each having a country assigned to him, continues : 'And India fell by lot and division to Judas Thomas (or the Twin) the Apostle ; and he was not willing to go ;' no further mention is made of the other Apostles. Now the oldest record of the division of the world among the Apostles assigns Parthia to Thomas. This was stated by Origen (A.D. 200–254) in his Commentary on Genesis, now lost, but the passage has been recovered for us by Eusebius who, before A.D. 337, incorporated it in his *Hist. Eccl.*, lib. iii. c. i. :—

Apostoli et discipuli Domini ac Servatoris nostri per universum orbem dispersi Evangelium praedicabant. Et Thomas quidem, ut a majoribus traditum accepimus, Parthiam sortitus est.

The same is repeated by other authorities. The statement, therefore, that India fell to Thomas's lot when the Apostles first assigned to themselves the countries they would evangelise, cannot be accepted. We feel bound to reject it as part of the work of one of the several hands that manipulated the text.

The Latin *De Mir.*, probably Gregory's work as has been seen, says nothing of the first division, but opens the story :—

Cum saepe a Domino commoneretur beatus Thomas ut partes citerioris Indiae visitaret, et ille quasi Jonas a facie Domini fugiens ire differret, &c.

The older Latin *Passio* also commences with our Lord's admonition to Thomas, that he wishes him to go to India with Hâbbân, the messenger of King Gondophares of India.

It becomes clear on reflection that the opposition of Thomas to go to India did not arise on the first dispersion of the Apostles. When might it have arisen? It could only have been years later, after Thomas's first mission to the Parthians and neighbouring nations was fulfilled. It would thus have occurred on his second Apostolic tour. The reader is here referred to Chapter IV. of the book for additional information on this point.

Besides, it can by no means be accepted that our Lord was forced by Thomas's conduct to sell him as a slave to Hâbbân. Such a thing, on the face of it, is inadmissible. This and the journey from the 'south country' by ship must be ascribed to facts inaccurately reported to the original writer, or to a subsequent compiler of the present form of the narrative. The same should be held in regard to the mixing up of King Gondophares' name with the building of the palace. For the rejection of this latter point sufficient grounds will be produced in the sequel.

21. Story of the Dream-Vision

But it is possible, nay probable—under the circumstances of the case—considering the obstinate and self-opinionated character the Apostle displayed during his apprenticeship in the apostolic school, and specially at the last stage, that he may have objected to proceed to India.

His objection, it may be incidentally observed, would be grounded on some knowledge of the difficulties he would have to meet in this future field of labour. 'Whithersoever Thou wilt, O Lord,' he says, 'send me; only to India I will not go.' All barbarous nations must have stood much on the same level to the Jew of Palestine. May not this special objection to proceed to India be based on what Thomas had learnt regarding India proper when, during his first mission, he visited the country over which Gondophares ruled?

The conduct of Thomas brings us to the vision-admonitions he received of his future destination to India.[1] Intimations of the Divine will were received by Peter in a similar manner. The visions of Thomas disclosed to him that he was to erect a palatial building in India, and that his work would redound to the honour of God and the good of souls.

When Peter was similarly to undertake a new sphere of work, quite different from what his own national ideas would have suggested, he had a vision just before the messenger sent by the centurion Cornelius knocked at the door and reported his object. It was only then that Peter caught the meaning of the dream-vision he had just had (read Acts chap. x. from 1 to 23 verse; and verses 26 to 43, as also 44 to 48). If close attention is again paid to what is written of Peter (Acts xii. 9–11) on his delivery from prison at Jerusalem, 'And going out he followed him (the angel), and he knew not that it was true which was done by the angel, but thought he saw a vision;' and again, 'Peter coming to himself said, Now I know in very deed that the Lord hath sent His angel,' &c., it must strike the reader that Peter had become so accustomed to communications through such a channel that it took him some time to realise that what had passed was a reality and not a dream-vision. The Scriptural incident is here introduced to point to the line adopted by

---

[1] See text, pp. 146–47, last and first line, and *De Mir*, p. 97 l. 5 f.

Divine Providence in communicating its will even to the chosen leader of the Twelve.

The book mentioned above written by St. Gregory of Tours, *De Miraculis B. Andreae*, offers two similar instances in the case of that Apostle. In a night-vision (c. xx. p. 837, *op. cit.*) which the Apostle had, mentioned therein, it is said that Peter and John intervened; the latter said to Andrew, 'Andreas poculum Petri bibiturus es.' Next morning Andrew informed his disciples of his passion and death now imminent; he prayed for them and took leave of them. Again in cap. xxii.–xxiii., p. 838, the following occurrence is narrated :—

Duodecimo die Patras Achaiae civitatem adpulsi sunt, &c., cum eum multi rogarent, ut in domibus eorum ingrederetur, dixit (Andreas) vivit Dominus quia non vadam nisi quo praeceperit Deus meus. Et nocte dormiens nihil revelationis accepit. Altera vero nocte, cum esset ex hoc tristis, audivit vocem dicentem sibi, Andreas ego semper tecum sum et non te derelinquo, &c.

This also, although of far lesser weight than the quotation in Peter's case, will go somewhat to confirm what has been said. Such intimation, when given, required of course active co-operation, but left the will a free agent to acquire merit by following up the suggestion made, or the command conveyed. In such cases what is true of one Apostle would be true also in the case of another. This appears to be the one rational explanation to give of the message to Thomas that he was required, under the image of a stately palace which he was to build, to establish the Church of Christ in the souls and among the people of India.

With the rejection of the story that Thomas was sold as a slave by Christ, the whole of the introduction and the journey by sea from the 'south country' entirely collapse, the vision-admonition alone surviving. As the Acts of Thomas do not embrace his whole apostolic career but deal only with some incidents of his mission to India, the vision story had naturally to precede this narrative. The bungling and the addition of inaccurate and erroneous statements can thus be also explained in part. The contact of the Apostle with King Gondophares must remain based on its own historical grounds, but its place belongs to the omitted portion of the Apostle's history concerning his mission to the Parthians, of which unfortunately no details have survived. It was during that Apostolic tour that Thomas had the easiest opportunity of entering the kingdom of Gondophares, and it probably formed part, or was an offshoot, of the great Parthian domination which overshadowed the whole of Central Asia during the first century of the Christian era. A trace of this journey of the Apostle survives in the *Acta Maris*, from which a quotation has been given in Chapter II., pp. 36–37.

Though we reject the introduction as having any historical basis, its origin is susceptible of some explanation. It may be based on a traveller's report, who, when asked how Thomas got to India, may have suggested the incident, basing it on his knowledge of the vision-admonition, and of Thomas's reluctance to proceed to India; all this he might also have heard. The thought of the 'south country' would naturally arise from personal experience, as the traveller would have made the journey thence to India by sea. Any narrative, besides, must have a suitable introduction, and if the original be lost, another is usually found substituted by Orientals. This has occurred, as a matter of fact, to the narrative of the Arab travellers of the ninth century, published by Reinaud. A bare narrative concerning a stranger to India and of his doings there could not well be put forward without introducing him to the country. The events that follow would be related orally, but the prologue, for want of correct information, was devised to answer the purposes of an introduction.

22. SYRIAC TEXT OFTEN ALTERED

The doctrinal development given to the Acts is probably not the work of one hand, but rather of three successive revisers. A comparison with the *Acta Theclae* will show how the first interpolator was careful to follow closely on the lines of his predecessor in similar work, and he probably limited his work to a few aptly inserted passages. The comparison of the two texts which we give in No. 29 will show similar passages yet retained in the story. But these have been followed up by set speeches and much additional doctrinal matter quite irrelevant to the subject and circumstances treated. In more than one place there are as many as three speeches put in the mouth of the Apostle or other person, very often two; these may fairly be taken to be the work of successive hands, who have endeavoured to embellish or strengthen the narrative with their own thoughts. Our

Western readers most probably are unaware that a Syrian transcriber, if at all educated, considers himself fully entitled to
enlarge the subject he is copying wherever it suits his taste, 'de
suo cumulans,' to adopt Tertullian's phrase.

From the high praise bestowed on the composition of the
present Syriac text by Professor Burkitt for its literary excellence,
it would be fair to conclude that the final polish must have been
given while the Syriac language was yet in its best age; this
would bring us to the fourth century, and from the connotating
name, Mygdonia, given to the most prominent female character
in the story, we may further infer that the work, at least of final
revision, was done in the vicinity of Edessa, Mygdonia representing the Seleucian form of the name of the district in which
Edessa was situated. M. Duval (*Litt. Syr., ut supra*, p. 100)
says that Noeldeke holds that the Acts were written at Edessa
by the school of Bardaisan. Find quotation from St. Ephraem
bearing on the subject at the end of No. 28.

We add the following historical data in support of the former
statement.

The name *Edessa*, borne by the ancient town of Mesopotamia
(known to the Aramæi as *Orrhei*, to the then Arabs as *or-Roha*,
now as *Urpha* or *Orfa*), was given to it by Seleucus Nicator,
B.C. 303, when he rebuilt the city in remembrance of the ancient
capital of Macedonia. This latter name they pronounced
Mygdonia, hence the district in which Edessa was situated was
called Mygdonia. See article ' Edesse,' in *La Grande Encyclopédie*,
Paris, 1892, tom. xv. pp. 552–53; and Rubens Duval, *Histoire
politique, religieuse, et littéraire d'Edesse*, Paris 1892, ch. ii. pp.
22–23. The district was called also *Osrhoe*, and *Osrhoena* by
Greek and Latin writers. Edessa, once the capital, remained
the chief town of the whole province under the Romans—and
Nisibis the next important city—till Constantius in 349 divided
it into two; Amida, which he rebuilt, becoming the capital of the
second province. But proof is forthcoming that the province
of Edessa, even after this, continued to retain the name of
Mygdonia[1]: 'Urbs autem Nisibis, quae eadem est Antiochia
Mygdoniae, et ab hortis et pomariis quae ibi sunt nomen ducit.'

---

[1] *Chronica Minora*, of *Scriptores Syri*, series 3a, tom. iv., Paris, 1903,
2nd *Chron. parvum*, p. 17, l. 18 *seq.*—'Corpus Scriptor. Christianor.
Orientalium.'

23. Acts Dramatised—Act I

'Act I. Judas Thomas the Apostle, when [Our Lord] sold him to the merchant Hâbbân that he might go down and convert India.'

It includes the introduction already dealt with. The story then proceeds to what occurred on the landing at Sandarūk (or Sanadrūk), the Greek has Andrapolis instead; both Latin versions omit the name. Gutschmidt thought he found here an allusion to the *Andhra* race. This race, according to Caldwell, formed the western branch of the Telegu race, but between it and the sea lay the Konkani on the western shores of India (see the excellent map of ancient India by Reinaud, *Mémoire sur l'Inde*). The change of Sandarūk into Ἀνδραπολις, Andrapolis, comes about by dropping the sibilant letter and adding the termination πολις. But the town referred to in the text ought not to be in India, for in two succeeding passages we are led to know that it was later the Apostle entered 'in the realm of India': the passages are at the close of this and the beginning of the next Act. The poem of Jacob of Sarug, which, as we said, incorporates the first two Acts of the story, also supports the interpretation that the wedding feast which comes after the landing occurred before the Apostle had entered India, based no doubt on the Acts.

If the reader follows us, we can, perhaps, place a different construction on the whole of the narrative given at the Apostle's first landing. Above we pointed out, No. 21, that the Introduction and the sea voyage from the 'south country' should be rejected as inaccurate. The Apostle on this, his second mission, would be approaching India from the island of Socotra and not from the 'south country' (the estuary of the Euphrates), he would then land on the western shores of India. Hence the contents of Act. I., whatever the present form of the text may say, should refer to India, as well as those of Act II.

The narrative recites that on arrival the townspeople were found keeping the bridal of the King's daughter; the newcomers were made to take part in the rejoicings, and a Hebrew flute girl is brought on the scene. She attracts Thomas's attention, and she makes the discovery of a countryman in him. An attendant at the feast strikes Thomas, and he foretells his imminent punishment: the man, who is a cup-bearer, is killed by a wild beast—a lion(?) prowling in the neighbourhood—when he went to fetch water; dogs tore the body to pieces, and one of these brought into the banquet place the right arm which had struck the Apostle. All were amazed at the occurrence: the king urged Thomas to come in to the bridal chamber and bless the new couple. The opportunity is here promptly seized to insert the first dose of Gnostic poison into the tale. The young couple in the sequel vow chastity; on hearing this, the king is indignant, and orders Thomas 'the sorcerer' to be arrested, &c.

The story of the cup-bearer and Thomas's part in the same is commented upon by St. Augustine in three passages of his writings.[1] We have these passages before us, and from their perusal it appears that the Manichaean version of the event agrees with what the text offers. The great Doctor of the Church considers the part attributed to the Apostle unbecoming and savouring of revenge; we may therefore dismiss the detail in the form it is presented by the text. But suppose the Apostle, when smitten on the cheek, in place of resenting it with a tinge of revenge, offered the other meekly to his assailant, not forgetful of his Master's counsel, would this not as well have promoted a general movement in his favour among the assembly? As the wedding incident might be true, the more so as the text says that at a subsequent stage the young converts joined the Apostle in his field of labour in India, and since it would not have occurred, according to the present form of the text, at any great distance from Mesopotamia where the writing to all appearances originated, there is a greater probability it was not a pure fiction. This Act closes with the statement that Thomas had left, and ' news was heard of his being in the realm of India.' The Latin *De Mir.* confirms the narrative and the latter statement; yet most inconsistently says at the opening of that narrative, 'Exeuntes de navi ingressi sunt primam Indiae civitatem,' &c. According to what has been shown above, the account of the bridal should belong to India.

---

[1] These are (i.) St. Augustine Opera omnia, edit. Benedict. Venetiis, 1730, tom. iii., pars ii. col. 194, *De Sermone Domini in monte secundum Mattheum*, lib. i. c. xx. n. 65; (ii.) tom. viii., ejusd. edit., *Contra Adimantum Manichaei discipulum*, c. xviii. n. 2; and (iii.) tom. viii. *Contra Faustum*, lib. xxii. c. lxxix. col. 409.

24. THOMAS'S SECOND MISSION DISCUSSED—ACTS II., III., IV., V., VI., VII

'Act II. When Thomas the Apostle entered into India and built a palace for the King in Heaven.'

We are inclined to accept the story of the palace building as true, not because the Acts contain it, but because St. Ephraem accepts it, and Jacob of Sarug writes of it, entering into details; it must therefore have had ecclesiastical tradition to support it. It may interest the reader to read the imaginative description of the plan, traced for the Apostle by Jacob, on the ground selected for its erection.

Thomas accompanied the king to the place assigned for the building.

'He measured with the measuring rod and left place for windows to give light and for windows to let the wind pass; he measured the rooms for summer and the chambers for winter; the house for the bakers [he traced out] towards the sun (south) and the spot for the reservoir of water. He marked out the place where the artificers of the royal palace should dwell, and the halls in which the weavers, the coiners in gold, and the silversmiths should carry on their trade. He measured off the house for the smiths and the house for carvers in wood, and the house for painters, and the stables for the horses and the mules. He measured the strong-room for the treasury, situated in the centre of the building plot on account of the danger to which it is exposed, leaving but few window openings for light and making them small.' (From Vatican Codex 118. 'He measured thus upon earth in order to show his art, whilst he knew the Lord on high would lay the foundations of the palace.') 'The king saw all this and rejoiced.'

While we accept the story of the palace building, to our way of thinking the event could not have occurred at the court of King Gondophares in northern India, but elsewhere in India. And why? Because it could only have happened after the vision-dreams, and not before: and these latter, for the reason assigned above, would not belong to the first period of Thomas's apostolate—which was to Parthia and the surrounding countries of Asia—as tradition handed down by Origen and Eusebius demands (see No. 20), supported as it is by the general tradition

R

of the East recorded in Chapter IV., p. 145. The tale, or the figurative incident of the building of the palace in India, falls necessarily during the second period of his mission, when, after passing through Ethiopia and Socotra, he landed on the shores of India according to the tradition shown in Chapter IV., pp. 135–140.

The reader should be prepared for dislocations in the story owing to the circumstances under which the original facts were obtained, as he has been warned in our preliminary remarks; hence owing to the above incident being wrongly placed, it becomes impossible to locate the part of India to which the proposal to erect the building belongs. If the tenor of the narrative be any guide it would be in the second country visited by the Apostle. But we are on safer ground when we say that the sea voyage from Socotra would land the Apostle on the west coast of India, and would not take him to the borderland of Afghanistan, Gandhara.

'Act III. Regarding the black snake.' The Greek has the story, but neither Latin version contains it.

'Act IV. The ass that spake.' The Greek of this story was for the first time published by Bonnet; both Latin versions omit it. Both these incidents are not only fabulous but even ridiculous, and probably obtained the favour of insertion for love of the marvellous which has quite an attraction of its own for the ignorant.

It is as well to take note of the peculiar introduction to Act III. of the text: 'And the Apostle went forth to go whither our Lord had told him.' The *Passio*, which, from what St. Gregory tells us, is the older of the two Latin Acts, after giving the tale of the palace, mentions that the fame of the miraculous cures worked by the Apostle had gone forth (p. 143): 'Cum exiisset fama apostoli per Indos quod esset in provincia eorum,' &c., of his preaching to large gatherings of people, besides healing the sick and baptizing many; it adds (p. 147): 'Profectus est autem apostolus ad Indiam superiorem per revelationem.' The text and *Passio* retain here clearly a detail of the ancient text, they are in fact insertions which no interpolator is likely to have made in such odd form. The Latin expression 'superior,' used above, is susceptible of various meanings, and can equally be applied whether the Apostle proceeded further to the north, or to the south, or to the east; it is a generic form of expression, therefore inconclusive for the purpose of indicating the direction taken. But

the recital in the text, first given, is somewhat more definite—
'whither our Lord told him.' This further corroborates the idea
that up till then Thomas had not entered that particular section
of India to which by revelation he had been directed to proceed.

'Act V. The demon that dwelt in the woman.' The Greek
has it, as also the *De Mir*. It recites the cure or delivery of
a woman possessed by an evil spirit. Casting aside the fictitious
incidents given in the tale, all that can be said is that it may
have occurred.

'Act VI. The young man who killed the girl.' The Greek
has it as well as the *De Mir*. The substance of the story told consists of this:—The Apostle received or asked for bread to be
brought to him, for the poor; this he blessed and distributed to
the people. There was a young man in the crowd who also
came forward to have his share; something then happened which
drew the Apostle's attention to him—possibly because of the crime
he had committed, to be presently disclosed. It may be, as the
text says, he was unable to reach the blessed bread to his mouth,
or he may have been seized with sudden illness when attempting
to eat of it. The Eucharist is here needlessly introduced by
the Gnostic hand: it could never have been indiscriminately
given, though bread blessed after a celebration was distributed
to the people—a custom yet surviving in most of the Oriental
rites and retained also by the Greek; or it might have
been ordinary bread. Under the circumstances, the Apostle
asked the young man under what weight of sin he lay, and
this led to the disclosure of his crime. He acknowledged he
had killed the woman with 'whom he had lived,' clearly not
his wife. In self-justification, he added, he had heard the
Apostle teach that no adulterer could enter the kingdom of
heaven, and since she would not live a clean life with him, he
had committed the deed. The circumstances, however, imply
that he took her life through a motive of jealousy. The narrative tells us the Apostle went to the place where the woman was
lying, and raised her to life. The opportunity was too good to
be left unutilised by the Gnostic scribe for his purpose. The
people are struck with admiration and wonder; multitudes
believe, the report goes abroad, and from villages and the
country 'the sick, those under possession by a spirit, lunatics
and paralytics, are brought and placed by the roadside: and the
Apostle went healing them all by the power of Jesus.'

'Act VII.   How Judas Thomas was called by the General of King Mazdai to heal his wife and daughter.'   The Greek version of this Act as well as the rest of the book was published for the first time by Max Bonnet.   The *De Mir.* has it and the rest of the story on the lines of the text.   The *Passio* omits it altogether and passes to describe what is given in the following Act.

We hold Act VII. to be substantially historical, barring a romantic incident treated separately.   A certain man of import-ance is introduced, called the General, whose name is not given in this, but only in the following act when, after a number of incidents, different persons are brought on the scene and names are assigned to all; then also the General bears a name. This shows plainly that this individual bore no name in the primitive text of the narrative; and discloses the fact that when the tale came to be dramatised, as we now find it, the necessity arose of assigning names to one and all the principal persons brought on the scene.   A narrative of this description, coming from India to the valley of the Euphrates as an oral narrative, would have been told without personal names, except perhaps of one or two of the principal personages.   It is well to re-member that besides Hâbbân the messenger, Gondophares the king, Gad, his brother, Xanthippus the deacon, no names occur in the book till we come to the full dramatic effort produced in Act VIII., where the last scenes are described.   The names occurring in the Acts are treated separately under No. 34.

25. ACT VII.—DISCUSSION CONTINUED

We now return to the contents of Act VII.   The General, having heard of Thomas's preaching 'throughout all India, came to him' to ask him to his house.   The text recites that the Apostle, after taking leave of his converts, whom he placed under the charge of Xanthippus the deacon, set out with the General, who had come in a cart drawn 'by cattle,' as the text expresses it, to seek the Apostle.   It should be borne in mind that horses are not in use, rather, we should say, were not in common use in early times, and are not even now in Southern India; while in Upper, and Northern India especially, they have been in general use at all times.   The country cart drawn by oxen is commonly employed throughout Southern India, not only for the transport of produce, but also for personal conveyance from

place to place both in town and country even to this day, except
where Europeans dwell in numbers. In Native States hardly
any other vehicle is procurable, but the state of things must
be now rapidly altering with the introduction of railways; and
if even now it be still so, in ancient times it must have been the
general, almost exclusive, means of conveyance. So the detail
of the General travelling in a 'bullock cart,' as they call it in
India, gives a touch of local colouring to the scene. Had the
incident anything to do with Northern India, where Gondophares'
kingdom was situated, the horse would have been introduced on
the scene, and the General would have been mounted on a steed.
Gondophares on his coins is figured riding a horse, not seated in
a cart drawn by oxen. The local colouring offered by this incident will be strengthened by other incidents which will be
noticed in No. 33.

We return once again to the story. The General had a wife
and daughter; both are said to be possessed by evil spirits. It
was this misfortune which had induced him to seek the Apostle's
aid. The possession, it would appear, was of an impure form, as
implied by what is narrated; this could but be the sequel, or
the result of their having led an impure life. The Apostle, on
arriving at the house, found the two women in a frightful condition; it is unnecessary to go into details, they would besides
not be reliable. They were delivered, and must have been made
to do penance in atonement for their conduct, and were placed
under instruction. In such cases the conferring of baptism would
be deferred for a considerable time. This in fact is what we find
had been done in the case; they were only admitted to it shortly
before the Apostle's martyrdom.

26. A Romantic Interpolation

This Act offers a characteristic specimen of the embellish-
ments introduced by foreign hands. On the drive the travellers
meet a troop of wild asses, four of these allow themselves to be
yoked to the cart, replacing the cattle, and thus the Apostle, the
General, and the driver continue their romantic journey. The
tale of this incident was not, most likely, carried from India to
the Mesopotamian reviser of the text. The one place in India
where the wild ass could exist, and where he is still found,
is the great sandy expanse stretching from the east of the Indus

below its junction with the Sutlej, to within a few miles of Delhi, and extending from the Rann of Kutch northwards to Ferozepore and Sirsa, known as the Indian or Bikaneer Desert. The writer was informed by a friend that in the cold season these wild, fleet denizens of those sandy plains visit the salt licks of the Rann; and when he was at Ferozepore in the Punjab, he possessed the skin of a wild ass shot a day's journey from Fazilka, on the Sutlej, on the outer limb of this desert. The species, however, is well known in the sandy tracts of Persia; and Marco Polo mentions wild asses when on his homeward journey from China, *en route* from Yezd to Kerman. So we may take it that a Gnostic or other hand introduced the incident as an illustration from a scene near home to enhance the charms of the narrative to his Eastern readers.

It will be most opportune that we here point out to the reader, not to have to break the sequence of the narrative too often, that the *Passio*, after giving the substance of what is recited in the next Act, reproduces not only the first ordeal before his martyrdom to which Thomas is subjected, but also a second, and then narrates a striking scene at the temple when at the Apostle's prayer the idol is suddenly destroyed. The reader is informed that after the first ordeal—*de laneis ignitis;* the text omits entirely the second—*de fornace*, and the incident—*de templo solis*, with the destruction of the idol. Both the missing parts are reproduced *verbatim* in *De Mir.* from the *Passio*—a proof that the unnamed text from which Gregory took what he incorporated in *De Miraculis* was bereft of these scenes. This important subject will receive separate treatment under No. 32.

27. ACT VIII.—NARRATIVE

'Act VIII.—Mygdonia and Karish.' The title covers only part of the story given in this Act. The Greek version, which closely follows the text, subdivides it: (1) the doings of the wife of Charisius; (2) the story of Mygdonia's baptism; (3) the doings of the wife of Misdeus; (4) the doings of Uazanes, the son of Misdeus; (5) the martyrdom of the holy and blessed Apostle Thomas who suffered—ἐν τῇ Ἰνδίᾳ—in India. The text has a following but short section, with the sub-head—'The consummation of Judas Thomas.' Wright's text of the Acts is divided into eight, while Bedjan's gives as many as sixteen acts. The summary here given shall be brief, as several of the details will demand separate treatment.

Karish is a kinsman of the king and Mygdonia is his wife. She hears of the arrival of a preacher of a new god and of a new religion: from what she learns from the General's family, she is desirous of hearing the prophet of this new faith. She is conveyed in a *palki*, or palanquin, to the house of the General, where the newly arrived preacher is staying; the *palki* is lowered to the ground near to where he stands. At the close of Thomas's discourse she comes out of the palanquin, approaches the Apostle, and addresses him. Her husband Karish is awaiting her at home. She, on her return, excuses herself for the evening. Early next morning Karish goes to see the king, and Mygdonia betakes herself to the Apostle and receives further instruction. Karish going home for the day meal [the midday repast] finds his wife absent; she also returns home, but only late in the evening; this gives rise to a difference between the husband and the wife; she denies herself to him. Early next morning the husband lodges a complaint with the king against the preaching of Thomas and the painful sequel it had developed in his home. The king then sends for the General—whose name is here introduced for the first time—and he is questioned about the new preacher. In reply, he informs the king of the great benefit Thomas had conferred on his family. The king orders a guard to be sent to fetch the Apostle; but they, on arrival, finding Mygdonia there and a great crowd, hesitate to execute the order and think it better to return and report how matters stand. On their informing the court of this, Karish, who was there awaiting the development of events, proposes to the king to go himself. He went with the guard, and, pulling off the turban of one of the servants, threw it round the Apostle's neck, and caused him to be dragged into the king's presence. The Apostle gives no reply to the questions put to him; he is ordered to be whipped, and one hundred and fifty lashes are inflicted, and he is led to prison. The text here very significantly reports what would seem in substance to be a relic of the primitive narrative (p. 237): 'But Judas, when he went to prison, was glad and rejoiced, saying : " I thank Thee, my Lord Jesus the Messiah, that Thou hast deemed me worthy not only to believe in Thee, but also to bear many things for Thy sake," ' &c.

After this Karish returned home rejoicing: but he finds his wife in great grief. During the night she goes to the prison, taking with her money to bribe the keepers and obtain admission. To her astonishment, on the way she meets the Apostle and takes him to her house. She awakens her nurse, Narkia, and tells her to fetch certain things which were necessary for baptism. This is administered to her by the Apostle; the nurse also, at her own request, is baptized. Thomas then returns to his prison.

Karish rising again early in the morning, goes to Mygdonia, whom he finds in prayer with her nurse and still opposed to his wishes. He starts at once for the court and lays his complaint once more before the king. The king in reply said: ‘Let us fetch and destroy him.’ But Karish thought it better to suggest that he should rather be utilised to influence Mygdonia to change her conduct. The king fell in with this view, and Thomas is sent for. The king sets him at liberty and tells him, ‘Lo, I let thee loose, go and persuade Mygdonia, the wife of Karish, not to part from him.’ Karish accompanies the Apostle to his house. Thomas is, by the Gnostic interpolator, made to say to her, ‘My daughter, Mygdonia, consent unto what thy brother Karish saith unto thee.’ At this she quotes his own words—put into the mouth of both by the Gnostic—against himself. Thomas leaves them and goes back to the house of the General. The latter asks for baptism for himself, wife, and daughter; they are instructed further, and then baptized.

Then follows the story of King Mazdai’s family and their conversion.

The king, after dismissing Thomas, communicated to Tertia, his wife, what had befallen Karish. Tertia goes next morning to visit Mygdonia; she finds her seated in penitential robes bemoaning her fate. Tertia expostulates with her at what she beholds. Mygdonia then discloses to her the new life, and she is at once fired with the desire to see and hear the prophet of the new faith. She goes to the Apostle at once and converses with him; she returns home full of the new ideas she has imbibed. The king inquires of her why she returned on foot—a thing beneath her dignity. Tertia passes the remark by and thanks him for sending her to Mygdonia. She adds, she had heard the new life and had seen the Apostle of the new God, and avowed her change of mind.

Her husband’s astonishment needs no description: he rushes out, meets Karish, upbraids him for dragging him also into

'Sheōl,' and says: 'He had bewitched Tertia also.' They go to the General's house and assault the Apostle; he is ordered to be brought to the seat of judgment. While Thomas is detained there by the guard, the king's son, Vizan, enters the hall. He takes Thomas aside and converses with him. Thomas, brought to judgment, is interrogated. The king becomes enraged and orders plates of iron to be heated, and the Apostle is made to stand on them barefooted. Whereupon a copious spring of water suddenly gushes out from the earth; the fire is extinguished, the plates are immersed, and the executioners fly in terror. The Apostle is then remanded to prison, and the General and the king's son accompany him; the latter asks leave to go and bring his wife Manashar. Tertia, Mygdonia, and Narkia, having bribed the guard, also enter the prison, when each narrates the trials she had to endure.

On hearing all this Thomas offers thanks to God; Vizan is told to go and prepare what is needful for the service which is to follow. On the way he meets his wife Manashar; Thomas overtakes them, accompanied by Sifur, his wife and daughter, also Mygdonia with Tertia and Narkia. They all entered the house of Vizan; it was then night. After praying and addressing them, the Apostle asked Mygdonia to prepare the women for baptism. They are then baptized, and when they had come up from the water the Eucharist is celebrated, as is stated to have been done at the two preceding administrations of baptism. All received holy communion; the Apostle left them and returned of his own accord to be re-imprisoned; 'they were grieved and were weeping because they knew that King Mazdai would kill him.'

28. ACT VIII. DISCUSSED—GNOSTIC SECTS IN ASIA

We ought now to take up in succession various questions affecting some of the details of the narrative reproduced; but it will be advisable first to give a short sketch of Gnostic sects, to enable the reader to follow the leading features of the numerous interpolations introduced into the text.

Gnosticism and the sects that embraced it originated within Christian communities in certain parts of Asia, but at root it was a foreign error (see article, 'Abrasax,' *Dict. d'Archéol. Chret. et de Liturg.*, Paris, 1903, col. 132) which some early Christians in a spirit of false rigourism and affected severity had adopted.

(*a*) Tatian, born in Syria between A.D. 120–130, once a disciple of St. Justin, the Roman martyr, left Rome after the death of the latter between 172–173, and had already lapsed into heresy. Among other errors, he held marriage to be no better than an impure life. He settled in Mesopotamia (Epiphanius, *Haeres.*, xlvi. n. 1) where he composed *The Diatessaron* [1]—'the four gospels in one.' The use of this book was forbidden in the churches by Rabbula, Bishop of Edessa (A.D. 411–435); and by Theodoret, Bishop of Cyrus or Cyrrhus, near the Euphrates, in whose diocese over 200 copies were destroyed (A.D. 423–457). In support of his tenets, Tatian excluded from his compilation of the Diatessaron the genealogy of Christ, and opened with the words: 'In the beginning was the Word.' He became also the founder of a sect named the Encratitae (Ephiph., *ut supr.*, and Jerome, *Chron. of Eusebius*, 'Tatianus haereticus agnoscitur a quo Encratitae.')

(*b*) Bar-Daisan of Edessa, a convert from heathenism, was born An. Gr. 465 = A.D. 154[2], and lapsed into Gnosticism. He and his son Harmonius composed in their native Syriac tongue many hymns tainted with their doctrinal errors. The father, as St. Ephraem (*Oper. Syr.*, tom. ii. p. 553) says, composed also 150 psalms in imitation of those of David. To prevent the further use of their hymns by the faithful, Ephraem composed his hymns and set them to Harmonius's tune. The name *Bar-Daisan* means 'child of the river Daisan,' which flows by Edessa, as his mother is said to have given birth to him on the banks of that river.[3] Bar-Daisan was known to Julius Africanus, who met him on his visit to the court of Abgar IX. of Edessa (who reigned A.D. 179–214), and styled him 'the Parthian,' and to Porphyrius, who called him 'the Babylonian.' The Acts of Thomas, Syriac text, contain the Gnostic hymn by him, 'The

---

[1] The original text of the Diatessaron, the Syriac, has not been yet discovered, but the work exists in an Arabic form and was published with a Latin translation by the late Cardinal Ciasca from a Vatican codex and a more complete Egyptian copy; an English translation was given by the Rev. J. H. Hill, Edinburgh, 1894, see *Introduction*, pp. 6–7.

[2] See Assemani, *Bibl. Oriental.*, i. p. 47, and *Chron. Edessen.*, ibid.; also No. viii. of same in Guidi's *Chron. Minor.*, p. 4, *Scriptores Syri*, ut. supr.

[3] See article, 'Bardesane,' in new *Dictionnaire de Théologie Catholique*, Paris, 1903, by Mangenot, now in course of publication. The article treats very fully the history and teaching of this early leader of a sect, and reproduces the result of the latest researches.

Hymn of the Soul' (translation, pp. 238–245), of which Professor Burkitt has given an English rendering in verse. There are also German and French versions of the same. Bedjan's edition does not contain this hymn.

(c) Marcion was the son of a bishop of Pontus, and had been excommunicated by his father for the seduction of a consecrated virgin. He went to Rome, c. 190, and sought re-admission to the communion of the church, but was refused until he first obtained release from the censure he had incurred. While there he came to be acquainted with and eventually joined Cardo, a Syrian Gnostic, with the object of inflicting a deadly blow on the Church. He became the founder of the sect named after him, the Marcionists : his followers were enjoined to abstain from marriage.

To the Gnostic, matter was essentially *evil* and the product of the demiurge : on this point the sect adopted the earlier error of the Docetae. In the celebration of the Eucharist they made use of water and abstained entirely from wine. See Alzog's *Hist. of the Church* (American ed.) vol. i. chap. ii. p. 304; also Assemani, *Bibl. Or.*, tom. i., *ut supr.*; Bardenhewer, *Les Pères de l'Eglise*, vol. i. § 17, p. 167, 'Tatien.'

These Syrian Gnostics who reprobated marriage were the heretics who corrupted the text of our Acts and made them a vehicle for the diffusion of their peculiar views in regard to the married state. This one concept permeates the entire Syriac text : that married life is debasing and sinful; that abstinence from it is the proper duty of a virtuous soul; and that those who happen to have contracted it should deny themselves. Every opportunity is taken to inculcate this; events in the story susceptible of a legitimate interpretation are purposely diverted to the cause that they upheld. Hence in and out of season exhortations and prayers are put in the mouth of the Apostle to forward this unnatural and unchristian tenet. The converts brought on the scene are shown to have a strong penchant for it, and develop into ardent and zealous promoters of the view. As the Syrian Gnostics manipulated the Acts of Thomas, so Marcion, the Pontic, made use of the gospel of Luke for a similar purpose. His edition of the text commenced with the opening words : 'In the fifteenth year of the reign of Tiberius Cæsar'—thus cutting off the entire first and second chapters of this gospel, containing the genealogy, the virgin-birth of Christ, and the birth of John the Baptist, &c. St. Epiphanius (Migne,

P. Gr.-L., vol. xxiii., *Haeres.*, xlii. cols. 359–419) gives a very full account, and almost the entire text of the altered sections by Marcion. An English translation of Marcion's gospel was published by the Rev. J. H. Hill from a recently discovered MS, but no allusion whatever is made to the older text given by Epiphanius.

In regard to our Acts Epiphanius mentions two Gnostic sects which in his time, A.D. 315–403, made special use of them in their assemblies, to the exclusion of the Scriptures. One of these had its chief seat at Edessa. When treating of the Encratites who succeeded Tatian, he says (*Haeres.*, xlvii.) that they added many more ridiculous errors to those they had imbibed from their master: they openly make the devil the author of marriage; in the celebration of the mysteries they make use only of water for they abhor wine and style it diabolical; 'among their primary Scriptures they reckoned the Acts of Andrew and John as well as those of Thomas,' &c. May not these have been the first to corrupt the text of the Acts of Thomas? In *Haeres.*, lxi., dealing with the 'Apostolici' 'who renounced all things and held fast to the principle of possessing no goods;' these, he says, came from the followers of Tatian, as the Encratites and the Kathari; they hold different sacraments and mysteries from ours; they do not receive back the 'lapsi,' and as to marriages they hold the same views as those mentioned above.

What St. Epiphanius distinctly says of the Acts of Thomas, that they were used by Gnostic heretics, is confirmed in a general way by St. Ephraem, who further lays on them the distinct charge of falsifying the Acts of the Apostles. A commentary of his on the Epistles of St. Paul has been preserved in an Armenian version; this, together with a translation in Latin, has been issued by the Mechitarist monks of Venice.[1] Referring to certain points of doctrine, he says (p. 119): Nam putant discipuli Bardezani, quod haec a Bardezano magistro suo adinventa fuerint—'the disciples of Bar-Daisan believe these things were discovered by their teacher, Bar-Daisan'; Atque ab ipsis omnino scriptae sunt Praxes Αὐτῶν [acta nimirum Apostolorum apocrypha] ut inter Apostolorum virtutes ac signa, quae conscripsere, scriberent in nomine Apostolorum iniquitatem quam

[1] *S. Ephraem Syrii Commentarii in Epistolas D. Pauli*, nunc primum ex Armeno in Latinum sermonem a Patribus Mekitharistis translati, Venetiis, 1893.

prohibebant Apostoli—'And by them have their acts been written, that among the signs and wonders of the Apostles which had been set down they might, in the name of the Apostles, write also vice and evil which the Apostles had forbidden.' This is an open charge against the followers of Bar-Daisan of propagating through forged Acts of the Apostles their master's errors. 'It is not too great a leap,' says Professor Burkitt (*Journal of Theological Studies*, vol. i., 1900), 'to say that he has the Acts of Judas Thomas in view.'

29. Doctrinal Additions to Acts of Thecla and Thomas

We propose to produce parallel passages of the doctrinal insertions found in the *Acta Theclae* and in those of Thomas. This will enable the reader to form an exact idea of the nature, origin, and relative dependence of these doctrinal interpolations, and will show that while in the former the Gnostic principles are gradually introduced, and put in the mildest form they can assume, they are in the latter openly stated, but yet so that they become framed after the model of what is found in the earlier work—the *Acta Theclae*. Quotations of the latter as well are given from Dr. Wright's translation (*Apocryphal Acts*).

The Acta Theclae	The Acts of Thomas
(1)	(1)
At the opening of the story, Paul, on entering the house of Onesiphorus, is made to speak 'words of God concerning the controlling of the flesh' (p. 118). The narrative discloses the betrothal of Thecla to Thamyris (p. 120); Paul's discourses are listened to with avidity by Thecla (p. 119). 'Thamyris is weeping because his betrothed had parted with him' (p. 121).	Thomas is taken by the king to bless the young couple; this he does in a long prayer (pp. 153–155). When all had retired from the bridal chamber, the bridegroom 'saw our Lord in the likeness of Judas [Thomas] who was standing and talking to the bride. "Lo, thou didst go out first," says the bridegroom in astonishment, "how art thou still here?" "I am not Judas," replies our Lord, "but I am the brother of Judas," and our Lord sat on the bed' (p. 155).
Thecla, after her condemnation at Iconium to be burnt, was looking out for Paul in the crowd. She saw the Lord Jesus, who was sitting beside her in the likeness of Paul (p. 128).	

THE ACTA THECLAE	THE ACTS OF THOMAS
(2)	**(2)**
He (Thamyris) complains, 'Who is this man within who leads astray the souls of young women and of virgins? Commands that there be no marriage feasts' (p. 122). 'This man does not suffer virgins to become the wives of men' (p. 124).	This is the instruction given: 'Ye preserve yourselves from this—— intercourse, ye become pure temples and are saved,' &c. (p. 155). 'The young people were persuaded by our Lord, and gave themselves up to Him; and were preserved from lust' (p. 156).
(3)	**(3)**
The cry is raised that he is a magician. 'Drag him along, he is a magician, for he has corrupted all our wives' (p. 124). 'The whole people cry out and say: Destroy this magician' (p. 127).	The king, on hearing of the determination taken by the young couple, rent his garment, and sent in haste through the city, 'Go and bring me that sorcerer' (p. 158). Mazdai's messenger says to the General, 'Dost thou sit and listen to vain words, whilst King Mazdai in his wrath is seeking to destroy thee, because of this sorcerer and seducer whom thou hast brought?' (p. 233). The king says, 'What is this story?—what doth he teach, this sorcerer?' (p. 235). The king, in his anger, says to Karish, 'Why didst thou not let me destroy that wizard before he could corrupt my wife by his sorceries?' And again, 'He had bewitched Tertia also' (p. 272).

THE ACTA THECLAE	THE ACTS OF THOMAS
(4)	(4)
A popular cry is raised— He separates young men from virgins, and virgins from young men' (p. 122). Thamyris' public complaint is this, 'Paul, thou hast destroyed the city of the Iconians, and my betrothed, so that she will not be mine' (p. 124). The hêgemôn asks Paul, 'What teachest thou? For they are not few who accuse thee' (p. 124). Paul replies, 'I teach a living God,' &c. ; 'and He has sent me that I might rescue them from destruction, and from uncleanness, and from all deadly lusts' (p. 125).	Karish, the husband of Mygdonia, complains of Thomas that he teaches, 'Ye cannot be children of this everlasting life which I teach, unless ye sever yourselves, a man from his wife, and a woman from her husband' (p. 233). The king reproaches Thomas, 'Why teachest thou a doctrine which gods and men abhor?' (p. 262). The poison is absorbed. Mygdonia, in reply to Judas, says her husband was angry with her, and meditated to punish her, 'because she did not give herself to corruption with him' (p. 234). Tertia advises the king her husband, after her first interview with Judas, 'I beseech thee to fear the God who hath come hither by means of this stranger, and to keep thyself purely unto God' (p. 271).
(5)	(5)
When Paul is sent to prison Thecla bribes the jailors, giving them her mirror of gold [Greek, silver mirror] to obtain admittance to him in the prison.	When Thomas was sent to prison, Mygdonia also, on hearing it, took money with her and went without any one perceiving her to the prison to give it to the keepers to let her in (pp. 255–256). This circumstance is interpolated into the text to no purpose, for she is made to meet him on the way ; yet it seems to have been introduced to follow up the lines of the prototype in Thecla's *Acta*. Another instance when payment was made also occurs (p. 284).

THE ACTA THECLAE	THE ACTS OF THOMAS
(6)	(6)

<table>
<tr><td>

Cause of Thecla's condemnation at Iconium. She is asked in court by the hêgemôn, 'Why art thou not to thy betrothed according to the law of the Iconians?' She gives no answer; her mother is made to cry out, 'Burn the fool in the midst of the theatre, that all the women whose doctrine this is, who see her, may be afraid.' The hêgemôn was sorry for her; then he condemned her to be burnt, &c. (p. 127).

</td><td>

Cause of Judas's condemnation. After the views disclosed by Tertia, the king rushes out and exclaims: 'May the soul of Karish have no rest, who hath brought this sorrow upon my soul.' And when he finds him, he says, 'Why hast thou taken me as thy companion unto Sheôl,' &c.; 'Why didst thou not let me destroy that wizard before he could corrupt my wife by his sorceries?' (p. 272). All this is said not because of any change of religion that had taken place, but because his wife also, as in the case of Mygdonia, was taught to deny herself to him. So, when the sentence of condemnation is passed, it is because of the Gnostic doctrine taught and upheld; see No. 32.

</td></tr>
<tr><td align="center">(7)</td><td align="center">(7)</td></tr>
<tr><td>

A list of thirteen Gnostic Beatitudes is given at pp. 118–119; they are a mixture of the special tenets of the sect with some of the eight Beatitudes of the Gospel.

</td><td>

The Gnostic Beatitudes in the text on virginity number thirteen, and are a great deal more explicit in their meaning than those in Thecla's *Acta* (pp. 226–227). As a rule, all the doctrinal insertions of the text are more pronounced than in the former, but the development runs on the same lines throughout.

</td></tr>
</table>

The details contained in Act VIII., which had been reserved, now demand separate treatment. The chief questions concern—the baptisms conferred, whether they were by oil; the different celebrations of the Eucharist; the ordeals the Apostle was subjected to, and the destruction of the idol, omitted in the text, and why; such points, if any, as may disclose Indian usages; whether any of the names that occur in the narrative belong to India; the age or date to which the Acts belong; the martyrdom; and what data, if any, can be given as to when the removal took place of the Apostle's Relics from India to Edessa.

30. BAPTISM, WHETHER BY OIL

Baptism of Mygdonia (pp. 257-258). She orders her nurse: 'Fetch secretly for me a loaf of bread, and bring a mingled draught of wine, and have pity on me.' Narkia the nurse answers, 'I will fetch thee bread in plenty, and many flagons of wine, and I will do thy pleasure.' Mygdonia rejoins, 'Many flagons are of no use to me, but a mingled draught in a cup, and one whole loaf, and a little oil, even if it be in a lamp, bring unto me.' The Greek has (p. 68, ll. 16-17), 'Measures I don't require, nor these many loaves, but only this (a cup of) mixed water, one loaf, and oil.' Text—'And when Narkia had brought them, Mygdonia uncovered her head, and was standing before the holy Apostle. And he took oil and cast it on her head and said, "Holy oil which wast given to us for unction," &c. And he told her nurse to anoint her, and to put a cloth round her loins, and he fetched the basin of their conduit (the *piscina*). And Judas went up and stood over it and baptized Mygdonia in the name of the Father, and the Son, and the Spirit of Holiness; and when she had come out and put on her clothes,' &c.

Baptism of Sifur's family (p. 267). Sifur asks for baptism for himself and family. Thomas before baptizing them, 'cast oil on their heads.' 'And he spake and they brought a large vat, and he baptized them in the name of the Father, and the Son, and the Spirit of Holiness.'

Baptism of Vīzān, Tertia, and Manashar (p. 289). 'After praying Thomas said to Mygdonia: "My daughter strip thy sisters." And she stripped them and put girdles on them and brought them near to him. And Vīzan came near first. And Judas took

S

oil and glorified God,' &c.; then followed a prayer, at the close of which 'he cast oil upon the head of Vizan and upon the heads of the others and said, In Thy name, Jesus the Messiah, let it be to these persons for the remission of offences and sins and for the destruction of the enemy and for the healing of their souls and bodies; and he commanded Mygdonia to anoint them, and he himself anointed Vizan. And after he had anointed them, he made them go down into the water in the name of the Father, and of the Son, and of the Spirit of Holiness.'

There can be no doubt that in all these three instances the text recites a valid baptism by water and not by oil. The unction by oil preceding the baptismal ceremony may belong to an earlier rite, perhaps for catechumens, but the words used at the third baptism also give reason to suppose this unction was a Gnostic form, perhaps, of initiation to the sect; anyhow it does not supersede baptism. It has been *obiter* said by some writers, and was taken for granted, that the Acts supported baptism by oil, but the text clearly rejects such a supposition.

31. EUCHARISTIC CELEBRATIONS

After describing a baptism the Acts generally mention the celebration of the Eucharist followed by communion given to the new converts (see pp. 166–167; pp. 188–190; pp. 258, 267–268, and 290: in the second of the passages communion is indiscriminately administered to all present). On the three last occasions the blessed Eucharist may really have been administered as the Apostle was nearing the close of his career; on the last of these occasions he was, so to say, on the eve of his martyrdom. But in some of the other cases the text may be representing what was perhaps only the custom prevailing among the Gnostic sects, and not the common usage of the Apostolic Church. The Catholic Church never sanctioned, as an usage and a rule, the giving of communion to converts after baptism, more especially so when they came from heathenism; neither would it be the custom to confer it too early on converts.

On two occasions, which appear to be the more striking instances, viz., the baptism of Mygdonia (p. 258), and at the general communion before the Apostle's martyrdom (p. 290), the wine used at the celebration is termed 'the mingled draught' in a cup, and 'the mingled cup.' We shall recur to these passages in No. 35.

32. Incidents Omitted in Present Syriac Text

The reader has been warned that the text omits two important facts concerning the Apostle, of which the Greek version as well retains no trace, but which have survived in the old Latin *Passio*, and have thence been incorporated bodily, without any change, into the narrative *De Miraculis*. Max Bonnet treats this insertion as an interpolation, and is inclined to make light of the facts themselves. But it strikes us very forcibly that the learned Professor has not studied attentively their bearing on the text itself, nor searched for the reason why they came to be excluded from the Syriac text, and are, in consequence, found missing in the Greek, which closely follows the former, even to details and phraseology.

The text, after giving the first ordeal of the heated plates of iron (pp. 275–276), passes on to the king's order, ' Drag him to prison,' to be followed up by the Apostle's martyrdom. The *Passio*, after giving the first ordeal, recites also a second to which Thomas was subjected, and then gives the attempt made by the king to force the Apostle to adore the sun-god idol, which ends with its destruction at Thomas's prayer. Are these two latter incidents so incompatible with the narrative of the story that they should be summarily dismissed? By no means. On the other hand, what is the result of their omission from the tale? What is the cause prompting the Apostle's execution? If the incident of the idol and its destruction be omitted, the narrative would disclose that the execution of the Apostle was ordered and carried out because of his holding and inculcating ideas unnatural to married life: or in other words—according to the reading of the text and of the Greek version—the Apostle Thomas was condemned to death, not because he was the apostle of Christ, the God-man, the preacher of His gospel, and the upholder of His divinity, but because he had merged himself into a Gnostic teacher upholding unnatural ideas as to married life. There can be no doubt on this point. We have already shown that it was on this account he was condemned according to the text (see No. 29, quotation 6) ; and in this the hand that manipulated the text for doctrinal purposes faithfully followed again, as has been shown, the lines of his prototype, the *Acta Theclae*, by making him a Gnostic martyr.

In addition to previous quotations we add one more to make

the point perfectly clear why King Mazdai, always according to the present Syriac text, condemned Thomas to death. At pp. 263–264, the king addresses him in these words: 'Now, therefore, if thou choosest, thou art able to dissolve these former charms of thine and to make peace and concord between the husband and his wife; and in so doing thou wilt have pity on thyself,' &c. 'And know if thou dost not persuade her, I will destroy thee out of this life.' The object, then, of the omission of the incident of the destruction of the idol becomes perfectly clear. The retaining of it would make him a Christian martyr, the omission an upholder of, and a martyr for, Gnostic principles. On the other hand, if the Apostle died a martyr, the incident of the destruction of the idol must form an integral part of the narrative of the Acts.

We return to the two suppressed passages. Under the second ordeal the Apostle was forced into the furnace of the baths, or the steam bath, to be killed; he issues out of this trial on the second day unharmed. Finding that this attempt likewise failed, the *Passio* narrates that Caritius—this is the form the name Karish assumes—suggests that he should be robbed of the protection of his God by forcing him to adore and sacrifice to the idol in the temple—*fac illum sacrificare deo Soli et iram incurrit dei sui qui illum liberat* (p. 156). The Apostle is made to follow a procession going to the temple with music and singing. Even at the present day the sacrificing (Brahman) priest is thrice daily accompanied by such a procession when he goes to sacrifice to the idol, early morning, noon, and evening. Arriving at the temple the king says to Thomas: *Modo faciam tundi arteria tua si non adoraueris et sacrificaueris ei*—'I will cause thy bones to be broken if thou wilt not adore and sacrifice to him.' The Apostle answers: *Ecce adoro sed non metallum; ecce adoro sed non idolum*, &c.—'I adore not a block of metal, nor an idol'; *adoro autem, meum Dominum Jesum Christum*—'but I adore my Lord Jesus Christ:' *In cujus nomine impero tibi, daemon, qui hic in ipso lates, ut nullum hominum laedens, metallum simulacri comminuas*—'In His name I command thee, O demon, who liest concealed in this idol, to injure no person but to destroy the metal of this image.' *Statim autem quasi cera juxta ignem posita ita liquefactum idolum resolutum est*—'The image of the idol is suddenly dissolved like wax before the fire.' The priests raise a howl, the king runs away with (Karish) Caritius, and the high

priest of the temple, seizing a sword, transfixes the Apostle, exclaiming, 'I will avenge my god!'

We may add that the idol was probably not that of the sun-
god, but, as will seem likely, was probably an Indian idol seated
on a car. The idea of the sun-god, likely enough, forms part of
a textual error because of the Acts originating in Mesopotamia.

The above reproduction of the destruction of the idol up-
holds, we venture to think, both points contended for: the
reason why it was omitted, and the necessity, on that very
account, of considering it an integral portion of the narrative of
the original Acts. This further proves that the text of the present Syriac by no means represents the original compilation or
writing in its primitive form; and that the *Passio* represents an
earlier text.

33. ACTS DISCLOSE INDIAN AND HINDU CUSTOMS

We now pass to inquire whether the contents of the Acts
offer any clue to fix the country where the scenes narrated were
transacted, since, in spite of the Acts mentioning 'the realm of
India' to which the Apostle had gone, there are yet many
Thomases who will not have it that it was the India 'of pearls
and gems' and 'of the Brahmans' of the ancients, but to some
other India that Thomas is supposed to have gone, which they
themselves are, of course, unable to designate or substantiate.

The reader will remember a small detail commented upon at an
earlier stage when the General was described journeying in a cart
drawn 'by cattle' to meet Thomas and invite him to his house.
That detail being peculiar to Southern India, would fit in with
that portion better than with the North-West of India. We now
take up some other incidents disclosing local colouring, and will
enquire how far they support the view of his martyrdom in the
India of the Hindus.

(1) Text, p. 218: 'Mygdonia had come to see the new sight
of the new god who was preached, and the new Apostle who was
come to their country; and she was sitting in her palanquin and
her servants were carrying her.' In a footnote Dr. Wright adds,
' *Pâlkî*, or *palanquin*, seems to be the best equivalent of the [Syriac
word] in the passage.'

In Southern India yet, to some extent, more so in the native
states of Malabar, the pâlkî among natives is considered a more

honourable means of personal conveyance than a carriage drawn by horses. It is used invariably at marriage ceremonies—indicating the older customs of the country; and in the States of Malabar the writer is aware that after the elephant the pālkī was considered the conveyance next in dignity. This, or its equivalent the *manchi*, a lighter form of the former, more in the style of a stretcher, is yet the common means of conveyance over long distances, especially for native ladies.

(2) Text, p. 227: 'Karish came to dinner and did not find his wife at home.' He was told, 'She is gone to the strange man and there she is; he was very angry,' &c. 'And he went and bathed and came back whilst it was still light, and was sitting and waiting for Mygdonia.' The Greek supports it, p. 57, l. 19 ff.

We would ask the reader if he knows of any country, outside of India, where it is the custom to bathe before partaking of the evening meal, or of any principal meal. He may perhaps know that this is a religious rite enjoined upon all Hindus in India that they should purify themselves by such an ablution before a meal. Another circumstance, which will escape the notice of such as are unacquainted with Indian native habits, is implied in the words, 'he went and bathed and came back whilst it was still light;' this implies the bathing was outside the house and before the evening meal. Every Hindu of a respectable position—especially in Native States—has generally a tank in his compound to which he resorts for this ceremonial bath; and this is precisely what the wording of the text implies that Karish had done.

(3) A prior instance of such a bath is mentioned at p. 223: 'Now Karish, the kinsman of King Mazdai, had taken his bath and gone to supper.' This further instance fully confirms what we have inferred; it is not a casual bath, but the religious bath prescribed by Hindu usage before the day's meal. The instances adduced disclose that we are dealing with Hinduism; that Karish was a Hindu, and he, being related to the king, it is a proof, for those who understand India's social life, that the king himself was no other than a Hindu Rajah. Both points will presently be further confirmed by what follows.

(4) The text, p. 225, recites: 'And when it was morning, Karish, the kinsman of King Mazdai, arose early and dressed,' &c., 'and went to salute King Mazdai.' The reader has here placed before him the customs of a Hindu court of Southern

India. Ministers, courtiers, and attendants are all waiting upon the Rajah at early dawn in court. Suitors and petitioners are waiting outside the court premises even from four o'clock in the morning to place their petitions and plaints before the Rajah. Court business in fact, in Hindu courts, is transacted from early morning until noon. The reason why Hindu Rajahs hold court so early in the day throughout the year is this—that they may have time to purify themselves with a bath before the midday meal. The above custom prevails to this day in the Hindu courts of Malabar, and must, more or less, be the same in other parts of India, where native Rajahs yet hold court. The writer is not personally acquainted with the exact customs of Hindu courts in Northern India, but believes they are much the same; and when he was present at an ordinary durbar at the court of Jammu, business was being transacted in the morning.

(5) A second similar occurrence in support of the court usage recurs at p. 232 of the text: 'Whilst Karish was meditating these things it became morning. And he rose early, dressed,' &c., 'but he put on sorry garments, and his countenance was gloomy and he was very sad, and he went in to salute King Mazdai.'

Here the custom of going to the Rajah's court the first thing in the morning is repeated. But a new detail is introduced— 'he put on sorry garments.' What can this mean? It indicates the Hindu custom that when a man is suddenly overtaken by a great misfortune, or by the death of a near relative, anxious to move to compassion and sympathy and to show his great distress to his superior, whether an official or his master, he appears before him in the garb of grief and with an unkempt appearance. The first question generally asked is, What has happened to you? Englishmen who have dwelt in India, and officials oftener, must have had experience of this usage in their private or official dealings with natives. This comprises the dress and the appearance, unkempt and distressed, which the person assumes, and which may be aptly termed that of grief. This is precisely what Karish has done; and in the king's question of inquiry both the garment and the personal appearance are referred to. He says, 'What is the matter that thou art come in this wretched plight? And why is thy aspect sad and thy countenance changed?' The Greek supports the text. The reader acquainted with India will realise that the customs described are purely Hindu; the court is a Hindu court, Karish is a Hindu, and his wife must also be one. The latter point is confirmed by what follows.

(6) There is yet one last detail of custom mentioned in the Acts that has to be placed before the reader. This is given in the text, p. 222. When Mygdonia first went to see the Apostle in her *pálkí*, she 'sprang up and came out of the palanquin and fell down on the ground before the feet of the Apostle, and was begging him,' &c.

Let the reader remember that Mygdonia is a lady of the court, related to the king, or Rajah; she is consequently not a poor, humble woman, who through an act of self-abasement would seek to obtain a favour, and may prostrate herself before a great man. But being a lady of high position, how could she behave in such manner to an utter stranger? the more so as this was the first time she had come in contact with the preacher of this new doctrine. Nothing but Hindu custom will offer a full explanation. Any Hindu, man or woman, who approaches a Brahman priest, when not influenced by the presence of Europeans, before addressing him, performs the same act of prostration on the bare ground as Mygdonia had done, with hands joined forward over the head, prostrate on the ground, in an act not only of supplication but of semi-worship, imploring a blessing and showing the deepest veneration for the person. The writer is informed that in Malabar even the Hindu Rajah performs this religious act to the chief Brahman priest in the temple at his religious installation on the *Guddee* (coronation ceremony), and when he attends any great religious ceremony at the temple. But the act is now so performed as not to be visible to the public. It is this act that the Hindu wife of Karish instinctively, and as if to the usage quite accustomed, here performs on her first appearance before the Apostle. The act, as we see, is the natural outcome of the first impulse in a Hindu woman who comes before the high priest of a new religion which has struck her intelligence and won her heart.

(7) The text at p. 265 gives a second instance of Mygdonia's homage to the Apostle in the Hindu form—and this in the presence of her husband and at her home: 'Whilst she was saying these things (to herself) Judas came in, and she sprang upright and prostrated herself to him.' The description is clearly by a narrator who had seen similar acts done; she does not prostrate herself from the seated position in which she

is, but stands up and completes the act, as those who have seen it performed, know. Then, again, how does her husband, with his intense animosity against Thomas, take her behaviour? Is he surprised? Does he rebuke her? Nothing of the sort; his approving remark to the Apostle is, 'See, she feareth thee,' hoping no doubt that the excess of veneration for Thomas he had witnessed would secure his own object.

(8) A third instance is also given at p. 287, performed by Manashar: 'And when Manashar the wife of Vizan (the king's son) saw him [Thomas who had entered her house] she bowed down and worshipped him,' no doubt according to Hindu religious usage.

34. Names Mentioned in the Acts

Another question reserved for separate treatment is that of the names found in the text of these Acts.

The first king whose name occurs in the narrative is Gondophares. This name was found on the coins belonging to the Indo-Parthian kings, who reigned over a large part of Afghanistan and some portion of North-Western India ; and in the inscription of *Takht-i-Bahi*, situated on the present borders of India in the ancient *Gandhâra*. The latter fixed the date of the beginning of his reign A.D. 20–21 ; and the date of the inscription itself, the twenty-sixth regnal year of the King Gondophares, brought us to A.D. 45–46. The tokens on the coins of Gondophares, according to best numismatic authority, demand a date not later than the middle of the first century of the Christian era. As Gondophares is mentioned in the Acts, in close connection with the Apostle, and the former was reigning from A.D. 20–21 to A.D. 45–46, and for what further period is unknown, it is historically quite possible that the Apostle visited that portion of India during the reign of this king. And since no other document has retained the mention of the name Gondophares except, and solely, the Acts of Thomas, until the recent discoveries mentioned above, it is quite legitimate to conclude that the mention of these two names, coupled as we find them in the Acts of Thomas, imply a well-grounded historical connection. The reader will find the question treated *in extenso* in our Chapter I.

In Act VIII. of the story quite a large group of names is introduced, and the name of the country, where the events described took place, is mentioned earlier in the Acts. From

the indications that have been already culled from the text, it has
become clear we are dealing with what not only was occurring
in India proper, as the text says, but also with events concerning
and passing among Hindu people, and in a Hindu realm. Without being thought guilty of rashness, we may therefore be per-
mitted to presume that the name of the king would, or ought
to be, Indian—viz., Hindu—and not foreign, as in the previous
case of Gondophares.

Having said this much, before entering into an examination
of the names found in the text, it will be very advisable to submit a few observations. Should any of the voyages narrated
by early travellers, say down to those of the early Arab travellers
of the eighth or ninth centuries, or even later, be taken up, with
hardly any exception that we can recall to mind, it will be found
that they one and all scarcely ever introduce personal names in
the narrative of peoples or events they describe. Even names
of towns are constantly omitted, rarely in fact given, except they
be of mercantile importance or of some principal place; they
may, perhaps, give the name of the country.

With regard to rulers of countries travelled through, they, as
a rule, are mentioned in a generic form, and if the name is introduced, it is either the popular form of the name or a name
coined from the country, or the country is found named after the
sovereign—instances of both can be found in the geographies ; in
the one by Ptolemy, and in that which goes under the name of
the *Periplus Maris Erythraei.* Oftener a generic form of description is adopted : the ruler is styled the king, the khan, the prince,
the great khan, &c. The names of ministers and courtiers with
whom the traveller has come in contact are similarly omitted, and
when indicated they are designated by their office.

Hardly ever does the personal name of an individual appear
in the narrative. Should the reader entertain any doubt on the
subject, we would refer him to Yule's *Cathay*, where he will find
quite a collection of early narratives of this description down to
even those of Christian missionaries in the Far East. The only
exceptions we would make to the above statement would be the
great Venetian, Marco Polo, in some instances, and the case of
Mahommedan writers when they have met a countryman holding
high position in foreign lands.

It may be asked, Why are personal names omitted by early
travellers ? Any one who has journeyed through foreign lands,

the language of which is unknown to him—which generally is quite different to his own—may fall back on his own experience in support of what is said. The language being foreign, the sounds quite unfamiliar, to him mostly unpronounceable—unless he were to go about in the style of the modern reporter with note-book and pencil in hand—he is unable to fix the sound perma-nently in his memory; even should he chance to hear the name oftener than once, he is likely to forget it. Hence, when a traveller is compelled to refer to individuals of the country, he falls back on the office held, or the service rendered, to designate him.

This is the true reason why proper names, even of rulers, rarely occur in such narratives, while those of individuals hardly ever appear in the older travels. When the name of a sovereign is given, it is the popular form of the name that occurs oftenest, not his distinctive personal appellation; this renders it, not rarely, a matter of considerable historical difficulty to identify the ruler.

Coming to our Acts, as to the names of female persons given in these—Tertia, Mygdonia, Manashar, and Narkia—we are of opinion that they should be summarily dismissed as fictitious, and that they were inserted only for the purpose of dramatising the tale. These are neither Indian nor Hindu names, as they ought to be, if they were the proper names of the ladies designated. Any one familiar with Indian Hindu customs and prejudices is aware that, owing to social opinions of seclusion as the proper thing for women, held by the people, and because of the usage thence derived, the mention of a woman's name—in the presence of foreigners more especially—never occurs, unless while she is a child. For that matter the case is largely the same throughout the East. But servants are, or may be, called by their proper names. When a girl becomes a wife, she is spoken of as the wife of A. (her husband by his name); as a mother, she is called the mother of B. (by her child's name); and if adult and unmarried, she is styled the daughter of N.'s wife. It is only among the lowest classes in India that a woman's name is heard pro-nounced in public. These are immemorial, unchangeable customs and social usages. The proper names of the Indian ladies so familiarly mentioned in the narrative, had they been their personal names, would never have been heard by a stranger.

On the general grounds stated above no importance should be attached to such names as Karish, Vizan, and Sifur, given in the text; they were introduced to give a scenic interest to the narrative, as the heading to each separate Act discloses. The text itself confirms this, as was suggested in the remarks on Act VII.; it gave the story of the General's family, but neither his personal name nor those of his wife and daughter were introduced to the reader, the first was simply designated by his supposed office. It is only about the middle of the following Act, VIII., when several persons appear on the scene, that names are assigned to them. Then it occurs to the embellisher of the story that the General had no name, and so a name is found for him and he is called Sifur; but yet he overlooked inserting the name in the previous Act, and has similarly forgotten to give names to the wife and daughter when they take part in the scenes of the next Act, and they are allowed to retain their original designation as the wife and daughter of the General. Besides, the remark occurs again these are not Indian names as they ought to be. These and the previous batch of female names are foreign to India, some perhaps are Persian—of Mygdonia the reader knows the origin, leaving a general trace of the hand that inserted it.

But out of this collection of names there survives that of the King Mazdai. On general grounds the name of the king who ordered the execution of Thomas ought to appear in the Acts of his martyrdom, and it would seem most probable that his name was inserted in the original composition. But Mazdai is thoroughly a Persian name, was borne by a satrap of Babylon (died B.C. 328), and it cannot be the true form of the king's name. This name appears under the following forms: Syriac text, *Mazdai;* Greek version Μισδαιος; both Latin versions, *Misdeus.*

M. Sylvain Lévi in *Notes sur les Indo-Scythes* (No. 1 of 1897, ninth series, tom. ix. p. 27, *Journal Asiatic*), section iii.: 'Saint Thomas, Gondophares et Mazdeo,' has worked out with considerable research a theory for this name. He starts on the supposition that the Apostle Thomas could have paid but one visit to India, and finding that connected with Gondophares in the north, he takes it for granted that the sequence of events given in the Acts took place in that section of the country. In a certain way the idea would naturally suggest itself to one who does not look for any other evidence regarding the Apostle but what is contained in the narrative, and, further, reads the latter without the benefit of a minute knowledge of Indian habits and usages. (The reader is referred to the second part of Chapter IV.)

M. Lévi's paper has appeared in an English translation by Mr. W. R. Philipps in the *Indian Antiquary*, vol. xxxii., 1903, pp. 381 ff., 417 ff.; and vol. xxxiii., 1904, p. 10 ff. where *Supplementary Notes* to the above will be found.

It will then be interesting to hear what M. Lévi has to say on the subject of the name Mazdai. The Ethiopian version happens to give the name of King Mazdai's capital, which is there named *Quantaria*. This reminds him of Gandahâra, and after having made a further reference to the text as to the probable direction of the journey, he makes the ingenuous remark, 'la connaissance exacte de l'Inde éclate dans les épisodes et les détails des Actes.' The opportune arrival of wild asses to convey the Apostle on his journey with the General to King Mazdai's capital which follows, lends zest to the view adopted.

Having so located himself, he takes up the name of Vasudeva, the Indian king (one, if not the last, of the dynasty established by Kanishka, who could not have been much posterior to the reign of Gondophares, and this is the one good feature in M. Lévi's discussion), whose legend-bearing coins have come down to us, and whose name in Sanscrit form appears in inscriptions as *Vasudeva*. The name in the Greek legends of his coins assumes the following forms (p. 38) BAZOΔHO, and BAZΔHO = *Bazodeo* and *Bazdeo*. The name Bazdeo passing under Iranian influences would, he suggests, easily be transformed into Mazdeo, and the latter form is the one, he continues, around which the varying forms or changes of the king's name are grouped. So the *Mazdai* of the text of the Acts is to him no other than King *Vasudeva* (ut supra, p. 40, end) who reigned from Kashmir.

We have a couple of observations to offer on the conclusions here quoted. First, it is not surprising that the sound of the letter *V* in the name Vasudeva is, in Greek, represented by the letter β, for the Greek alphabet offers no better correlative sound ; we need not enter into the question whether *beta* (β) had in ancient Greece the same sound as the modern Greek gives to it, making it the equivalent of our *v*; or whether the sound was rather that of *b* of the Latin alphabet. In either hypothesis, the name Vasuveda having to be reproduced in Greek letters, no other letter could replace the sound of the *v* than β. But when M. Lévi asks us to go further and to assume *m* as an equivalent for *v = b*, the name 'Vasudeva,' or his *Bazdeo*, becoming *Mazdeo*, the reader

cannot fail to observe that quite a new name is substituted for
the original. But, while demurring to accept this theory and substitution, we are glad to admit that there is an important point of
historical evidence disclosed in the argument—viz., that Indian
kings in and about the first century of the Christian era were in
the habit of incorporating the epithet of the divinity with their
own name, or of assuming it absolutely (if they did not already
bear the name).

Apart from the evidence here produced, we can offer similar
instances as to other kings of India. In fact, M. Lévi himself
offers a sample of this sort in section i. of the same paper.
This section will be found in the first part of the paper,
and appeared in the preceding vol. viii. of 1896 (see pp. 447,
452, 457, 469, and 472). He gives there translations from
Chinese versions of Sanscrit writings or poems regarding King
Kanishka—the Sanscrit text of which is now lost or at least has
not been recovered. The Chinese translations belong respec-
tively to the years A.D. 405, 472, and 473 (pp. 445–447). The
poems introduce the Scythian Buddhist King, Kanishka, in these
words: 'The King Devaputra Kanishka.' Devaputra signifies
'the child of god,' or 'born of god.' This denotes that, at an
age prior to Christianity, the name of the divinity was coupled
in some form with the name of Indian kings, indicating that
this coupling of names was so deeply rooted in the Indian mind
at that period that even the Buddhist Kanishka, a foreigner, is
made to assume it; or, at all events, it is popularly done for
him. It is relatively immaterial by which of the two above
ways the appellation was adopted.

It must further appear singular that even the founder of the
Parthian dynasty in India, the Maharaja Gondophares, who was
certainly no Indian and probably had not embraced the religion
prevailing in Upper India, should nevertheless find himself compelled to assimilate to the same Indian usage of appellation which
we have seen attributed to Kanishka, and adopted certainly by a
successor, Vasu-Deva; but it appears here in a modified form.
If the reader will turn to the coin plate of this king (Chapter I.)
and refer to the Indian legend reproduced in the text, coin 4,
he will find that it reads: *Maharaja*, &c., *dramia-devavrata* |
Gudapharasa; Coin 8, *apratihatasa devavratasa Gudapharasa;*
and Coin 9, *a pratihatasa deva.* . . . The term *deva-vrata*
signifies 'devoted to the gods.' It is clear that, though Gondo-

phares does not go to the extreme length, like Vasu-Deva, of styling himself a 'Deva,' he yet feels the necessity of introducing the term in a modified form and meaning on his legends. See E. J. Rapson's *Notes on Indian Coins and Seals*, Journal of the Royal Asiatic Society, April 1903, pp. 285–286.

Other instances, for a later period of kings reigning over part of the former territories of Gondophares who adopt the same usage, are available. The information is given in General Sir A. Cunningham's *Coins of Mediæval India from the Seventh Century down to the Mahommedan Conquests*: London, B. Quaritch, 1894, p. 55; 'Coins of Gandhâra and Punjab,' deals with those of the Brahman kings of Cabul. Among these occur kings bearing the following names: (1) Venka-Deva, A.D. 860; (2) Salapati-Deva, A.D. 875; (3) Samanta-Deva, A.D. 900; (4) Bhima-Deva, A.D. 945. In the list of coins of the Tomars of Delhi and Kanuj (p. 85) 'Deva' is again found joined to rulers' names: (5) Salakshana-Pala-Deva, A.D. 978–1003; (6) Ajaya-Pala-Deva, A.D. 1019–1049; (7) Ananga-Pala-Deva, A.D. 1049–1079; (8) Someswara-Deva, A.D. 1162–1166; (9) Prithri Raja-Deva, A.D. 1166–1192. Similar instances also occur in the list of the Tomars of Kanuj. The Sanscrit word *Deva* has the same meaning as *Divus* and *Deus* in Latin.

There is forthcoming also from quite a different part of India evidence of the prevalence of this Hindu custom even at a posterior age. Marco Polo (Yule's 2nd ed., vol. ii. p. 348) writes of the Kingdom of Mutfili, which Yule says applies to Telingana, or the kingdom of which Warangol was the capital; Mutfili, a port of the same, was visited by the Venetian, and in the language probably of traders he names the kingdom after the port instead of as more commonly by its capital. 'The kingdom,' he says, 'was formerly under the rule of a king, and from his death some forty years ago it has been under [the rule of] his queen, a lady of much discretion, who for the great love she bore him would never marry another husband.' Yule adds that the king's name was Kakateya Prataba Ganapati Rudra-Deva. The name *Rudra-Deva* means *Sun-god*. The queen's grandson was Prataba Vira Rudra-Deva, c. A.D. 1295, and he is called by Ferishta, the historian of Akbar the Great, *Ludder-Deo*. Here are two kings of the peninsula of India styled 'Deva,' of which the popular, or abbreviated form, is *Deo*, the same as was found to be the case in Upper India at a more remote period, in the case namely of Vasu-Deva, which name in its time was popularly rendered *Basdeo* or *Vasdeo*, according to pronunciation.

Again, Wilson (*Catalogue of Mackenzie's Collection*, Madras reprint, 1882, p. 77) treating of the kings of the above line, writes: 'Rudra-Deva, to expiate the crime of killing his father, built a vast number of temples, a thousand, it is said, chiefly to Siva,' &c. 'After some time his brother Mahadeva rebelled, defeated him in battle and slew him, and assumed the direction of affairs. He left to the son of Rudra the title Yuva Raja, heir and partner of the kingdom. Mahadeva lost his life in war with the Raja of Devagiri. Gunapati-Deva, the son of Rudra, succeeded, and gives the name to the family, who as Kakateya Rajahs, are often termed "*Gunapati.*"' We have here a plain and simple narrative of a dynasty of Rajahs bearing the name *Deva* in the southern portion of India, similar to what we have already seen was also the case in Cabul and elsewhere. This name 'Deva' becomes popularly abbreviated into Deo, and one of these Rajahs was also found named Mâhâ-Deva, whose name on the same grounds would be popularly contracted into *Mahdeo*.

Here the reader should be informed that Siva, a member of the Indian trinity, is the special divinity greatly venerated in Southern India, so that the majority of ancient shrines and temples are dedicated to Siva under one or another of his various titles. The worship, however, of Siva was by no means restricted to Southern India, for Gondophares' coin (see plate), No. 4, on reverse bears the image of Siva (see also E. J. Rapson *ut supr.*, p. 285). He is besides κατὰ ἀντονομασίαν the Mâhâdeva, 'the Great God' in Southern India. This name is borne by Hindus, and it is not uncommonly heard in the streets as a personal appellation.

Now if the name Mâhâdeo be passed through Iranian mouths, it will probably assume the form of 'Masdeo'; owing to similarity of sound with the Iranian name, Mazdai, the sibilant would be introduced, and the outcome of Mahadeo or Madeo would be Masdeo, and would appear in Syriac as *Mazdai:* the Greek version reads Μισδαῖος, the older Latin *Misdeus* and *Mesdeus*, and from this *De Miraculis* would borrow it. These forms would represent, approximately, the name of the Indian king who condemned the Apostle to death, and so would reproduce the characteristic divine epithet *deva* as well, retained in the abbreviated Indian form, *Mahdeo*.

The point need not be forced, we will leave it to the reader to assimilate the idea and judge of its probability on the strength of the parallel evidence adduced.

35. DATE OF THE ACTS

When treating of the Eucharistic celebration (see Nos. 30 and 31) we produced two quotations from the text—'a mingled draught in a cup,' and 'the mingled cup,' we then said they were reserved for separate treatment; they were also found supported by the Greek version when neither of the Latin translations — both abbreviations—contained any trace of the same. Considerable importance, in our opinion, is to be attached to the use of the phraseology. In the first place, it indicates that the age of the writing takes us back to the period when the *disciplina Arcani*, or the *lex Arcani*, regarding the mention of Christian mysteries, and more especially the Holy Eucharist, prevailed. In the second place, the phrase is one that belongs to the sub-apostolic age, reserved to express and denote the celebration of the Eucharist, or the holy mass ; yet so, that while understood by the faithful it was meaningless to the outsider. In proof of what we assert we shall introduce the reader to a safe authority, that of Abercius, Bishop of Hieropolis, in Phrygia Salutaris.

In the metric epitaph composed by the bishop—which belongs to the early date A.D. 180-191—an expression parallel to that quoted above is found employed to designate the Eucharistic celebration. The inscription itself was known long ago, for it is attached to a life of Saint Abercius in the Greek *Passionales*, and many MSS containing it are found in the Bibliothèque Nationale, Paris, and in the Vatican library. Tillemont, however, rejected it ; and in our days every attempt has been made, by Ficker in 1894, by Harnack in 1895, and by Dieterich in 1896, to explain it away as anything but a Christian record, just as many another ecclesiastical document had been treated, under a cloud of misapplied scientific erudition, but the native truth of its authenticity enabled it to triumph over all attempts to suppress it. It now becomes evident that the writer of the Saint's life had a fair copy of the inscription before him, if he did not write the life on the spot where the tomb stood. The copy that is attached to the life, though faulty in passages, yet in substance is now ascertained to be accurate, and

T

has been confirmed by the discoveries of the original epitaph, and of one of Alexander, moulded on the former, of the year 216.

By good luck Professor W. M. Ramsay recovered in 1882 the epitaph of Alexander of Hieropolis, the son of Antony, which he published the same year. This attracted the attention of the late ecclesiastical archæologist, De Rossi, and he suggested that the tomb of Abercius could not be far off, as the epitaph of Alexander closely imitated the lines of the known epitaph of Abercius. On a subsequent expedition of research, in 1883, Professor Ramsay alighted on two fragments of the original inscription of Abercius.

This had been engraved on three faces of a sepulchral cippus of white marble, the fourth bearing a crown and foliage. The cippus, according to the recital, stood over the tomb itself, and must have occupied the centre of a chamber, or open space. On the occasion of the Episcopal Jubilee of Leo XIII., 1892, the Sultan of Turkey made a present of this most ancient relic of Christian epigraphy to the Pope. Later the Professor kindly sent over the smaller fragment as well which he had removed to Scotland. The whole is now set up in the 'Christian Museum' at the Lateran Palace, holding also those discovered in the Roman Catacombs.

The translation of the Syriac expression given by Dr. Wright agrees with that used by Abercius in his epitaph, as we said. The quotation we give was first taken from H. Maruchi's *L'Eléments d'Archéologie Chrétienne* (General Notions), Paris, 1899, p. 296, but it has been compared with that given in the article, 'Abercius,' by Dom H. Leclercq, *Dictionnaire d'Archéologie Chrétienne et de Liturgie*, Paris 1893, edited by Dom Fernand Cabrol, of which the first six fasciculi are now published. The article reproduces the Greek original reconstructed on the text given by the fragments discovered, with a large plate reproducing the recovered fragments. The print shows distinctly what has been recovered from the fragments, and what is confirmed by Alexander's epitaph ; to this is added a Latin translation, which is quoted below. The article treats most elaborately all questions concerning this early epitaph, and supplies a complete list of literature on the subject.

Abercius, speaking in his own person, tells us he ordered his tomb, dictated the inscription, was a follower of the Shepherd,

visited Rome, passed through the cities of Syria, went beyond
the Euphrates, saw Nisibis; then continues :—

Fides vero ubique mihi dux fuit
Praebuitque ubique cibum, piscem e fonte
Ingentem, purum, quem prehendit virgo casta
Deditque amicis perpetuo edendum,
Vinum optimum habens ministrans mixtum cum pane.
Haec adstans dictavi Abercius heic conscribenda
Annum agens septuagesimum et (vere) secundum &c.

The expression *mixtum* reproduces the Greek κερασμα
(*vinum aquae*) of the original—the 'mingled draught,' or
'mingled cup' of the Acts, used in the celebration of the
Eucharist. Etienne (Henricus Stephanus) in his *Thesaur. Gr.
Linguae* (ed. Dindorff, Paris, 1841) has *ad voc.*—κερασμα,
'Mixtura; de mixtura vini Eustathius; item mixtura aquae
frigidae et calidae.'

The entire epitaph is enigmatic, owing to the prevalence of
the 'lex Arcani.' The reader may perhaps know that under
the emblem *piscis*—the fish—Christ is symbolised, as shown by
several mural paintings found in the Roman Catacombs. A
similar allusion to *Ichthys–piscis* is found in the epitaph of
Pectorius of Autun quoted by Leclercq, *ibid.*, col. 83. The
'mixed' or 'mingled cup' denotes the consecrated element of
wine slightly mixed with water, as is used to this day in the
Catholic Church; and the *panis*, 'bread,' represents the body.

The coincidence of the ancient expression found in the epitaph
of Abercius and repeated in the Syriac of the Acts of Thomas
justifies us in seeing therein a trace of an original remnant of the
earlier text, sufficient to conclude on this ground what the writer of
the article 'Thomas' says on his own account (Hastings's *Dictionary
of the Bible,* Edinburgh, 1902, vol. iv.) that 'the Acta Thomae
is a work probably going back to the second century.' The
writer speaks of it as of Gnostic origin, but the reader will
have found sufficient evidence to consider it instead only
subjected to very extensive interpolation and adaptation for
Gnostic purposes, yet so that all trace of the original text has
not disappeared. Fortunately a German scholar, who has made
a special study of Gnostic writings and is considered a great
authority on the subject, von Carl Schmidt (*Die alten Petrusakten
im Zusammenhang der Apocryphen Apostellitteratur*, Leipzig, 1903)

has arrived at the conclusion that of the Acts of Peter, Paul, John, Thomas, and Andrew, which in the time of Photius were attributed to Lucius Charinus, all, even those of John, are by more or less orthodox Catholics; certainly none are of Gnostic origin (p. 129): Der gnostiche Apostelroman, he says, ist für mich ein Phantom— 'In my opinion a Gnostic romance [Acts] of the Apostles is a phantom.' It is satisfactory to find others coming to the views we hold.

The passages 'a mingled draught in a cup' (text, p. 258), and the 'mingled cup' (p. 290) we maintain are survivals of the primitive writing; for since the Gnostic sects abhorred wine and did not use it in their celebration 'of the mysteries,' it becomes undeniable that these expressions were not inserted by them. Besides the use of wine and bread on the above two occasions, the use is also mentioned at a third celebration on p. 268; these offer ample evidence that the expressions have come down to us from the original text in which they stood before Gnostic manipulation took place—and this proof of itself would be sufficient to fix the date of the composition as anterior to the development which it now presents—to the latter portion, at least, of the second century.

Perhaps the reader would like to see a quotation of the oft-repeated phrase, as used half a century later, by another bishop, St. Cyprian of Carthage, A.D. 250–268. The extract we are going to give is taken from a lesson of the office for the octave of *Corpus Christi; Epist. ad Caecilium :*—

Ut ergo in Genesi per Melchisedech sacerdotem benedictio circa Abraham posset rite celebrari, praecedit ante imago sacrificii, in pane et vino scilicet constituta. Quam rem perficiens, et adimplens Dominus panem et calicem mixtum vino obtulit : et qui est plenitudo, veritatem praefiguratae imaginis adimplevit.

36. THE MARTYRDOM

We now pass on to the closing section of the Acts, the martyrdom.

The narrative of the Acts was interrupted at the point where the Apostle Thomas was remanded to prison after the one ordeal mentioned in the text. We found him administering baptism to the last of his converts while detained in prison.

The king ordered Thomas to be brought up for judgment.

Mazdai questioned him whence he came and who was his master. The king hesitated what sentence he would pass, or rather how he should compass his death without causing popular excitement. The reason for his hesitation is given, 'because he was afraid of the great multitude that was there; for many believed in our Lord, and even some of the nobles.' So Mazdai took him out of town, to a distance of about half a mile, and delivered him to the guard under a prince with the order, 'Go up on this mountain and stab him.' On arriving at the spot the Apostle asked to be allowed to pray, and this was granted at the request of Vizan, the king's son, one of the two last converts. Arising from his prayer, Thomas bid the soldiers approach and said, 'Fulfil the will of him who sent you.' 'And the soldiers came and struck him all together, and he fell down and died.'

The burial is described in the following words: 'And they brought goodly garments and many linen cloths, and buried Judas in the sepulchre in which the ancient kings were buried.'

The narrative also states that the grave was opened in the king's lifetime and by his orders, when the bones were not found, 'for one of the brethren had taken them away secretly and conveyed them to the West.'

The Greek version and the Latin *De Miraculis* generally agree with the text, but both say, as to the manner of death inflicted, 'four soldiers pierced him with lances.' As to the disappearance of the Apostle's bones, the former says: 'One of the brethren having stolen him, removed him to Mesopotamia.' The latter is more explicit: 'Quoniam reliquias sancti apostoli quidam de fratribus rapuerunt et in urbe Edissa a nostris sepultus est'— this tells us the removal was to Edessa, where the Apostle's bones were again buried.

The *Passio* places the death at a different period, and assigns its occurrence to quite a different cause, as shown in No. 32. The same is made to take place immediately after the miraculous destruction of the idol: 'The priests raised a howl, and the chief priest of the temple seizing a sword transfixed the Apostle, exclaiming, "I will avenge the insults to my god."' As to the removal of the bones from India it also gives a different version: 'The Syrians begged of the Roman emperor Alexander [Severus, A.D. 222–235], then on his victorious return from the Persian war against Xerxes [Ardashir], and petitioned that instructions should be sent to the princes of India to hand

over the remains of the deceased [Apostle] to the citizens. So
it was done; and the body of the Apostle was transferred from
India to the city of Edessa.'

37. THE REMOVAL OF THE APOSTLE'S RELICS FROM INDIA

A few general remarks are demanded by the differences disclosed between the text and the *Passio*. The difference on two
points is radical. The local tradition of Mylapore (see Chapter
IV.) coincides with the text that the Apostle was put to death on
the great Mount St. Thomas, while *Passio* makes it occur suddenly, and inflicted by the hand of what would be a Brahman
priest.

As to the removal of the relics to Edessa, the text and the
versions agreeing with it, the Greek and *De Miraculis*, say it
occurred during the lifetime of King Mazdai, while *Passio* distinctly asserts it to have taken place long after, viz., after the
close of the first quarter of the third century. We shall find
that the version given by *Passio* will demand acceptance, while
that by the text is inadmissible.

The Apostle would probably have lived considerably past the
middle of the first century before he could have completed the
mission assigned to him. Keeping this in mind, we will place
before the reader all the available historical data to show exactly
on what basis the question can be solved.

According to historical data, Abgar V., surnamed Ukkama
(the Black) King of Edessa—to whom the Apostle Thomas had
deputed his colleague the Apostle Thaddeus (see No. 7), confirmed, as explained above, by Eusebius and the *Doctrine of
Addai* (*infr.*), and whose conversion after the miraculous cure we
uphold—reigned, during his second term, from A.D. 13 to A.D. 50,
which gives a period of thirty-seven years and one month (see
Duval's *Edesse*, pp. 48–50). He was succeeded by his son
Manu V., who reigned for seven years, to A.D. 57; he again was
succeeded by his brother Manu VI., who reigned for fourteen
years, down to A.D. 71. It is during this third reign that
Aggai, mentioned in the *Doctrine of Addai* (Philipps, p. 39), was
put to death by the prince (pp. 48–49): 'And years after the
death of Abgar (Ukkama) the king, one of his rebellious sons
who was not obedient to the truth, arose and sent word to
Aggai,' &c. 'And when he saw that he did not obey him, he

sent and broke his legs, as he was sitting in the church and expounding.' This discloses that after the new faith had been followed by Abgar and his son Manu V., after the year 57, when Manu VI. obtained power, he not only rejected the faith—if he had ever accepted it—but started an open persecution against the nascent church, and killed the chief priest or bishop who then presided over it. As his reign was prolonged to fourteen years, and he was succeeded by his son Abgar VI., who reigned for twenty years, down to A.D. 91, and would have been a heathen like his father, the faith that had commenced to bud would in all probability have been crushed out under persecution, to revive at some later date.

Now, had the remains of the Apostle come to Edessa during the reign of Abgar Ukkama, or the short reign of his son Manu V. (whose conversion, together with that of his father is mentioned, see *Addai*, p. 31 and note *a*), there is not the slightest doubt it would have been loudly proclaimed by Edessan scribes and by St. Ephraem. It not having taken place then, we may assume that the ground at Edessa would not again have been ready for such removal until Abgar IX. had ascended the throne, and had embraced the Christian faith. He reigned thirty-five years (A.D. 179–214). Besides this local improbability, there arises another objection. The route from India *viâ* the Euphrates was not open to dwellers within the circle or bounds of the Roman empire except after Trajan's expedition, A.D. 114–116 (Mommsen, *Römische Geschichte*, vol. v. p. 395; see also Duval's *Edesse*, p. 53); and again after the victory of Alexander Severus (see date given above) over the Persians. So the removal, said to have taken place during the lifetime of Mazdai, must be summarily rejected as untenable.

Abgar IX., mentioned above, styled on his coins Μεγαλος, after his return from Rome—which is by Gutschmidt (*Untersuchungen über die Geschichte des Kœnigsreichs Osrohœne*)placed not earlier than 202—embraced the faith. This would be the second time that the ruler in Edessa submitted to the preaching of the Gospel. The details of this conversion have unfortunately not come down to us. This is the same Abgar of whom the compiler of the *Chron. Edessen.* (Guidi, *Chronica Minora*, p. 3, l. 15 f.), quoting from the city archives, says that he witnessed the great flood that destroyed the walls and a great part of the city in November, 201: 'Abgarus rex stans in magna turri, quae Persarum

vocatur, aquam (exundantem) collucentibus facibus conspexit'—
the Chronicle includes among the buildings destroyed, the
'temple of the Christians'—'in templum aedis sacrae christianorum (aquae) irrupuerunt.' The document from which the
details of the great flood were taken is an attested notarial
document which had been placed in the archives of the city of
Edessa; the wording shows that at that period the State was still
pagan although there existed a church within the city.

Eusebius (*Hist. Ecl.*, lib. v. cap. xxiii. col. 490-491, Migne,
P. Gr.-L. tom. xx., Eusebii, tom. ii.), supplies an earlier date for
the existence of churches in Osrhoena. Writing of the Synods
which were held in the West and in the East in the days of Pope
Victor, A.D. 192-202, regarding the celebration of Easter, he
adds : There were also Synods held 'in Osroene and in the
cities of that country' of which synodal letters exist. Mansi
(*Concilia*, tom. i. col. 727), in the *Ex libello Synodico*, which contains in brief a collection of principal synods held on this question, gives the following : Osroena. Synodus provincialis in
Osroene, cui Edessa et Adiabenorum regio subjacet, collecta
episcopis octodecim, quorum praeses memoriae traditus non est :
de sancto pascha idem statuens, Commodo imperante [A.D. 180-
192]. A double entry of this Synod, differing slightly in wording, is given, and a comparison of the two will show them to
have been the same and not separate Synods. M. Duval (*Edesse*,
p. 114, note) has arrived at a wrong conclusion on this point, based
on the grounds that Mesopotamia was not divided into two
provinces until 349, under Constantius, and rejects the synodical
ruling as spurious. In reality the question of the division of
Mesopotamia into two separate provinces has no bearing on
the case; besides, the second province under Constantius had
Amida for its capital and not Adiabene. There is no distinction
implying two provinces in either of the synodical entries : one
mentions the number of bishops, the other does not; one is
spoken of as the provincial council of Mesopotamia, the other
as of Osroene ; both names were applicable to the same province. Even after the time of Constantius, Socrates, the Church
historian, writes of Edessa as being in Mesopotamia (*Hist. Ecl.*,
lib. iv. cap. xviii., Migne, *P. Gr.-L.*, tom. lxvii. ; the quotation is
given in Chapter IV. p. 105). The data obtained from Eusebius
and the Osroene Synod (A.D. 192-197) show that there were
assembled bishops and rectors of churches to the number of

eighteen before the close of the second century. But Christianity had not yet become the adopted religion of the country, neither had the court or the wealthier classes joined it. It would only be after the conversion of Abgar IX., after A.D. 202, when influence and wealth were at the command of the Church, that a merchant would be forthcoming who could have brought to his native city the relics of the Apostle. When a few years later, Alexander Severus reopened the door of Eastern commerce to the empire *viâ* the Euphrates, it is then that we have all the conditions required for such a transfer. Edessa was then thoroughly Christian, the trade route to India was opened, peace would facilitate commerce, and backed by wealth the citizen of Edessa, 'Khabin,' trading with India, was able to bring the precious Relics to Edessa (for evidence see Chapter II., note p. 23). It is only then that this transfer was practicable.

Some writers have fixed upon the year 232 as that of the removal, Lipsius among others, but there are no further data available to fix the time with precision. The transfer would probably have been between the dates 222–235, or a little later; but it cannot be placed after 241, for in that year Ardashir (the Xerses of the *Passio*), accompanied by his son Sapor (Duval, *Edesse*, p. 70), invaded Mesopotamia and threatened Antioch, so the trade route to India by the Euphrates was once again closed to commerce, and continued so for a long subsequent period.

As to such details as that the body was buried in linen cloths and was interred in the tomb of the ancient kings, they are mere specimens of faulty information or incongruous ideas introduced into the narrative. In the India of those days linen cloths would not be readily forthcoming; and as to tombs of Hindu kings—for such they would have been were the details accurate —there never were any to receive the holy remains of the Apostle, for Hindu rite has rigorously prescribed from all time the cremation of the dead.

INDEX

Printed by BALLANTYNE, HANSON & Co.
Edinburgh & London

Printed in the United States
87868LV00007B/1/A